IBSEN

A CRITICAL STUDY

COMPANION STUDIES

IBSEN

A CRITICAL STUDY

JOHN NORTHAM

CAMBRIDGE

AT THE UNIVERSITY PRESS

1973

Published by the Syndics of the Cambridge University Press
Bentley House, 200 Euston Road, London NWI 2DB
American Branch: 32 East 57th Street, New York, N.Y. 10022

© Cambridge University Press 1973

Library of Congress Catalogue Card Number: 72-80297

ISBNs:
0 521 08682 5 hard covers
0 521 09733 9 paperback

Printed in Great Britain
by W & J Mackay Limited, Chatham

CONTENTS

ACKNOWLEDGEMENTS

I wish to express my indebtedness to the Delegates of the Oxford University Press for permission to quote from Jens Arup's translation of *Love's Comedy*; to the Old Dominion Foundation for making it possible for me to work in peace at Berkeley College, Yale University, for three months during the formative stage of this study, and to Charles Walker, Master of the College, and Bernice, his wife, for their unobtrusive but sustaining kindness and hospitality; to Sheila Sibson-Turnbull not only for coping with a well-nigh impossible manuscript but for driving me on to keep her fully occupied at a time when an incentive was invaluable; and to all those specialists in the field of Ibsen studies who have encouraged the adventures of an outsider by their sustained interest and sympathy; none will be offended if I single out two families, the Haakonsens and the Høsts for my special gratitude.

John Northam

1

INTRODUCTION

'My book is poetry. And if it is not, then it shall be.' Ibsen's declaration of faith in *Peer Gynt* is one he could as well have repeated at the end of his working life: all of his books, early or late, in verse or in modern prose, are a form of poetry. Some recognition has been paid to this fact, but for the most part the picture of Ibsen the poet is still a little out of focus.

Poet in his earlier career, certainly. Whether writing there in verse or prose Ibsen demonstrates in play after play before *Pillars of Society* a consciousness that his principal artistic tool is language, and the twin climaxes of that period are fittingly his great dramatic poems *Brand* and *Peer Gynt*. But poet in the second half of his career as author of the series of modern prose plays? Here recognition has been given grudgingly. Poet in intention and ambition perhaps; his use of symbolism and of that peculiarly sporadic, heightened language of his is obviously an attempt to express intensity of experience beyond the normal. But is it real or pseudo-poetry?

The problem is twofold since the form of poetry cannot be divorced from the vision it expresses. Ibsen's later dramatic poetry has been judged imperfect because it has been applied, so the judgment runs, to a form loosely termed naturalistic that is by its very nature hostile to poetry. His symbolism and heightened language are seen as attempts to rectify this inherent deficiency of form but only at the expense of artistic integrity: there is a manifest straining of the fabric of the plays. His poetry is imposed and not organic, his plays neither fully naturalistic nor fully symbolic. And by this assessment Ibsen's work, viewed as a whole, is broken-backed. In the first half of his writing career he was a true poet in the sense that he gave full and free, even if immature, expression to his imaginative vitality in words and situations untrammelled by the restrictions of naturalism; for his later work, either by deliberate surrender to an alien but convenient form of drama or by a decline in creative fertility, he subdued his inherently poetic genius. The break is represented as abrupt and is usually located in the appearance of the first important play of the modern prose series, *Pillars of Society*.

The other half of the problem concerns Ibsen's vision of life. This has dated; in short, Ibsen is no longer, in any serious sense, relevant.

I believe both these estimates, of form and vision, to be mistaken. There exists an important continuity that joins the apparently disjointed halves of Ibsen's career and it is one whose elucidation may lead to a slightly more adequate understanding of the modern prose plays. They may appear not as artistic aberrations, but as the consummation of prolonged exploration, discovery and development along two lines which eventually converge. The easier line to start with is the development of Ibsen's vision of life in the earlier half of his career.

Ibsen's work falls into two approximately equal halves: the plays that precede *Pillars of Society* (published 1877) and those that follow. The earlier plays are far less well known than the later, and properly so; there are no neglected masterpieces among them. They can reasonably be seen as the work of an apprentice in drama. From his first play, *Catilina*, onwards, Ibsen shifts his dramatic style from play to play, responding to models from imitation or adaptation of whom a young dramatist might learn the secret of success – Shakespeare, Scribe, Schiller, Goethe, Holberg, Hebbel, and others. And yet, amid the din of varying styles there runs one single, continuous note. Whether he writes of the Roman malcontent, or of Viking chiefs, of young lovers or a parish priest, Ibsen seems constantly fascinated by what can only be called man's potentiality for heroism. His studies are not all positive; Earl Skule in *The Pretenders*, Ibsen's finest history play, is an example of a man who lacks the essential ingredient of self-confidence; yet of play after play, and regardless of form or model, it can be said that Ibsen felt impelled to create situations that gave opportunity for his characters to show how much or how little they are truly possessed of the capacity to rise to great challenges.

It could be argued that the earlier works are for the most part not comparable in worth with the later for the simple reason that in them Ibsen chose too direct a method of indulging this interest of his. Heroism is most easily depicted in the past, and most of these works depend upon the synthetic glamour of great personages in great events of real or fictional history. The gestures are easy, but they remain, in the limiting sense, theatrical. Ibsen's vision extended beyond the theatre into contemporary life. Through the past he could depict heroism with ease; what he could not do through the past was portray heroism in the life of his own times.

That this was a nagging preoccupation of his throughout the earlier half of his career can only be presented as a working hypothesis; there is not enough evidence to constitute proof. But there is evidence. For one thing it seems reasonable to deduce dissatisfaction in Ibsen himself with his own plays from the fact that, even after some modicum of success with one kind, he moved to another, different model for his next. His own achievements did not satisfy him; hence the constant and restless trying-on of styles and forms, to find one that could fit his vision. There is, furthermore, the fact of his own youthful and active involvement in contemporary politics, ideas and events. This seems, to judge by his letters and his biographers, to have been submerged during his years of poverty and discouragement by the more immediate and limiting concern of keeping a job and a family, yet that period too can be judged as one in which his earlier, more theoretical ideas about contemporary society took on the substance of actual, first-hand experience. Though most of his plays of this period were set in the past, Ibsen was living painfully in the present and out of that experience his vision was forming.

There is, of course, no reason why a play set in the past should not present an image of contemporary life. Another fact to be taken into account is that some of the earlier plays seem, sometimes demonstrably are, fables of modernity in period costume. *Catilina* turned the Roman into a symbol of rebellion against any corrupt society past or present; Earl Skule's rivalry with Haakon in *The Pretenders* may be seen as a representation of Ibsen's rivalry with

Bjørnson; when Bishop Nicholas' ghost in the same play moves to the footlights to accuse the audience of being vacillating, shrivel-hearted cringers there is no mistaking Ibsen's desire to use a historical play to convey directly his sense of the quality of life in his own times. It could be done and Ibsen tried to do it; but the effect is either muffled by the historical disguise, or discredits the disguise by thrusting through. Oblique presentation, it seems, could not satisfy Ibsen.

The most convincing fact emerges from observing a rhythm that gradually builds up during this earlier period – the rhythm of modulation from history to modern or near-modern times as a setting. From almost the beginning of his dramatic career, Ibsen gave warning that he wanted to write directly and openly about his own generation. After *Catilina* (1850) and the Viking play *The Burial Mound* (1850) comes *Norma, or a Politician's Love* (1851), a Gilbertian skit on contemporary political absurdities; a satirical parody of Bellini's opera, not properly a play, but a tentative in the direction of a modern play. And that was followed, in 1853, by *St John's Night*, a comedy in modern setting and colloquial language interspersed with lyrical poems. Again, hardly a success-ful play, but another significant attempt. But neither of these little works seems able to concern itself with heroism. The modern forms seem too fragile to entrust the vision to. Significantly Ibsen retreats to the past to make his large affirmations again, as though at that stage it was the idea of heroism that it mattered most to him to keep alive in his imagination. After *St John's Night* he wrote *Lady Inger of Østraat* (1855), *The Feast at Solhoug* (1856), *Olaf Liljekrans* (1857), itself a development of an earlier treatment of 1850 called *The Grouse in Justedal*, and *The Vikings at Helgeland* (1858) – all plays set in distant times whether historical or imagin-ary, and all concerned, in one way or another, with heroism.

Then, after a significantly long pause, came *Love's Comedy* (1862), a remarkably self-assured verse play set firmly in Ibsen's own times. Unlike the earlier attempts it is a fully achieved work with a consistency that extends throughout its structure and texture; a true play, a truly modern play, and one, moreover, which has the self-confidence to at least attempt to investigate the

4

possibilities of heroic response to circumstances as apparently trivial as an engagement to be married. There are many objective reasons why Ibsen should have taken so long to give the play its final form – he began to think about it as early as 1858; it comes towards the end of one of the most distressing periods of his career, a time of disappointment, penury and humiliation. But nonetheless something drove him on to write *this* first, a modern play, rather than another history play that was germinating during the same period. Perhaps two subjective difficulties also intervened to prolong the period of creation: the problem of imagining, in terms of situation, crisis and character, what heroism in contemporary life might actually involve, and the concomitant problem of creating a dramatic form that could accommodate the vision. The play is not a great one, but it is a great advance towards solving those problems, and from it Ibsen may have derived the inspiration to change rhythm. From this point on, instead of modern works making sporadic appearances amongst works set in the past, the reverse becomes the case. Ibsen wrote only two more history plays.

The first of these two, and the greatest, was *The Pretenders* (1863). It was, in many ways, Ibsen's most substantial achievement to date and it was a success, but it was not one Ibsen cared to repeat. His next three works were all modern in setting. The first two, *Brand* (1866) and *Peer Gynt* (1867) are usually taken to represent the climax of Ibsen's earlier and more truly poetical period. They can also be seen as decisive stages in the clarification of one of his twin problems, that of defining for himself what modern heroism would amount to. Ibsen deliberately avoids the other problem of dramatic form by writing these works not as plays for performance but as dramatic poems, dramatic in texture but not for the theatre, as though, once again, understanding took precedence over form. If no dramatic model could yet provide a form that would allow him to explore fully what heroism in his own day meant, then he must at least temporarily abandon strict dramatic form. He used his freedom not just to write his greatest poetry, in the formal sense, but to give his fullest versions of the obverse and reverse sides of the one thing that fascinated him continuously. *Brand* is a study of the heroic; *Peer Gynt* of the unheroic in the recognisably modern world; these dramatic poems represent the furthest penetration so far of Ibsen's imagination into that complex of tensions.

The next play marks Ibsen's return to the neglected second problem. *The League of Youth* (1869) is a very well-made play. It is entirely modern in language, setting, situation and character. Ibsen has learned how to construct a modern play, but he has not been able to carry over into it what he had discovered in *Brand* and *Peer Gynt*. They were about modern heroism without being plays. The *League of Youth* is a modern play without heroism. Ibsen has moved along the second line of advance but there has not, as yet, been a junction effected with the first. And his response is to return, for the last time now, to the past for his most extensive investigation into the crises that men must face in their lives; he wrote his World-Historic Drama, *Emperor and Galilean* (1873).

Though an historical play, it is similar to *Brand* and *Peer Gynt* in escaping the limitations of normal dramatic form. It is a vast work in two parts; in the Oxford edition of translations the text occupies approximately 250 pages; *The Pretenders* takes up approximately 120. It is, in fact, another attempt by Ibsen to clarify his vision further, this time without even the limitations of having to represent either dramatically or non-dramatically the circumstances of his own age, of the essential spiritual conflicts that must engage men who are not dull or evil or supine. *Emperor and Galilean* is a vast portrayal of spiritual trial.

It is, in my sense of the word, about heroism, but it is set in the distance of the past; it does not advance Ibsen's art as a dramatist. It may develop his vision, but it does not bring new form to vision. Ibsen thought very highly of this work, but clearly it did not satisfy him. He did not write again in that mode. Not another history play, nor another modern play like *League of Youth*, nor another modern work in non-dramatic form like *Peer Gynt*, but silence followed until 1877, when he published *Pillars of Society*; and thereafter he modified but never again radically changed his dramatic form. He was satisfied at last.

The implied argument must by now be clear: that the modern

prose plays by which Ibsen is best known amongst foreigners are, for him, the fusion he had been searching for between form and vision: fully dramatic representations of modern life that are also capable of expressing his sense of the heroic potential that exists even in modern man, for whom there are no large gestures to make, no great events to confront or grandeur of status to be assumed. To justify this estimate will indeed be one of the purposes of this book but the case will be demonstrated, not argued here. For the moment it is time to return to the starting-point of poetry. In what reasonable sense can these plays of the later period be thought of not merely as culminating statements of Ibsen's vision but as statements in poetry?

The idea is not difficult to accept provided that the commonplace is accepted that a good play, any good play whether in verse or prose, is more than the sum of its words. Ibsen's plays, from the earliest onwards, show an instinctive awareness of this. Rudimentary though some of them may be, examples abound of Ibsen's understanding that a play contains imagery that is not only verbal but visual; that is to say not merely words which by association and controlled expansion of meaning help to enrich the significance of particulars, but also effects that work through the eye in performance, or through the eye of imagination, to the same end. From the beginning the verbal and the visual co-operate, though at first it is the verbal that predominates. As his art matures, so the co-operation of the two kinds of imagery becomes integration; when he enters upon his series of modern prose plays, the emphasis moves away from the verbal to the visual as more and more is left unsaid because unsayable. The shift of emphasis is decisive and should not be minimised; yet it is a shift and not an abrupt change. In the plays of this later period of his life, Ibsen may have adjusted the elements of his dramatic poetry but he has not ceased to write poetry; the modern prose plays are, even more decisively than the earlier plays, works whose essential experience is conveyed not through plot or character study but through complex, and, by now, highly structured patterns of unified dramatic imagery. If the later plays are looked at in this way, then the notorious symbolism may cease to appear as a pseudo-poetic excrescence on prose works and be seen for what it is, special, structural concentrations of imagery forming within a generally imagistic structure. This book attempts to justify these suggestions, but again they must await substantiation through demonstration rather than theoretical discussion.

As for the language of the plays: for those who have no Norwegian, translations, however good, can never be adequate. This is inevitable. But it is particularly unfortunate in Ibsen's case, and therefore sad that so little has been done to tell the non-Norwegian reader at least something about the characteristics of Ibsen's mature prose style. A good translation of, say, *Brand*, can give some notion of the kind of poetry that lies behind; even a good translation of *Ghosts* will necessarily obscure subtle distinctions in manners of speech and the full characteristics of the moments of high rhetorical utterance. This is a task that cries out for volunteers, for experts who will condescend to the level of description and explanation that, however simple and banal to them, might illuminate these difficult works a little more brightly for the great, inexpert majority. I am no such expert, but I have hazarded some observations about Ibsen's use of language in the plays that I have selected for analysis. If these clumsy attempts of mine do no more than provoke someone better qualified to do the job better, then they will not be without their justification.

To illustrate the poetic character of these plays means working by close attention to detail. The method has its dangers. It is not fashionable at a time when large generalisations seem more impressive and acceptable; it runs the risk of producing tedium; it may seem to imply that I, the critic, am presuming to establish for all readers what the one right reading is and what are the right responses. The risk of outmodedness and tedium I must accept; I can only work by the method that seems to me best for the subject and I must bear the consequences. Any didactic tendency will be more apparent then real. Though they may be presented with some confidence, all of my readings are tentative; they make no claim to define or exhaust meaning. They aim to do little more than draw attention to the workings of imagery where it might be overlooked, and to the structural nature of that imagery. No account of mine could possibly remove from each reader or spectator of an Ibsen play the freedom to experience, explore and respond to the full richness of which these analyses are but poor and scanty indications.

It follows from the method of analysis that I have chosen that, to keep within the limitations of length set by editorial policy, I have had to limit my attention to only six of the plays. I have chosen to write on *Love's Comedy* as at once a verse play and Ibsen's first substantial attempt at his theme of modern heroism; on *Brand* as arguably the greatest poetical work in the formal sense; on *Ghosts* as the most impressive of the modern prose works before, as I see it, he achieved full mastery of form and vision in the later period; *The Wild Duck* represents for me the threshold, and *Hedda Gabler* the heart, of his maturity; while *Little Eyolf*, that strange, delicate play, represents a partial failing of Ibsen's heroic vision. That all of these are worthy of attention I am certain. I hope that in conjunction they will help convey some idea of the continuity of development that I have referred to in this introduction.

Finally, since Ibsen always felt the close relationship between his plays and life, I have thought it right in a brief concluding section to hazard some general and perhaps unduly personal opinions about the relevance of Ibsen to our own lives.

2

'LOVE'S COMEDY'

For a play that Ibsen himself thought so highly of – some ten years after completion, and after the production of *Brand* and *Peer Gynt*, he could still rank it amongst his finest creative efforts – *Love's Comedy* is insufficiently known to those who depend upon translations. For even if the translations are read, they do not convey the flavour. The difficulty is to preserve two contradictory elements: the general colloquial vitality of the language and, at the same time, the formal ingenuities of the rhyme-schemes. Translators have usually managed to represent one or the other but not both. C.H. Herford follows the rhyme-scheme quite closely but he pays the price of artifice. 'Hope's own singer young and fain...sorrow in its train'; 'a chord united...youth's memory benighted' are fair samples of what can go wrong. He is also forced into liberal recourse to ''tis' and 'nay'. Jens Arup's version (in the Oxford edition) has the vitality but drops the rhyme, and that is a loss.

I am not myself a translator, but I have tried to hammer out versions that represent closely the rhyme-schemes without falling into too false a poetic diction. I cannot pretend that the result is tolerable as poetry, but it is not intended to be. It is rather an indication of the sort of thing that Ibsen is offering than a full reconstruction of it. If the versions read, as I am sure many do, stiffly and stiltedly, the balance can be struck by re-reading the Oxford version. The original is as formal in structure as my version, but as lively as Arup's.

It seems to me important to preserve the rhymes because they constitute the prime source of wit and variety in the play. The basic unit of the verse is predominantly the iambic pentameter in rhyming couplets, but there is a great deal of flexibility in its use. Rhythm is not dominated by the line or couplet form; caesuras break the flow of lines, the voice is carried over by single or double feminine endings; single lines are frequently subdivided between two or even three different speakers, and couplets too are often shared. But the most important variations are to the basic couplet form. It constantly expands into quatrains and sestets; sometimes, even, by combination, it comes close to the sonnet form. Appropriately enough, the nearest comparison I can find in English is with certain passages in *Love's Labours Lost*. And yet we are constantly reminded of the basis from which the variations depart; one of the most agreeable features of the play is the way in which one's ear is kept cocked for the next strict couplet that will, without warning, put an end to an extended set of variations. One never knows when the next rhyme is coming.

Rhyme also serves in the play as a useful index to mood and character. It can represent sententious platitude or impassioned conviction; where the rhyming is desperate enough, it can suggest banality; where sharp and inventive, wit and intelligence.

I do not propose to place much emphasis on the humour in this play. Either it will make something like its proper impact even in translation (for Ibsen's humour, though genuine, is never very complicated) or it will not; talking about it will compromise such chance as it has of survival. I shall concentrate more on trying to bring out the tension between this self-evident humour and the inherent seriousness of the theme. This may be *Love's Comedy*, but even at comedy Ibsen looks with the eyes of tragedy. If the analysis makes it appear a solemn play it is because that is its underlying character; the humour looks after itself. But it must not be forgotten.

Certainly there is a blitheness about the opening of Act I which is unmatched in any other play by Ibsen; for this, and for what indications it gives of the way Ibsen's creative imagination is working, it is worth quoting a few lines:

(*The stage presents a pretty garden of irregular but tasteful layout; in the background the fjord can be seen with islands beyond. To the spectator's left, the main building of the house with a veranda and an open dormer-window above; to the right, in the foreground, is an open summerhouse with a table and seats. The landscape basks in strong afternoon light. It is early summer; the fruit-trees are in blossom.*)

(*When the curtain rises, Mrs Halm, Anna and Miss Skjære are sitting on the veranda, the first two knitting, the other with a book. In the summerhouse Falk, Lind,*)

Guldstad and Styver can be seen; punch-mugs and glasses stand on the table. Svanhild sits by herself in the background by the water.)

FALK   (*stands up with raised glass and sings*)
Sunshine in a garden fairly
beckons us to dance and sing;
why reflect that autumn rarely
keeps the promise of the spring?
Apple blossoms, snowy flowers,
were created for our mirth;
why repine about the showers
that will bring them down to earth?[1]
(*the men in Chorus*) 'why repine' *etc.* . . . .

FALK   Well, there's the song you asked me for; be kind;
there wasn't one real thought inside my mind.

GULDSTAD   Who cares, so long as it's a song that swings?

MISS SKJÆRE   But Svanhild, who seemed thrilled right to the bone –
as soon as Falk began, she spread her wings
and now she's gone.

ANNA   No; sitting there; alone.

MRS HALM (*sighing*) That child! God knows, she's getting worse and worse!

MISS SKJÆRE   But tell me, Mr Falk, your final verse
was less rich – well. . .in poetry perhaps
which did appear elsewhere in snips and scraps.

STYVER   Quite. Surely it's a pretty simple thing
to put a bit more in towards the ending.

FALK (*touches glasses with him*) Just fill the cracks and blemishes with plaster
to look like marble, sleek as alabaster.

There is more here than just people in front of a background. People and setting interpenetrate through the words of the song. The setting – trees in blossom, sunshine – gives body to what the men are singing about, it is the physical equivalent of their light-hearted philosophy. And by their location under an open summer-house out there in the garden, the sense of identity between the men, their philosophy and the setting is strengthened.

The women have their own setting. They sit as a separate group on the veranda of the main house; they do not carouse, but occupy themselves with domestic tasks; nor do they celebrate the beauty of the fleeting moment; before long they show their disapproval. The first scene already begins to suggest potential oppositions and

---

[1] I cannot improve on Jens Arup's version of this song.

tensions through imagery that is both verbal and visual: male versus female, nature versus domesticity, spontaneity versus social decorum – the terms are vague but some such possibilities are there. And one other suggestion drifts across – that Svanhild, sitting alone in the background, belongs to neither group.

Not that Falk's group shows much solidarity outside the song. It is true that when Falk begins to elaborate his philosophy, Lind (Falk's theological-student friend) does not dissociate himself but he seems privately bemused by some obsession of his own. Styver, once a poet but now a clerk, once a lover but now a fiancé, is comically inadequate in actual behaviour to the sentiments he sang. Whereas Guldstad, the middle-aged man of wealth, actually ridicules the moral of the song:

> Do you call that economy? To let
> the birds strip all the blossom off the tree
> and eat your fruit before it's ripened yet
> and then allow the sheep and cattle free
> to graze the garden later in the summer?

Guldstad's argument is not exciting, but at least he is aware of trees and gardens as facts in nature, not just as words in songs. The setting backs him up.

These desertions do not shake Falk; he becomes more aggressive, verbally and physically. He moves across to confront the women over the veranda railing to give a paradoxical twist to his philosophy – it is not instant joy that he wants, but any intense experience, even tragic, so long as it is immediate:

> With blindness blank the mirror of my eyes
> and then I'll sing the brightness of the skies.
> Let me, if only for a month's term, borrow
> some torment, some gigantic, crushing sorrow,
> and then I'll celebrate life's joyous fling.
> Or, ma'am, why not a bride, complete with ring,
> to be my light, sun, God, my everything?
> You mustn't think I'd plan a life of leisure,
> of fair-ground visits hand in hand – believe me,
> right in the midst of wild pursuit of pleasure
> for deserts of eternity she'd leave me.

13

I need a little spiritual P.T.,
and that might be the finest thing for me.

It is a flippant speech, of course, but it is consistent with what we have heard of Falk's thinking. Certainly Svanhild takes it to be basically sincere as she comes out of her isolation to challenge Falk's sincerity – she hopes, mockingly, that he will be man enough to endure his own philosophy. She suddenly seems hostile, especially when she joins the ladies on the veranda and Falk returns, thoughtfully, to his summerhouse; but it is evident that though Svanhild is with the ladies, she is not of them. She stands amongst them 'cold and mute'.

Now that the tensions have begun to show themselves as fundamentally an opposition between Falk and the rest, with Svanhild's position interesting but uncertain, we begin to take sides. But this the play makes it difficult for us to do. It is easy to feel that Falk's case against society is made during all the chatter about the expected guest, Pastor Straamand, a man of promise ruined by domesticity. It is funny, but there is enough that is also disturbing to explain why, when Falk finds a second opportunity to talk with Svanhild, he drops his bantering tone. His condemnation of the modern age is deadly serious – it is small, petty, unheroic. His own heroic name, Falk (Falcon) seems suddenly appropriate. Svanhild (named after the heroine of the Volsungasaga) is equally serious in her agreement with him; serious enough to attack him for confining himself to heroics on paper only. Their enthusiasm is attractive and well justified.

But then, just as the play seems to be about to simply endorse Falk and Svanhild, it shocks us out of sympathy. Falk throws a stone at Svanhild's favourite song-bird and kills it. He has, or fancies he has, a reason. He believes Svanhild is engaged to Lind; if so, she has killed the song-bird in his breast; he is entitled to this revenge. It is not merely the petulance that is disgraceful here, but the destructive nature of the deed. The wanton killing comes just after Falk and Svanhild have extolled the need for heroic action; this is Falk's action, his sole action so far. Falk seems suddenly very inadequate by his own standards and his philosophy of instinctive, impulsive living very nasty and destructive when translated into deed. A song is one thing, a stone is another.

Svanhild is prepared to forgive and forget when she discovers that Falk loves her, but it seems somehow fitting, after this display, that the sun has been going down and that it is now dusk. Without ceasing to be comic the comedy has become serious. It is still funny to see how nervous the heroic rebels are when they hear somebody coming, but that does not cancel out the thought: is *this* what Falk's philosophy can lead to?

Then the play swings back the other way. The arrival of Straamand with his grotesquely large family, the defection of Styver, immersed in financial worries and subservient to his fiancée, the whole display of domestic decadence is funny too, yet it registers a valid hit on the society Falk opposes. And Falk has to face it alone – Styver has ratted. Lind is about to; Guldstad remains critical. And Falk is much more sadly aware now of the power for degradation of what he is up against. Towards the end of the Act he stands alone for a moment out in the garden that has grown quite dark, staring at the brightly-lit windows of the house. There is no jaunty aggressiveness in his voice as he says:

> All burnt out, dead – so squalid, sad and tame – !
> They go through life in couples, hand in hand;
> they huddle up like tree-stems, blacked with flame,
> left standing after fire on ravaged land;
> nothing but ashes, as far as eye can see –
> oh, is there no green life in anyone!

To judge by what we have witnessed, Falk is right: the situation behind the comedy *is* deadly serious. Marriage does this to people. And this lends a new intensity to his relationship with Svanhild. She is for him the only kindred spirit, as he is for her, now that he has dropped the mask of flippancy.

And yet there begins to show a great difference between them. It was lightly indicated at the beginning of the Act where Svanhild was neither wholly with nor wholly apart from either camp, but now it is amplified. The difference lies in Svanhild's greater experience of life. She may be hostile towards domesticity, but her own career makes her aware of its real power. She has tried to break away to become an artist or an actress, but society has beaten her. Unlike Falk, she has really suffered from the tyranny. Thus Falk may indulge his aspirations in verse that contains no recognition, in spite of his earlier dejection, of difficulty:

> No, triumph's what two souls as one can win.
> We won't attend St Mediocrity
> where only vulgar spirits enter in.
> The goal for self-hood is identity,
> and work for self-reliance, total, true.
> I'll face up to this challenge, so will you.
> Inside your veins a soul-life pounds away,
> your strong mind finds warm, vital words to say;
> you'll never tolerate convention's stays
> about your heart; no, your heart must beat free.
> Your voice will never chant banalities
> in common choir, like lines from hackneyed plays.

She knows better:

> I wanted to strike out in my own way...
> But then my aunts came with their good advice –

and got her a place as a governess!

It is this strongly developed sense of fact that makes Svanhild turn suddenly on Falk when he urges her 'be mine'. He makes no bones about his offer: he wants Svanhild so that he may be inspired as a poet; he does not pretend to offer any permanence of affection. His enthusiasm is fresh and attractive, but again it is questioned. Obliquely by his own language, directly by his fellow-idealist. Falk is callous enough to tell Svanhild that when he has done with her, her fate will be the same as the song-bird's which he killed. The reminder of that petulant destructiveness takes some of the gloss off his enthusiasm. Svanhild strips off the rest.

Falk asks her to be the breeze on which he can soar like a falcon. Svanhild turns the image to show how insubstantial, how self-ignorant Falk is for all his attractiveness. It is not through a sense of propriety or of self-interest that she turns him down, but because of the shallowness of his understanding. What he proposes as a philosophy of living reduces him to a mere paper kite, not free but dependent on the string that tugs him into the air. What Falk is really asking for is the freedom to go on indulging in easy, purely verbal protest, without true commitment. Her experience of life makes her insist that Falk can only truly soar, be truly free, through action in life. He must live his poetry and not just write it. Having insisted on fact, Svanhild withdraws into fact by going back into the house where she has learnt her experience.

Falk is left alone in the garden, a changed man. It is one sign of change that when the sound of a song floats in from the fjord – a song similar in sentiment to the opening song – Falk has nothing to do with it; he has other things to think about now. And yet, for all that has happened in Act I to make Falk see his own immaturities, he remains comically unimpressive. For it is absurd that a young man of Falk's heroic ambition and rebellious nature should try to meet Svanhild's challenge by turning to the middle-aged Guldstad for advice:

> Oh, Guldstad – just a word before – please wait!
> Pick out a mission for me, one that's great – !
> a life-and-death —

Guldstad's reply is justified and salutary:

> (*with ironical emphasis*) Why not try tackling life?
> That's quite a life-and-death affair, you'll find.

And even when Falk seems to be convinced:

> Not words from now on, only deeds, just deeds!

a touch of absurd bathos creeps in through his language. He likens himself to the Creator; he will create a new world; as if that were not enough, he implies a special distinction for himself; he will create his new world on the Sabbath. His arrogance is astonishing in itself, but what truly demolishes it is the effect of language here. His boast is expressed in the form:

> Tomorrow, Sunday – I'll create my world!

which repeats the shape of another forecast that he has just made:

> Tomorrow, Svanhild, we'll become engaged.

The pointed similarity brings the two lines into comparison; and equates the high-sounding 'create my world' with the petty 'we'll become engaged'. When it comes to translating his high aspirations into social action, Falk is ridiculous. He has a lot to learn. Nonetheless he is now prepared for some degree of commitment. As he leaves the darkened stage, and we hear the unheeded song fade away, we feel that we have come a long way from the superficial brightness of the opening scene. But, because of the shifting of the balance, we are a long way from any secure assessment of the parties in conflict. The play inhibits simple judgment.

At the beginning of Act II domesticity seems to have taken over. It is Sunday afternoon; the scenery and lighting are (presumably) the same as for Act I, but all the emphasis is now on the house. The veranda and the room behind are filled with ladies and gentlemen drinking coffee in their Sunday best. It is from inside the house that the opening song can be heard, and it is vastly different in spirit from the other opening song:

> Now you're engaged, you really belong!
> Now you can publicly love without fear,
> Now you can cuddle the whole day long,
> Now you can kiss when the impulse is strong; –
> not worry that someone might hear —

Soon the guests spill out into the garden itself. The air is full of trivial chatter arising out of Lind's engagement to Anna. Society, based on domesticity, seems to engulf everything.

By contrast, Falk seems lost. He wanders about in the garden, but he has no base of his own now and no supporters however fickle. He says little. He watches while the pressures of domesticity destroy Lind's sense of mission in life. The only thing Falk has done so far in fulfilment of his great resolve of yesterday is to wreck the little hut he used to write his poetry in. Once again, Falk's philosophy has emerged in trivial action of a destructive kind.

He does not, nonetheless, run away from the opposition he promised to face, even though it seems overwhelmingly strong. He takes his place on the veranda now, right in the middle of the opposition, the tea-drinking guests, to make his first act of commitment – he attacks by comparing love to tea. It is Falk's best speech so far, but it is not a deed. It is not even an original speech, in the sense that it says nothing that we have not heard before in other forms from him. The impression that nothing truly new is happening is strengthened by the restoration of the original groupings of Act I. As Falk is carried away by his enthusiasm, he removes himself from the veranda and takes up his familiar station in the garden. The shocked company withdraws into the house. The old positions have been resumed.

And yet, although Falk cannot be said to have *done* anything, his speech has done something. It has produced proof of his rejection by society; his friends have broken with him formally and he has been asked to leave his lodgings in the house. The confrontation, though in itself not of great significance, has produced a significant sharpening of the issues and a significant change in Falk. His first response is bitter cynicism – for a moment he mistrusts even Svanhild's loyalty. But when she dedicates herself to his mission, his faith in it flares up again. Only now his experience gives a new definition to it. He refuses to accept the isolation he once demanded for himself. His new mission is not merely to act heroically, but to act heroically within society, to live like others and yet fight the prejudices by which society lives. Falk has made a great advance in the direction of relating his idealism with the facts of modern life. But only in words. They are, as usual, impressive, but they carry less than total conviction. For when these youngsters talk of their heroic campaign within the modern world, their vocabulary is drawn from the romantic past. Svanhild offers to be Falk's squire in battle. Falk will ride into battle like St Olaf to fight his duel with the lie. It is heady stuff, but it is rhetoric that leaves us wondering what it will all mean when translated into modern terms. And there is not much of an answer given us. It seems bathetic again that these high words should produce, as their only outcome, the giving of the engagement ring as token of the change in Falk's philosophy. Falk and Svanhild, who throws herself with gay confidence into his arms, are convinced by themselves. We, as usual, have to suspend judgment.

In Act III, the house has usurped the garden. It is night-time. What takes the eye is not appleblossom but little coloured artificial lights strung up in the trees. There are tables standing around the garden with drink, food, glasses etc. The house is lit up; sounds of piano-playing and singing come from within. The only touch of nature is the strong moonlight. Domesticity is dominant, and Falk is in retreat. He comes on with his belongings and takes a passionate farewell of Svanhild. As in Act I, the imagery of his speech interpenetrates with the imagery of the set:

> We have one hour, Svanhild, all our own
> in light of God and this night's summer-stars.
> Look at them shining through each leafy crown...

Falk is rejecting the petty artifice the garden has become and appealing to nature's distant beauty beyond. It is elevating, but not encouraging as a prelude to meeting society on its own ground as they had resolved to do. And indeed both of them seem to have forgotten what they undertook. They seem rather to luxuriate in a sense of their isolation. Falk indulges in mighty comparisons between himself and the tribe of Jacob setting out into the desert, whereas he is, after all, simply looking for new lodgings. Svanhild betrays a mixture of something suspiciously like self-pity and complacency when she says:

> I was a stranger in my mother's house,
> I was a solitary in my self,
> a guest unbidden at joy's bright carouse –

and when she expresses pity for her sister Anna; not because she is destined to dull domestic life, but because she will have to share her soul amongst many friends, whereas Svanhild has pledged herself to one alone. Falk expressed the mood they seem to share when he says:

> Yes, you and I, the world's unfriended pair,
> we are the wealthy ones; we have joy's treasure,
> we, standing out here in night's silent air
> looking through window-panes at others' pleasure;
> let the lamps shine and let the music sound
> and let those in there dance and swing around; –
> look upwards, Svanhild – up into the blue; –
> up there a thousand tiny lamps shine too –

It is ludicrous, but salutary after this heated stuff, to see Falk fall into a panic at the mere thought of meeting Svanhild's mother. As for actually announcing the engagement, that must wait.

If Falk's, and Svanhild's, philosophy seems at once to insist on confrontation and to make confrontation intolerable, that does not mean that confrontation can be avoided. It is now thrust on Falk. It comes in the form of his meeting with Straamand. If anything could swing the balance of our sympathy in Falk's direction it is this episode, for Straamand exemplifies everything that is demoralising and demoralised in domestic and social living. Falk must be right to despise it and him. But slowly Straamand begins to emerge as more than a clerical clown. This is where Falk has to confront facts he did not suspect. It happens when Straamand talks about home life:

> My home –
> You do know, Mr Falk, what that means – home?
> FALK (*shortly*) I've never known one.
> STRAAMAND   I can well believe you.
> A home is where, for five, there is ample room
> though without love it would be small for two.
> A home is where your thoughts can all run free,
> like children playing round their father's chair;
> where, if your voice taps at another's heart,
> prompt answer of a kindred song sounds there —

Falk tries to brush this aside with mockery but it is forced. And the attack continues to develop through Straamand:

> All right, I'm grasping, stupid, dull – oh yes;
> but grasping just for those God gave to me,
> and stupid from my battle with distress,
> and dull from sailing loneliness's sea —

Straamand is not aware of attacking Falk. His tone is defensive, apologetic. Yet he threatens the basis of Falk's philosophy simply by showing that the society Falk despises is not, after all, utterly contemptible. Straamand is and remains a social scarecrow, but he becomes also a man of humble self-awareness, of toughness of a kind, of endurance for the sake of his wife and children. It is not so easy to scoff at marriage by the time he is finished.

No sooner has Falk recovered his wind – as he does by the end of the interview – than Styver confronts him in much the same way. Contemptible at first, he too reveals a new dimension under a hectoring attack from Falk:

FALK   I know one life can be lived well by two,
          enthusiasm fresh, faith strong as new;
          but you have followed where a mean age beckoned,
          and preach its doctrine: 'the ideal comes second'!
STYVER No, it comes first: because it ends its term,
          like appleblossom – once the fruit's set firm. . . .
          And when our love eventually ends,
          and dies, and we are resurrected friends,
          that song will still bind then and now together.
          And if my back grows, like my desk-top, slant,
          my daily toil becomes a fight with want,
          I'll still return at day's end cheerfully
          to home where memories live in harmony.
          A brief hour there at evening – just us two –
          – then I'll have come off well, I think. Don't you?

Certainly there is nothing in this that could be called, in any way, distinguished, but there is enough to place Styver, and marriage even on conventional terms, beyond the reach of automatic contempt. Marriage, even Styver's, is more than a bad joke: it commands some sympathy, some respect. And this is a threat to Falk's position.

Svanhild shows that she recognises the danger more directly than Falk by throwing herself 'pale and agitated' into his arms after listening in attentive silence – she wants to run away; but even Falk shows by the sheer unjustness of his reaction that he too has been affected:

          Just look at Styver, Lind, the priest, his wife, –
          like painted actors imitating love;
          truth in their mouth but lies within their breast, –
          and yet they're decent people for the rest.
          Each to himself and to each other lies
          but the lies' substance none dares criticise.
          They're shipwrecked past salvation, yet each counts
          himself a Croesus, blessed as a god.

This simply does not square with what Straamand and Styver have

just said about the sober, sad reality of their lives. Falk is being
forced by his sense of the weakness of his own position into over-
statement, and Svanhild is even more afraid now.

At least it can be said that Straamand and Styver know how
degrading life can be and yet what happiness can be squeezed out
of it. The youngsters do not have this kind of experience, not even
Svanhild, and the deficiency shows in their language – as, for
example, when Svanhild says:

> Oh, there's no easier path that can be trod
> than bible's bidding: forsake hearth and home
> and seek the love that leads us on to God.

It is elevated – self-aggrandising would not be far off the mark –
but what does it point to by way of intended action? What *do*
they mean to do? withdraw? stay and fight? stay and criticise?
So far they have expressed noble thoughts about commitment but
have done nothing to commit themselves. They have their
justification – the play has provided it liberally through its many
examples of domestic degradation – but admiration is heavily
tinctured by the feeling that they are still cut off from real experience. And ranged against them now is a domesticity, a society,
that cannot be defined as simply degrading; it has proved itself
capable of generating at least some dignity even in those who
submit themselves to it.

At long last the young couple is forced into commitment by
having the choice between ideal and society presented to them in
immediate terms. Guldstad challenges them in a way which
precisely formulates the ambivalence that by now fills the play.
For he defines the choice not, as once it appeared, as between an
obvious right (poetic heroism) and a manifest wrong (prosaic
domesticity), but between two different but comparable sets of
values. He challenges poetry with poetry, Falk's kind with his own.
He begins by picking up a brief reference to something he said in
Act I:

> Last night I told you I was pondering
> some sort of poem.
> FALK   Yes, one that faces fact.

It is not verbal poetry that is in question. Just as Falk's is less important in itself than as an index of Falk's sense of a poetry of living, so Guldstad's poetry indicates a way of life.

It is one that has much in common with Straamand's and Styver's, but it is purged of their sad, comic meanness. Guldstad speaks as a deeply experienced man. He has known youth and not forgotten it; known love and its degradation and not grown embittered. He loves Svanhild because he knows her and has observed her development carefully. Experience leads him to reverse the values of Falk's poetry. Love, in his scheme, is less important than marriage. Love is blind, it does not take enough into account. The trouble with Straamand and Styver is that marriage means for them just love and nothing else.

So far Guldstad's case sounds more ingenious than truly impressive, but then it takes on weight as he defines positively, both in word and deed, what his kind of factual poetry, the poetry of marriage as distinct from the poetry of love, can mean:

> It is the quiet, the warm-hearted stream
> of tender care that could exalt its object
> as surely as adulation's fevered dream.
> It is a sense of happiness in duty,
> fond sympathy, a home that's quiet and still,
> of wills deferring each to other's will,
> of watching that no stone may bruise the beauty
> of her beloved foot, walk where she will.
> It is the gentleness that soothes each smart,
> male strength sustaining with a willing shoulder,
> the time-resisting steadiness of heart,
> the arm that will support and safely hold her –
> That is the offer, Svanhild, I can make you
> To build your happiness upon; now answer.

This is the most impressive challenge Falk has had to face so far: not from the banal prose of life but from an alternative, practical poetry. For that is what it is. Poetry in contrast to the degraded prose lives of Straamand and Styver, retaining and elevating what was fragmentarily valuable in them and purging all the grotesque imperfections. And practical in sharp contrast to Falk's unspecific idealism. Guldstad defines the poetry that can be created by living

in and through society, by commitment to the facts of life.
The deed that follows turns the thought into action. Guldstad
leaves the choice between himself and Falk entirely open:

> If you can vow to me, with hand and lips,
> that you can offer friendship such as mine,
> such comfort in distress, such firm support
> as I myself can give her – (*turns to Svanhild*) well, that's fine;
> cancel my offer, don't give it a thought.
> I'll still have won a secret victory:
> you will be happy; that's enough for me.

He goes on to divest himself of all unfair advantage by promising
to make over his fortune to them if Svanhild chooses Falk. This is
his poetry, and it leads to immediate action.

Svanhild, by virtue of her keener sense of fact, responds more
quickly than Falk to this challenge. She asks Falk the essential
questions:

> But all the same, if something should destroy
> this love that is supposed to carry all –
> could you provide some other prop for joy?
> FALK   No, when my love died, everything would fall.
> SVANHILD And dare you, solemnly, before God, swear
> that it will never droop, will always smell
> as freshly as today? that it will wear
> throughout a lifetime?
> FALK (*after a brief hesitation*) It will wear quite well.
> SVANHILD (*painfully*) 'Quite well', 'quite well' – oh what an abject phrase!
> what can this 'quite well' signify for love?

The verbal form of Svanhild's painful outburst indicates the
reversal that has taken place in the play. In shape and sentiment it
repeats an outburst of Falk's in Act I.

> 'The next', 'the next' – oh what a nauseous thought
> lurks just behind that flabby phrase 'the next'.

There Falk was distributing the contempt; now it is he who is
being accused of hiding behind words. At long last he is being
made to justify himself.

In the event, neither kind of poetry is discredited. Svanhild is
suddenly inspired to recognise that permanence can be achieved

through loss. Their love can never be permanent in Guldstad's sense because Falk cannot tolerate commitment, but it can be permanent as a sublime inspiration if it is terminated now, in its young glory. To break now is to inspire Falk and to set him properly free, dependent on no person but on memory alone which cannot be defaced by time or habit. When she has brought him to understanding, Svanhild renounces Falk for ever and he her.

The scene restores to Falk and amplifies all the significance that he has ever embodied. The imperfections of his poetry are accepted as necessary conditions of his being his kind of poet and the value attached to that is sublime. Yet the play would be untrue to itself if it ended on that single affirmation.

The loss is painful as Svanhild throws her ring into the fjord. She may see gain in loss when she says:

> Now I have lost you for this earthly life, –
> but I have won you for eternity!

but the loss is more measurable than the gain. Yet she gains elsewhere – that other kind of poetry. Even Falk now – it is the sign of his maturity at last – can see that poetry and living are not impossible for other men to combine:

SVANHILD And you'll strive upwards to your goal as poet?
FALK As poet, yes; for every man is one,
　　　 whether in schoolroom, office, church or kirk,
　　　 whether he's called to high or low condition,
　　　 who glimpses the ideal behind his work.
　　　 Strive upwards, yes; my winged steed waits for me;
　　　 you've touched my whole life with nobility.

Every man *can* be a poet – in the schoolroom, like Lind, in government service like Styver, in the church like Straamand. It is not impossible. And with Guldstad it is certain. We accept what he says:

> I'm starting on a poem of simple beauty –
> about a man who lives for humble duty.

His poem will be his life with Svanhild.

The final balance is very hard to strike. Svanhild has lost so much; as Guldstad says

Something has surely broken in her soul.

She postpones her marriage until autumn as a fitting time. When
she says:

> Now I have finished with my outdoor life;
> the leaves are falling; – let the world now take me.

it takes her in a way that confirms loss – she and Guldstad are
immediately surrounded by the social scarecrows in high glee at
the defeat, as they see it, of Falk. And yet, on the other side, we
know what it is that Guldstad offers. And in any case life is bigger
than Svanhild. She may have lost one kind of poetry and gained
another, but life goes on. And life contains a poet inspired and
liberated by her love; kindred spirits to that poet, other students
like him; and even in the uninspired, in those who may well find
themselves trapped like their decadent elders in the artifices of
domesticity, there is vitality and the same promise that Falk
showed. The young guests who dash out of the house to dance
and sing in the garden speak his language:

> Let's dance in the garden.
> > Life is meant for dancing.
> A dance with fresh spring garlands, sweet, entrancing.
> Let's dance, let's dance!
> > And never cease from dancing.

The joy may seem ironical since we can see what life has done to
others and will do to them. The threat is eternal. But so too is the
vitality. While that exists, while youngsters can believe in spring,
the promise is as eternal as the threat. They speak Falk's language
and Falk has come through – the singing-party he went with into
the mountains can be heard singing their song above the sound of
the dance. Svanhild's loss must be weighed against that gain. And
against the lesser but vital gain represented by Guldstad.

Ibsen has not invited us to take sides. He has explored the greatness and the limitations of idealism, the smallness and the humanity
of society. That they are incompatible, and that the greater cannot
be combined with the lesser is less important to him than that both
are necessary, both in their different ways essentially valuable. The

27

true sadness of the play resides in the fact that the two kinds of poet cannot be combined in one person, the true comedy in the fact that two kinds of poet can, in fact, exist. The play ends not in the initial tone of conflict, but of harmony. As the students' song drifts in from the fjord, most of the guests, the social beings within the house and garden, raise a cheer. Only then does the curtain come down.

The play pleased Ibsen, but he never attempted another of the same kind. Certainly it shows deficiencies. Its irony is uncertain. The use of irony is in itself a strength since it shows Ibsen's refusal to fall into sentimentality over his hero, but, as critics have shown by their responses to the play, it is impossible to be sure where the irony stops. There can be little doubt over many of Falk's weaknesses, but there remain some inadequacies in him which Ibsen seems not to recognise as such, and the same may be true of Guldstad and Svanhild; but we cannot be sure. All that we can be certain of, from the structure and tone of the play, is that, when all reasonable ironies have been entertained, Falk and Guldstad represent concepts that are, in the final analysis, important to Ibsen and Svanhild portrays the perplexity of choice between them. Irony does not entirely cancel out the impression of seriously heroic confrontation between a young idealist and society, however absurd may be many of the incidents and motives in the conflict. The most serious deficiencies of the play lie in its failure to explore the full dimensions of that conflict.

To put it simply, Falk cannot be a satisfactory protagonist in such a confrontation because he is never seriously involved in it. In a play in which Ibsen displays his glee at being able to define his characters as social beings through the language of their professions and social standing, and to show how character and behaviour are moulded by consideration of salary, tenure, and advancement, Falk is left singularly ill-defined in such terms; indeed in any social terms at all. To make him a student was, no doubt, neat tactically, since it gave him the requisite independence; but strategically it is damaging. For Falk, not being subject to the pressures of society, cannot really be in conflict with them. He is not an idealist *in* society, but an idealist who stands, a special and not a convincing case, outside it, having no ties or obligations, no economic or social identity. Ibsen satirises his callow inexperience; but the vagueness of Falk's social identity is something else, and for this Ibsen is responsible. He does not locate Falk firmly within modern society.

The same is true of Guldstad. His dramatic function is to represent the best that can be evolved out of living by the conventions of society; he represents a man who has resisted the degradation that most of the others have submitted to. Yet he, like Falk, is not really called upon to resist; he is exempted by his wealth from the ignoble pressures. In later plays Ibsen recognised clearly enough that acquisition of wealth could itself constitute the closest and most damaging involvement with society, but not here. Guldstad is rich and unmarked by the effort to become so. His magnanimity strikes us more as that of a fairy godfather than as that of a man who has evolved a practical morality through intimate experience of life.

Thus, although we are left in no doubt as to what Falk and Guldstad are meant to represent, namely different relationships with society, neither is truly related. They express ideas, but they do not communicate experience.

If they are not located socially, neither are they temporally. Ibsen's concern in the play is almost exclusively with the present; past and future barely interest him. The three main characters are all in their different ways exceptional yet there is virtually no indication to explain how they have come to be what they are. Such hints as there are are few and they are not developed; Guldstad had to work hard for his money and he was disappointed in love; Falk never knew a home; Svanhild felt a stranger in her mother's house. All of these are potentially important factors in their lives, but Ibsen does not, in this play, see that the past is important.

He is similarly incurious about the effects of the present upon the future. The irony makes conjecture dangerous, but on balance the play seems to suggest that the future will be a simple extension of the final state of things in Act III: Falk will remain for the rest of his life a blithe, free poet, suitably inspired by his experience; Svanhild will remember her sacrifice but will live in subdued and unembittered content watched over by Guldstad's unfailing devotion. Ibsen seems not to have asked himself: 'What would it *really* mean to a girl like Svanhild, or to a young man like Falk to go through so traumatic a renunciation?'

Perhaps it is when we ask 'renunciation of what' that the lack of definition in the play becomes most disturbing. The play evolves into a choice between two kinds of poetry which amounts to choice between two modes of living, one centred on marriage, the other on love. They are presented as being mutually exclusive, so that when Guldstad defines marriage in terms of warm affection, a deep and abiding loyalty, intense and sustained respect, selfless devotion, these terms are denied to love. What, then, can love signify if it does not contain these? when it seems, by definition, incapable of sustaining the strain of any actual relationship? The choice that faces Svanhild is symmetrical but only theoretical and Ibsen, not Falk or Svanhild, is responsible. He cannot give substance where it is most needed.

Falk is the central problem. He is presented as a poet out in the open; acknowledged, forthright, fully articulate and, finally, free to act as poet; indeed his poetry only matters insofar as it is indicative of a poetry of living, a style of being. Falk has no difficulty in demonstrably being a poet; and yet it is impossible to feel fully persuaded by Ibsen's account of him. However heavily modified by intentional irony, his portrait seems not to be free from a certain assertive vagueness that is Ibsen's rather than Falk's. Most important of all, his freedom to be a poet, in either significance of the word, has to be engineered by the dramatist. It is Ibsen who gestures with disarming enthusiasm towards an ill-defined poetry of living, and Ibsen who sketchily and insubstantially creates Falk's relationship, or lack of real relationship, with the society he is supposed to be challenging. Ibsen's first modern hero is a poet of living in modern society only because the circumstances have been specially contrived for him.

My impression overall is that Ibsen has come to formulate an idea of heroism within modern society but has not yet succeeded in turning either component of the idea into imagined experience. The imagery bears this out by its unvarying predictability. Springtime, birds, flowers, stars are repetitiously the images of youthful idealism; mountain and fjord of freedom. Most indicative of all, the language of heroic endeavour does not suggest modern heroism at all; it is carried over from Ibsen's romantic/historical portrayals of heroism of the past. It is the archaic imagery of swords and plumes and banners, squires, single combat and chargers. It looks as though Ibsen was writing about modern heroism without yet being able to feel and express what specifically modern heroism would entail or to understand the make-up of a modern hero.

Yet, compared with the earlier plays, *Love's Comedy* is moving in that direction. Its setting is Ibsen's own Norway; its people and its situations are modern; the language draws upon the idiom of everyday speech; and in that milieu Ibsen is at least trying to give expression, however imperfectly, to his sense that heroism is possible there too as well as in the colourful past. But perhaps the most encouraging sign in the play is its irony. It is not perfectly managed, yet it already makes clear beyond doubt that Ibsen will not fall fatuously in love with his chosen theme. Modern heroism it may be, but *Love's Comedy* shows Ibsen's ability to resist seduction by what most interested him: not by a coldness or remoteness, but by a rigorousness of examination that tests and probes the false spots, the absurdities, the material failures of heroic endeavour, yet leaves him in the end with something intangible yet genuine to justify his admiration, the heroic spirit.

3

'BRAND'

Brand is a work that invites extreme responses. Stark in its situations and characters, it has induced a similar starkness in its critics. It should serve as a warning that these assessments have often been totally opposed. Bernard Shaw, for example, took Brand to be a terrible warning about the destructive inhumanity of idealism; Gathorne-Hardy sees him as a second Christ. The poem is, in fact, far too subtle to support either of these judgments, but the proving of the case is difficult because the work develops through its imagery, rhythm and rhyme, much of which can be blurred or even lost in translation.

The main problem lies in the verse form. The four-stress line, patterned, as *Love's Comedy*'s pentameters were, into flexible variations of the rhymed couplet, has acquired additional expressiveness through marked alternation of rhythm; transitions from iambic to trochaic passages help to characterise a person, a change of emotion, a development in situation. The translator's task of giving some idea of the nature and quality of this organisation of the verse, its formality and variety, without sacrificing the bite and the clean, simple cogency of the language has not, so far, been satisfactorily done, and perhaps it never can be. For there is a further difficulty. To a far greater extent than *Love's Comedy*, *Brand* is intricately architectural. It is full of internal and external echoes, repetitions and references. It may prove relatively easy to translate a key word or phrase and at the same time adhere to the rhyme and rhythm patterns when it first occurs; but it is often wellnigh impossible to retain the same word when it recurs in the context of a new pattern of rhyme and rhythm. The temptation to adopt a slightly different word for the sake of local rhyme or rhythm is strong, but the cost is a weakening of the echo or repetition or reference.

C.H. Herford's translation, which was included in William Archer's set of versions, is wonderfully ingenious. It retains the four-stress line, and keeps close, though not absolutely, to the rhyme schemes. But it does so at the cost of drawing for its rhymes on words and phrases so overtly poetical as to give false colour to the simplicity of the original.

G. M. Gathorne-Hardy has more recently tried to capture the essential poetry of the piece but avoid the frightening difficulties of close reproduction of a form which, in any case, has never become a major poetic form for serious purposes in English, by using what he sees as an equivalent form – iambic pentameters, without rhyme. This attempt fails too. The simple choice of a five-stress line increases the length of the work by a quarter. The extra syllables are sometimes needed to contain the compressed syntax of the original, but often they amount to padding; an adjective, an adverb added here or there may serve the translator's convenience but weakens the intensity. The extraordinarily powerful sense of strong emotion being packed into sparse, clipped utterance is lost. It is also significant that Gathorne-Hardy seems to show, by omissions, that he did not see the importance of the visual imagery.

To recognise both of these attempts as, in the final estimate, only partial successes may seem to recommend the use of versions such as Michael Meyer's, that sacrifice poetical formality to prose-like directness. Here again, the essential structure can be lost. Poetic form, especially rhyme, can invest a word with a kind of memorable prominence that prose or near-prose cannot convey, and without it echoes fail to register.

Because it seems to me that the only answer to oversimple interpretation must be an understanding of the poetical organisation of the whole work, I have provided my own versions. I have not been able to retain in full measure the directness and simplicity, but I have tried to keep as much of it as I can, without being driven to depart from the metre, rhymes and patterns of the original. Thus, where I refer to identity or similarity between words and phrases or to rhythmic effect, it is because it exists in the original and not just in my translation. I have no doubt that in most ways my versions are worse than any that I have referred to; but paradoxically they may be better for the purposes of analysis.

There is nothing in Ibsen's work more decisively characterised than the opening of this poem and yet it is here, in the first few seconds, that subtlety of estimate is called into play. It is a scene of oppressive mist, encroaching darkness, ice and snow, natural violence and danger from ice-falls and storm and from the hidden peril of crevasses. Brand, pressing on without fear through this terrifying place, demonstrates great courage and confidence and the source of these: his equal faith in his mission as God's messenger. Compared with the scared peasants his stature is, from the start, gigantic.

And yet the setting helps to modify this estimate of stature by suggesting for it what might be called a very special temper. Brand as a person, clad in black, harsh and bleak in sentiment, physically violent towards the Peasant, seems as it were part of the nature which surrounds him and in which only he seems to be able to survive. The vague sense of identity between man and environment does not diminish Brand's stature, but makes that too seem to be of hard, inhumane and above all gloomy temper.

Brand has little to say in this first episode – less than the Peasant. To be laconic seems part of his nature. And yet as soon as he is left alone, he expands into a long soliloquy. He behaves like the natural solitary, reticent in company, free to give full expression to his thoughts only when alone. And his thoughts too are indicative of the temper of his idealism. He falls at once into condemnation of the frailty of his fellow-men in terms of broad and confident generalisation. He reveals his notion of a joke, and a very bitter kind of humour it is: he remembers how he used to chuckle at the thought of an owl afraid of darkness, a fish of water, and man of his natural condition. It is the assessment of man's condition that is most disturbing. Towards the middle of his speech, Brand says:

> Each last Norwegian, sick or spry,
> is owl or fish respectively.
> To labour in the deep's his doom;
> he should accept life's murky gloom –
> yet nothing terrifies him more.
> He squirms in panic towards the shore,

his proper star-chamber he flies,
for 'Air and light of day' he cries.

This is a forbiddingly negative estimate. According to Brand, man is absurd in his longing for air and light. And this cannot be accepted simply as a normal severity of moral judgment: it is so unnatural, so exclusive of the essentials to natural human existence, that it emerges as a kind of perversity of judgment. Brand's stature, his courage, drive and tenacity, remain unchallenged; but already he appears to be a strangely twisted character.

If the first confrontation, with the peasants, turns out to be less clearly and simply indicative than might be expected, so too does the second when Brand's thoughts are disturbed by the approach and arrival of Einar and Agnes. Here the stern moralist meets the feckless aesthete and his girl, another conflict of stark opposites. In fact something much more interesting takes place.

When Brand first hears and then catches sight of the young lovers and their friends dancing and singing across the moor, his verse changes character. From the short-clipped, tightly-rhymed verse of contempt, he modulates suddenly into a gentler rhythm and a more lyrical verse form, almost that of a sonnet:

What's that? is it the sound of song?
Yes, song, and with it laughter blends.
Now cheers – and, hark, as first one ends
the next – third – fourth – fifth floats along.
　The sun is rising. The mist lifts.
I glimpse the white peaks through the rifts.
Ah, there the cheerful party stands
on the high ridge, in mornbeams dressed;
their shadows fall towards the west;
exchanging goodbyes, shaking hands...
　Look how light glitters round that pair –
as if the mist had yielded way,
the heather dressed the moor all gay
and heaven smiled on him and her.
Must be her brother. Hand in hand,
look how they bound and leap together.
She scarcely seems to touch the heather,
and he's as supple as a wand.
She's pushed him off; yes, he may try

to catch her, but it's all the same –
she slips him – chase turns into game,
their laughter turns to melody.

For a man who has just delivered himself of that harsh denial of
light and air, Brand's uncensorious interest and aesthetic delight in
this bright scene is remarkable. He is fascinated, he can enjoy it.
Somewhere in the stern moralist lies a capacity to enjoy the side of
life his morality rejects. Brand is already far from being a simple
figure.

So too are Einar and Agnes, though in a different sense. Their
words, taken alone, might suggest a light-weight, frivolous couple
and no more, but they are defined by more than words. Brand's
description of them is amplified and reinforced through the
imagery of the setting: as they approach, '*The sun gradually breaks
through and disperses the mist*'; as they enter, '*The mist has gone; a
clear summer morning covers the mountainside*'. Whatever else they
may be, Einar and Agnes arrive as youngsters who dispel the
terrifying gloom of the first scene; they command an instinctive
welcome from us. The attractiveness does not cancel out the
fecklessness; it co-exists with it; and it is indicative that Brand
should abruptly suppress his instinctive responses to their warmth
and vitality as soon as he finds himself in company again. Thus the
confrontation is far from simple. On the one side the stern, vigorous moralist is also a man who can entertain more clement feelings
which he will not acknowledge and whose refusal gives to his
idealism a bleak quality; on the other, the frivolous youngsters at
least remedy, in part, his deficiencies.

Brand's bleak rigour is given some brief explanation as he talks
to Einar. Speaking of their schooldays, Brand says:

> But I was homeless amongst men,
> yet I believe I loved you then,
> though all you southerners, unlike me,
> were smelted from a different ore;
> I grew on rock beside the sea,
> in shadow of a treeless moor.

Brand's boyhood enters momentarily into our assessment of the
grown man.

The episode ends as ambiguously as it began. Brand reminds us
of his greatness as he describes his call: a world-wide mission to
revive in men's minds a God who is a storm, vigorous and
demanding of total commitment; to piece together fragmented
man into a being God could recognise as his glorious child. Brand
is impressive as he speaks; but when his black-clad figure leaves
the scene, he has become positively identified with the bleakness
that earlier had vaguely characterised him. It is done through
Agnes's uneasy responses:

AGNES The sun has set?
EINAR   No, just a rain-
    cloud passing; now it's out again.
AGNES It's blowing cold.
EINAR   A puff of wind
    that's coming from the pass behind.
    Here's our way down.
AGNES   Never so black,
    that crag that blocks our southward track.
EINAR You couldn't see it while we played
    until his talk made you afraid.
AGNES   Did you notice...
    How, as he talked, he seemed to grow?

The imagery makes Brand seem to act upon Agnes like nature
itself – the grim, harsh nature of the first scene. He eclipses her sun,
chills her like a cold wind, stands like a black crag in her way to
happiness, grows huge. Brand seems elemental; great, but hostile
to natural living.

The setting of the next scene seems to suit Brand's character too,
though its implications become wider. Brand is walking along a
mountain path through wild and dangerous landscape, with no
sense of fear. Looking down from this height into the dale where
he was born, Brand's reaction is familiar – harsh censure of the
place, the people and his home. But on this occasion Brand is not
able to sustain his posture of remote, superior censoriousness.
He hates the place. The dale is small, even smaller than he remembered it; and the fjord is ugly and narrow – but he can
control his feelings towards the merely physical conditions.
His composure breaks, however, for the first time, when he

re-experiences the spiritual conditions that the physical epitomise.

> By that shore, amongst that stone,
> my infant-soul grew up, alone.

His verse registers the impact on him of returning to this place. The rhythm becomes trochaic and the effect here is of greater emotional, less intellectual pressure. Sentences are longer, less firmly controlled by the line unit, giving the impression of feelings too involved to be simply organised into expression. The verse reinforces what Brand says in the central passage of this long soliloquy:

> Crushing burdens bear on me,
> weight of consanguinity
> with a soul bent always down
> earthwards, alien to my own.
> All my glorious plans now fail,
> waver as behind a veil.
> Courage, power, sink and drown,
> heart and soul lose strength and sap;
> nearing home where I was born
> strangeness weights me, dull, forlorn, –
> I awake bound, tamed and shorn,
> Samson in the harlot's lap.

Where physical danger, opposition and seductive alternative have failed, Brand's recollection of childhood has succeeded in shaking his confidence. He is, after all, vulnerable at this particular point. He feels he cannot hope to succeed in his mission in such a place and turns to leave.

The intervention of Gerd may seem a strange interlude. She nearly hits Brand with a stone intended for a hawk which she says is persecuting her. She draws Brand out of his reverie. The verse moves back into a lighter, freer, iambic rhythm and becomes more colloquial. Tension seems to lighten. And yet something of importance, and related fully with the development of the poem, seems to be hinted at in this scene. This is Brand's third confrontation and again it seems to be between simple opposites – sane man with a Christian mission confronting a wild, tormented pagan girl. And yet, as the scene expands, a strange kind of affinity seems to be hinted at. When Brand asks Gerd where she is going, the answer is 'to church' – there is that link between them. When Gerd pours contempt on the church down in the dale, she uses words that Brand employed to describe his birthplace – it is 'small' and 'ugly'. Her church is the ice-church, a natural formation in the mountains, cold, dangerous and deadly – Brand's mission has led him through such territory. When Brand warns her of the physical danger, she warns him of the spiritual danger of the dale, and we know that Brand shares her opinion. Brand himself finally accepts her as more than a mad creature:

> A weak man stays weak; well, he would;
> but evil *can* change, into good.

He sees in her a capacity for commitment, though to the wrong thing, which he respects. His final words about her suggest again some measure of approval:

> That was a church-goer, like the rest.
> In dale, on mountain, who does best?

The question cannot, by now, be an open one. And Brand shares with Gerd a preference for the mountain.

After all that has happened in Act I, Brand's concluding speech in it comes as a shock. It is so inadequate. When Brand defines his future mission as battle against the three trolls of frivolity, weakness and wildness, he seems to see these as qualities in other people, enemies standing outside himself, offering clear and easily identifiable targets. This is a very simple understanding (expressed, incidentally, in revealingly formal patterns and mechanical rhythm) of what we have seen in this Act. It is true that Brand has had three encounters, and that one of his newly-named trolls was involved in each: weakness in the Peasant, frivolity in Einar and Agnes, wildness in Gerd. But we have come to suspect what Brand himself does not, that he himself is not so free of the trolls as he imagines. We remember his moment of unconscious surrender to the charm of frivolity; his moment of weakness as he felt the pressures of his birthplace build up around him; the strange, vague affinity between his very special kind of idealism and the wildness of Gerd. May not Brand find himself with a different kind of battle on his hands? The very neatness of Brand's summary, its formal shapeliness, its simplifying use of abstractions, make us want to see its validity tested in action. And it is towards action that Brand moves, for he moves off downwards to give battle, down into the dale where people live.

Act II begins with a large-scale manifestation of weakness in a setting which at once symbolises it and helps to explain its genesis. In Brand's birthplace, a narrow dale by a narrow fjord, hemmed in by steep crags, served by an old, dilapidated church, the dispirited people queue for their dole of food, but their true poverty is spiritual. When a desperate woman seeks help for her husband who is dying by his own hand, no-one will stir.

Brand is there. His victory over this poverty of spirit seems straightforward, exhilarating. He agrees to sail across the fjord in a gathering storm to absolve the husband; his courage persuades Agnes to leave Einar in disgust and help him handle the boat. If Brand cannot be said to have defeated weakness in this encounter, it has not been one that has revealed any in himself, and at least he rouses the people to shame. But the signal deed receives a more complex colouring from its context. Brand's spiritual temper shows in his tongue-lashing of the folk; less directly in the imagery that identifies him with storm and danger. As one of the peasants says:

> A storm is breaking on the fjord
> as if he'd raised it with his word.

And another:

> As black as raven's wing his hair
> streams drenched in the wild stormy air.

Less directly still, yet powerfully because unexpectedly, through the second intervention of Gerd. She is reported yelling and throwing stones from the cliff. Brand's great demonstration of the power of his will is coloured by imagery of storm, blackness, and tumult; and it is juxtaposed with the actions of the person who epitomises wildness. Brand has, in this scene, confronted weakness and, at least in a preliminary skirmish, frivolity; but wildness he has not come face to face with; and yet so much of it appears in his own actions.

After the storm, the smooth, bright fjord landscape suggests peace following strife. Brand has succeeded in his task; he and Agnes now discuss the event. And yet there is no moment of relaxation in the scene. Brand speaks in a pounding, trochaic rhythm where a feeling of passionate obsession is created out of repetition. Translation defeats me here; I can only reproduce a fragment of the speech where even in the Norwegian the patterning is obvious to the eye. The italics are Ibsen's own, and so are the dashes:

> ...*de* som bare så og så –
> skjønte ikke selv hvorpå –
> *de* hvis sjele fikk en plett
> etset inn som ei de skrubber
> av i tidens slit og tvett,
> selv som bøyde sølvhårsgubber –
> *de* hvis livsens-elv skal rinne
> ut fra dette stygge minne –
> *de* som nu skal gro i lys
> av hans nattegjernings gys –
> *de* som aldri ut kan brenne
> denne tankes åtselbål –
> *dem* han mektet ei å kjenne
> som de to der har i hende
> just det store eftermål –

...*those* who simply gazed and gazed –/could not comprehend at what –/ *those* whose soul received a strain/etched too deep to be erased/by time's cleansing friction/even as bowed and silver-haired old men –/*those* whose stream of life must issue/forth from this hideous memory –/*those* who now must grow up in the glare/of his shuddering deed of night –/*those* who can never burn out/the carrion-pyre of that thought –/*these* he could not recognise/ as precisely the pair afflicted by this terrible manslaughter.'

The cause of Brand's passionate concern is not the dead man but his two children who sat in the hut and watched him die. Their souls will bear the imprint of this experience; perhaps their father's sin will work through them unto further generations. Why? Because it is man's fate. We are our fathers' sons. We inherit sin. And yet we cannot plead this in mitigation. This is the great human mystery. How great a mountain of sin, says Brand, rears up out of that little word 'life'!

This is moral reflection of a different kind. It involves Brand more deeply and more personally than on any earlier occasion. There is no explanation for this, though we may recall that in Act I Brand had showed himself sensitive to his own involvement through kinship:

> Crushing burdens bear on me,
> weight of consanguinity (etc.).

The agitation is strong, remarkable – all the more so for the deceptive tranquillity of the setting – and disturbing. Brand himself is coming under pressure.

It increases with the unspectacular arrival of a nameless man who begs Brand to stay and be the local priest. The folk are putting pressure on Brand now, not he on them; and since this involves not merely the surrender of Brand's world-mission but remaining in a place of painful memory, he does not find the encounter easy. He wins. He refuses and sends the man away; but his reaction is unlike that of Act I. Then he poured scorn on his fellow-men as he watched the peasants crawl away; now he watches this man and his friends go home with a sense of failure in his heart. They go like wretched exiles from Paradise; Brand sees that instead of creating them as images of God, he has made them images of guilt. He tries to revive himself with thoughts of his greater mission, but he has been shaken and, it seems, defeated by this innocent-seeming demand made upon him. Contact with people and their lives is not proving easy for Brand.

It is Agnes who opens a fresh way forward. She speaks almost as though she were in a trance of contemplation, expounding a vision. She speaks of a greater, wider world waiting to be shaped, waiting to be peopled. The world she defines is much like the one we have seen in this poem: of seas and tides, sun-gleam through mists, lurid light on cloud-capped peaks, keen winds and wilderness. She interprets for Brand. This uncreated world, this stirring of the waters, this new dawn is all within; within the heart. The heart is itself a great world. And she hears a voice saying '*this* is the earth that you shall people'. She senses the presence of God brooding over this inner world and she hears a voice proclaiming: 'Perform your task, the heavy burden.'

Brand is swept away. He echoes her word when he says:

> 'Within! within! that is the word'

for she has shown him how he can bear his mission to a world as spacious, harsh and challenging as any he contemplated, without ever leaving this place. He suddenly realises that his world, his sphere of operation, must be his own heart. That is where the new Adam must be created.

It is significant that this new sense of direction comes from Agnes. He seizes on her words, but she utters them first. More significant still is the indication that Brand is wrong in assuming that he has identified himself with Agnes's visionary ideas. When Agnes refers to her brooding God, she gives some idea of what she thinks his nature is:

> And I rather sense than see
> Him who sits in heaven on high,
> feel Him gazing from above
> full of sadness, full of love,
> bright and mild as day's red dawn-glow
> yet filled unto death with sorrow...

A gentle vision, not one that Brand would have subscribed to earlier. But neither does he now. For though Brand imagines that he shares the vision, he goes on to describe his mission within the heart in his familiar terms of strife:

> there the will's vulture shall be slain...

and the relationship between himself and the outside world similarly:

> should we, though, confront as foes,
> should it try to wreck my labour,
> by heaven, I'll return the favour!

Brand has not really absorbed Agnes's vision. He has merely transferred his old militancy to another field. The inspiration he derives is strong but short-lived; he rises to the heights of:

Some place on this earth to be
wholly true to self and free –
that is each man's right in law,
for myself I ask no more.

but immediately crashes into the old, familiar obstacle:

True to self? But weight of sin,
debt inherited from kin?

Brand has used this cluster of terms before, when he brooded over the plight of the murderer's children. Then he asked:

When will they feel weight of sin,
debt inherited from kin?[1]

and the thought, in different words, goes back to his sense of the 'weight of consanguinity' pressing him down. The frequency, the intensity with which this thought seems to recur to Brand suggests how deeply and painfully he feels himself to be involved in the moral predicament he defines. Brand can be made very uneasy on this score, for all his outward strength and decisiveness; he is no longer the man of unchallengeable will he first appeared to be.

The episode that follows amplifies the intimations of this scene. Brand's mother arrives. She brings with her the darkness and cold that form so much of Brand's character. No word of affection passes between them; Brand seems hostile. And yet his mother's presence clearly shakes him. Amongst other indications, his verse slips for a while from terse, powerful trochaics into a looser, more colloquial iambic form introduced by his mother. But his lapse is only momentary. He begins to define his relationship with his mother in terms, and in verse, that make him sound himself again:

One matter must be cleared between us.
From boyhood up I've been rebellious; –
you were no mother, I no son
till you were grey and I a man.

---

1 The degree of correspondence between these two references is not easy to render accurately. My version makes it too exact, but the mere appearance of the Norwegian will show how nearly justified the exactness is:

(a)   Men vekten
     av ens arv og gjeld fra slekten?
(b) Når begynner ansvarsvekten
     av ens arvelodd fra slekten?

He can put his finger on the moment of crisis that broke all affection between them and left a scar on his memories of child-hood – the horrible moment when, as a child, he stood in his father's room, watching his mother ransack the deathbed for hidden money, swooping on it like a falcon on its prey – an image that may link her, though not unquestionably, with the hawk that persecutes Gerd.

This is more than narrative. It explains what Brand means it to explain, namely why he has known no love in his life. It explains what Brand himself cannot see, that his own lack of tenderness towards other people has its origin here; and it suggests, retro-spectively, the reason why Brand was so deeply moved by the sight of the children watching over their father's deathbed. He responded because their situation was once his own. Again, Brand cannot make the connection for himself, but the poem makes it. Partly through the mere juxtaposing of these two similar episodes; partly through a further echo from that cluster of terms that have obsessed Brand. As she tries to get Brand to think about the wealth he will inherit from her, his mother says:

MOTHER Don't probe your mother's mind, son; you
take heritance when it falls due.
BRAND And debt?[1]

Brand's completion of his own, earlier phrase ('arv og gjeld') shows how active it is in his mind, and thus how the plight of the murderer's children has become fused with his own.

Brand is deeply involved in the experiences he narrates – his verse shows acute disturbance – yet he speaks as though he were outside them. He does not see himself as we do, as so deeply scarred by a cold, cheerless, loveless childhood as to be in his maturity cold, cheerless and loveless; so sickened by his mother's surrender to expediency for the sake of wealth that he now wages obsessive war against expediency. Brand is so sure of his own freedom from contamination that his words, besides showing his

[1] MOTHER ...men ta din arv når den blir din
BRAND Og gjelden?

lack of self-understanding, show too a disturbing indication of spiritual arrogance:

> Your son takes all your debt on him.
> God's image, so defiled by you,
> in me shall, cleansed by will, rise new.

Brand is in danger of seeing himself as Christ. But without that essential quality of Christ, love. It is true that Brand promises that he will be 'warm-hearted son and gentle priest' to his mother, but only if she will first meet his essential condition of giving away all that she possesses. Until then Brand will not be warm and gentle. Brand is not like Christ; he is a man who sees himself as Christ yet lacks Christ's compassion.

And yet that impression is not left to stand without modification. For all his hostility, Brand is involved by his filial feelings. As soon as his mother leaves, he speaks in a very gentle trochaic rhythm:

> Yes, your son will stand close by,
> wait your message 'I've amended',
> warm your hand, so cold and dry,
> whensoever it's extended.

Brand does not, after all, lack compassion for his mother; he can feel it, but he insists on subordinating it to his will. That is the peculiar temper of his idealism, and the scene has explored the reasons why it should be so.

In different terms, the scene is another confrontation with weakness; not in strangers now but in a mother. Brand's ideals are being tested in particular and more intimate circumstances, and he is not finding the process easy. He wins in that he maintains his idealistic stance and shakes his mother's complacency, but he shows too that he is very poignantly involved, in ways that he himself does not comprehend, in the relationship he thinks himself able to reform from the outside.

This inner conflict seems at last to purge Brand of some of his hardness. The coda to the Act, when he and Agnes talk together, is gentle, formal – the rhythm becomes trochaic again as soon as the Mother leaves. Einar's intervention when he comes to reclaim

Agnes produces little heat – he is brushed off. Brand wins against frivolity with ease this time. The ending is serene with his acceptance of this new, inward sphere for his mission – the heart – and with the vision shared between himself and Agnes. And yet the imagery casts, almost literally, a shadow. Musing over her experiences, Agnes says:

> Morning's pale compared to evening.
> Then I wanted lies and laughing...

Brand defines the life he can offer her:

> Now I stand where dusk grows grey
> long before true end of day –
> stand between steep scree and sound,
> to the thronging world an alien,
> glimpsing just a streak of heaven –
> yet I stand on my *home's* ground.

Agnes accepts it in preference to what Einar offers; she ends the Act with:

> Into dark night. Through death's shadow. –
> Day shows faint beyond in dawn-glow.

Meanwhile the light is fading on the scene. These images of darkness and night and death colour the serenity of the ending. Life with Brand still means negation. Agnes, it is true, sees with eyes of faith beyond night and death to a new dawn but this is her vision, not Brand's. Indeed that prominent word 'dawn-glow', emphasised by its being the concluding word to the Act as by its intrinsically poetical quality, is another of the echoes in the poem. It is part of her vision of God who was, for her,

> bright and mild as day's red dawn-glow

Agnes has faith in the new dawn, in the tender mildness of God; we have had proof that Brand's idealism remains still fundamentally negative in temper. The imagery leaves the relationship between the two of them unresolved, in spite of the apparent, sure serenity, and in spite of Brand's recent victories over two of his trolls.

Three years later, when Act III begins, Brand has been drawn

47

into even more intimate contact with the realities of living. He has graduated from his position as spectator on the heights, through his closer but still not truly close proximity to others in the dale, to a situation now of complete intimacy. He is married to Agnes and has a son. But more than closeness is implied. With the relationship comes new restriction; Brand and Agnes live in a vicarage overshadowed by a high cliff and surrounded by a stone wall. The fjord is narrow and shut in. It is a terrible place, bleak, sunless, cold, confined.

The setting becomes at once an image of the kind of society Brand is trying to reform and of the effect that society has had upon his own nature. Agnes very soon uses the word 'hard' of him; it begins to chime in the dialogue like a refrain. He is still, as he judges and condemns others, the old Brand; but now only in part of his soul, for in another part, Brand has become more capable of feeling. The Act begins with a demonstration: after three years he is still suffering because his mother has not sent him word.

Agnes and his son have performed a more complete transformation. Brand, who in Act I insisted that it was man's doom to labour in the dark, unselfconsciously adopts the imagery he rejected then to describe the new warmth he has discovered:

> love entered in with you to bring
> my heart a sun-bright day of spring.
> Love new and unaccustomed came;
> my parents never lit such flame.

Brand seems to have accepted what he once rejected. And it seems to have informed his relationships with others. Agnes celebrates – we need some such word to describe her language – his tenderness to others:

> Each brother in want, each son of grief,
> each crying child, each mother's smart,
> at the rich banquet of your heart
> has found a place and sweet relief.

But the transformation is not complete. Agnes places the paradox:

> Your love is hard, though, nonetheless;
> you strike down where you would caress.

And Brand's reply makes it clear that though love has entered into his life it remains subordinate to his old concepts.

> What stands for love in the world's eyes
> I neither want nor recognise.
> God's love I know and understand
> and that's not weak or mild of hand;
> it's hard as death's last frightfulness,
> commands us strike when we caress.

Brand, who has discovered warmth, insists on hardness, and in this situation of conflicting impulses coins for himself and others a new slogan:

> Upon the whole flock, Agnes, lies
> one charge: no coward compromise.

As usual, he feels himself free from the taint, but then his staunchness receives its severest testing, when the Doctor enters.

The scene between them is fascinating not merely for the story – will Brand relent towards his mother, will he save his son's life by giving up his mission in that place? – but for the evidence it gives of the new tension Brand is under now that his hardness is in conflict with his experience of the warmth that love can bring. The Doctor chides him, gently, as a man deficient in love:

> Oh, human will, yes – large amounts
> stand entered in your credit book; –
> but, priest, what of your love accounts?
> that page is virgin, if you look.

– but Brand's behaviour shows otherwise. His mother's silence hurts him now:

> You she can send for; me, ignore; –
> I wait and wait, my heart grows sore.

And when he tries to oppose the Doctor's claims for love, he denounces it with an intensity that is new and hysterical – the last eight lines of his speech end either with the word 'love' or with words that rhyme with it. The effect is obsessive. In the argument Brand is making his case: will must come first, even though it lead to martyrdom; a man must first will his own crucifixion before he can win redemption; then love can come:

> Let will its strength in battle prove,
> and *then* the turn comes round of love,
> love *then* descends like a white dove
> bearing the olive-leaf of life...

The intellectual shape of the argument is clear. But Brand is no longer capable of simple assent to his own rigorous moral logic. His speech totters to a collapse where logic comes into conflict with his feelings:

> To man *here*, faint, degenerate,
> the best love we can use is hate!   (*in horror*)
> Hate! Hate! a war against the world
> lies in that little, simple word.   (*rushes into the house*)

– there to demonstrate the intensity in him of what he tries so hard to deny, for he rushes in to kneel by his son's cot in an agony of grief and anxiety. Brand's doctrine subordinates love, but his feelings do not.

Altogether this Act contains many lightly defined intimations of Brand's inner experience. For example, the moment when Brand returns to the stage. He has seen something in his son's appearance which made him leap to his feet, ashen-pale. Yet his first thought as he comes on the scene is:

> Has no message come?

Only then does he reveal his fears that Alf is ill. His intense love for his child, and his longing for a message from the mother who did not love him as a child are linked; and the fact that his own relationship with his mother comes first in his mind shows how inextricably involved he is, even now, in that relationship. There is much more to Brand than what he preaches.

The intimations proliferate as Brand becomes more and more the object rather than the subject of testing. The time when he could feel remote from those he preached at, or when his involvement was minimal has passed; he is now fully caught up, not merely through closeness of relationship but because his own inner contradictions are being tested. When other nameless men bring a series of unsatisfactory messages from his mother, offering to sacrifice more and more but never all of her wealth, the episode becomes more than a repetition of the earlier confrontation by virtue of the difference in Brand's reactions. Here he shows a new depth of feeling, a new tension between his doctrine and his feelings. The first offer he rejects '*firmly*'; the second costs him more pain; he '*clenches his hands*' to say:

> I daren't use different weights to try
> my kin and my adversary.

The word 'dare' is itself indicative of the temptation he labours under to do just that. Finally there are '*tears in his voice*' as he recognises that he is once again at war with the stubborn weakness of the world. Only now it is reluctant war. Brand has not defeated that troll of weakness as easily as he expected.

He is not all hesitation even so; he recovers his old tone and confirms his doctrine of All or Nothing; yet immediately his '*voice changes*' and he confesses to feelings of confusion; doctrine has become confused through conflict with a longing for tenderness. He yearns to be able to show love to those whom he afflicts with his demands; and again, by mere juxtaposition, a connection is made between this new desire to be tender to others and his tenderness for his own son. He moves directly from:

> I really hungered to embrace.

to:

> Go, Agnes; while he sleeps, watch over;
> and sing him into brighter dreams;
> an infant-soul is mild and bright
> like mountain-pool in summer's light;
> a mother can as lightly hover
> as bird in silent flight can keep
> its beauty mirrored in the deep.

Brand is again using as his own imagery that once he rejected; he does so because his own experience of life now embraces what he once denied.

The impression of dislocation in Brand – for that is what these frequent moments of abrupt transition amount to – is sharpest when Brand sees the Sheriff approaching. At one instant he is speaking poetry that betrays the strong emotion his mother can still evoke in him:

> Why does the sufferer, then, delay
> the word of willing sacrifice,
> of penitence that tears out vice
> by deepest root, by wildest spray?

in the next line:

> Look – ! no, it's just the sheriff coming,
> well-meaning, sprightly, brisk and blooming,
> both hands stuffed in pockets, like
> two brackets in parenthesis.

The sudden change in tone, the uncharacteristic joke, makes Brand seem to be welcoming with relief the appearance of an easier, less disturbing opponent. If this is so, it still does not prevent the scene from becoming one of the blemishes on the poem. It lacks tension. Its purposes are apparent: to provide a range of targets for Ibsen's own satire and, by matching Brand against so puny an opponent, to restore his stature so that, however much we may recognise his deficiencies and incoherences, we never forget that he is also great. The trouble is that by now this sort of confrontation, between Brand and weakness in a simple, external form, is insignificant compared with the inner conflict that has developed. In a sense Brand is not involved here; he has far less to say than the Sheriff and when he speaks it is with simple, undisturbed dogmatic certainty. The same cannot be said of his second meeting with the Doctor.

It begins with thoughts of his mother flooding back into Brand's mind after this relaxed interlude. He watches the departing Sheriff in much the same contemptuous way as he watched the peasants in Act I; but there is now a sudden transition back into involved emotion:

> (*with sudden fear*) The message! message! – No-one comes!
> The doctor, yes! (*rushes to meet him*) Tell me! My mother – ?

She is dead and the news brings out the contradictions in Brand.

Part of him censures her, part of him fights fiercely against the Doctor's advice to be humane; this is the old Brand. The new complexity shows in his inarticulate grief. He censures his mother, but sinks upon a bench and buries his face in his hands; he defends his hardness against the Doctor, but ends his speech by covering his head and sitting in dumb misery. And this is only a prelude to a more intimate probing of his strength of will.

When the Doctor warns them that Alf must be taken to healthier parts if he is to live, doctrine is forgotten, feeling takes over. Brand becomes simply a loving parent; they will go at once. But then he is forced to set his love beside his doctrine, to find that he cannot reconcile them; and finally he forces himself to choose doctrine. The process which leads him to this choice is in itself as significant as the choice.

Brand's natural emotional reaction is checked three times. First when the Doctor, in all friendliness, remarks that Brand makes lighter demands on himself than on other people. Second when a man dares him to abandon the flock that depends on him. It is the third check that is decisive. Gerd administers it; Gerd at her wildest, running, clapping her hands, shouting in wild exultation.

GERD Heard the news? he's off, the priest! –
   Out of caves and up from holes
   swarm the goblins and the trolls,
   big and little, ugly, black
   ow! – they know how to attack – !
   Nearly tore my eye out – beast;
   and they've stolen half my soul; –
   still I'll manage; cope at least
   with what's left me, though not whole.
BRAND Your fantastic mind spins lies;
   here I am, before your eyes.
GERD You? yes, you, but not the priest!
   Down my hawk swooped, from Black Peak,
   crossed the moor, a whirring streak,
   bridled, saddled, fierce and black,
   through the windvexed twilight hissed,
   and a man rode on its back –
   it was priest, yes, it was priest.
   Now the village church stands empty,

barred and bolted up completely.
Ugly church, here ends your story;
My church now comes into glory.
That's where priest stands, great and strong,
dressed in white and spotless vesture
woven of winter's rain and moisture.
Want to come? then come; join hands;
village church all empty stands;
my priest's tongue is like a gong
filling all the earth with song...

Hark, now all the bells together
over mountain-wastes ring out!
See that congregation gather
on its churchward way devout?
Do you mark a thousand trolls
village-priest consigned to sea?
Do you mark a thousand gnomes
until now condemned to be
sealed by him in rock-fast tombs?
Sea and grave no longer hold;
out they swarm now, wet and cold;
mourned for dead and lost, troll children
tumble rock-falls off in tons.
'Mother, father' – hear their cries;
men and women make replies.
Village men parade amongst them
father-like in flocks of sons;
village women clutch their dead,
give them breast that they be fed; –
they stood no more proudly when
they took babies to baptise.
When priest fled, life came again.

This is Gerd's greatest moment, dramatically speaking. She never secures quite so much attention as she does through this series of long speeches, and never has verse of such vitality elsewhere. It would be a mistake to reduce the effect to a simple impression that Gerd is at this moment a demon-figure exulting over Brand's surrender. She distinguishes between the village-priest that Brand has become – a man who works through the ugly little church in the dale, subduing trolls and demons – and her priest, the priest of the ice-church. She is not a demon; the trolls are her enemies, and her spiritual home is still a church; it is to this church that she now invites Brand to accompany her. What marks the speeches is their glee. Gerd is ecstatic that an end has been made to the kind of compromising mission Brand has subdued himself to, because it makes possible the new era of the ice-church; and if this means renewed and savage war with spiritual demons, so be it. Maimed or not, Gerd will cope. And she senses that Brand, now that he can no longer continue in his muted role, is ripe to join her in her wild religion.

Gerd's language is her own; nobody else in the poem could be given these lines; and yet her speeches have a familiar ring. Her contempt for the weakness of the village folk, expressed in those strong trochaics; her stance of spiritual superiority, her rejection of the dale for the wild heights and her claim for her religion of a kind of universality; all these are reminiscent of Brand as, for instance, he watched the disappointed delegation crawl away in Act II. Gerd may be her distinctive self, but she seems also to be an amplification of Brand's original temper. It is almost as though Brand were challenging himself. She represents, as it were, the impulses that had temporarily been subdued by events, Brand's essential self; and her wildness suggests that when Brand yields to the old imperatives, there is wildness of sorts in that decision too. This is the second occasion in the poem where Gerd's intervention has marked some great manifestation of Brand's will.

I find the scene that follows Gerd's departure almost intolerable. The situation is painful enough. Brand tries to force Agnes to choose whether to go or stay and finally decides himself. But the agony lies as much in the form of expression as in the events. Brand sees himself once more as Christ. He tries to drive Gerd away with 'Get thee hence' and similarly echoes the words attributed to Christ by Mark:[1]

> Take the cup of choice from me!

Yet he does not save life, as Christ so often did – he kills. Not only

---

[1] At least it can be said that of the three Gospel versions, St Mark's comes closest: cf. 'tag denne Kalk fra meg' and Brand's 'Valgets Kalk meg ta ifra'.

his son, but humanity in himself and Agnes. Kill is not the right word – suppress, repress intolerably would put it better. His implied decision – implied before openly declared – weighs upon Brand and Agnes to the extent that their last scene turns into a kind of terrifying ritual. They speak in language of extreme simplicity, both in vocabulary and in rhythm. I have not attempted to retain rhyme in my version because I think nothing must disturb the peculiar tension of this passage:

AGNES (*comes close and says in a low voice*)
 Let us go; the time has come.
BRAND (*stares*) Well, which way then? (*points first to the gate, then at the door of the house*)   This? – or this?
AGNES (*recoils in horror*) Brand, your child, – your child!
BRAND   Reply;
 was I priest first and then father?
AGNES Even if the thunder asked –
 there's no answer in this case.
BRAND (*follows her*) You're a mother, answer then;
 here the last word rests with you.
AGNES I am a wife; if you dare bid,
 I will yield and I'll obey!
BRAND (*tries to grasp her arm*) Take the cup of choice from me!
AGNES (*turns behind the tree*) I should be no mother then!
BRAND There's a sentence in that answer.
AGNES (*intensely*) Ask yourself if you *have* choice!
BRAND Sentence, reconsidered, stands.
AGNES Are you sure of God's command?
BRAND Yes. (*grips her fast by the hand*) And now you must pronounce sentence over life or death.
AGNES Go the way your God has bidden (*pause*)
BRAND Let us go; the time has come.
AGNES (*flatly*) Which is our way?
BRAND (*remains silent*)
AGNES (*points to the garden gate*) This?
BRAND (*points to the door of the house*) No – this!
AGNES (*raising the child high in her arms*)
  God! This offering you dare claim
  I dare raise towards your heaven!
  Guide me through life's horrors now! (*goes into the house*)

It is the numbness that is intolerable, the inability to express the feelings the occasion demands. Brand's assertion of will has reduced

two people, one all love and the other capable of love, to partici-
pants in an exchange of tight, clipped sentences that seem never to
dare approach the heart of the matter, their feeling for their son.
The feeling is there, but Brand has made a human event into an
inhuman issue. In a sense he wins. He has met the threat of weakness in himself and has overcome it. But at this cost. And the last
instant of the Act shows that the testing is not over for him. Brand
may suppress his love until the decision is made, but for all his
re-assertion of will he cannot save himself from a contradictory
despair. The Act ends:

BRAND (*stares in front of him for a moment, bursts into tears, strikes his hands
together over his head, throws himself down on the step and cries*): Jesus, Jesus,
give me light!

This is no triumph of will. It is the promise of further conflict.

From the solitude on the heights, to proximity in the dale, to
the family garden of the vicarage; now we see a setting that implies
full intimacy with the facts of practical living. It is Christmas Eve
inside the house. Ironically the light Brand pleaded for at the end
of the previous Act has not been granted. It is dark inside the room
and beyond the windows; Agnes is wearing mourning for her
dead son. She has, through her marriage with Brand, gone into
night, as she foretold when she accepted him.

Her verse is in the trochaic metre that by now marks most
moments of high intensity; heavily broken in rhythm, as she
longs nervously for Brand's return. She throws her arms about
him, begging him not to leave her again. Brand's reply is striking.
Not so much for what he says:

Child, you've got me back again.

– the words, though kindly meant, are neutral. It is the accom-
panying visual image that makes most impact. As he says the
words, Brand '*lights a single candle, which throws a feeble glow over
the room*'. The effect acts as a kind of assessment, almost as a judgment on Brand's deficiency in warmth at this instant, in power or
desire to dissipate the awful gloom.

Brand has no intention of dispelling it. When Agnes weeps for
her son, he orders her to dry her tears. As she baulks at the brutal

fact of the grave, he thrusts at her the word she fears – churchyard. He seems even harder and even stronger than before. And yet the tension that had grown in Act III begins to show itself again.

Agnes can see that his hardness costs him sweat and tears. That is an obvious sign. But there are more impressive though less direct indications in what he says.

> Agnes – why, then I see God
> nearer than I've ever seen him –
> oh, so near, it seemed he stood
> for me easily to reach him...
> And I yearn for heart to cast my
> long-lost self upon his breast,
> heart to be secured, held fast by
> his warm father-arm in rest.

Brand's language expresses his yearning for the gentleness he refuses to show. It is also all of a piece with his past experience; it is the language of a man who lost his father as a child. Brand is as he is because of what he was.

When he tries to force his feelings into subordination to his will, articulating his arguments, he attempts a new formula. Brand quickly rejects his own longing for God the warm, loving father; he must see God as he proclaimed him in Act I, great and strong; and Brand must be prepared to fight and be hard. But Agnes, he says, is a woman; it is her function to love; she may perceive God in this softer guise. Thus he can be hard in pursuit of will, she can be warm and loving. The formula is new but its aim is familiar. In Act III Brand insisted that will and love must be kept separate in time; first will, then love. Now Brand believes that one person can will and another, subject in a sense and inferior, can love. The argument is neat but unconvincing; it satisfies his doctrinal needs, but it does not match the portrait that is filling out of Brand himself, a man torn to bits by his inability to keep his human feelings from clashing with the demands of his will. Brand does not, or will not, understand his own nature or, indeed, human nature in general.

It is ironical that Brand's assumptions of superiority over his wife should be followed by demonstration of Agnes's superiority.

Brand's fixity of will prevents him from being a creative mind. In Act II it was Agnes who, with the word 'within', redirected his mission for him. She does it again now. Suddenly, and by pure intuition, she says that the old church is too small. Brand's reaction is prolonged, ecstatic – he calls her his angel sent by God; her word casts daylight over his work; he ends his speech by repeating the very words of dependence that Agnes used to him in the first scene of the Act: 'do not leave me, do not leave me'. To a remarkable degree, the man who claims that love must be secondary to will depends for inspiration and direction on the woman whose nature is greatly loving.

It comes as a shock to descend from the level of this scene to the following confrontation with the Sheriff. It serves the same purposes as before, to provide Ibsen with targets and to elevate Brand. It is only towards the end that Brand himself seems to be more than superficially involved. When he talks about paying for his new church, there is just a hint that he sees this as a way of cutting off from the past by using up every penny of what he has inherited from his mother. But then he discovers that the past is involved in ways more complex and terrible than that. The Sheriff tells him, as a joke, that Gerd is in a way his mother's offspring, begotten in despair by her rejected suitor. Brand is quick to interpret: his mother's sin against love produced Gerd; Gerd was sent by God at the moment of decision to persuade Brand to remain in the dale; therefore Alf was destroyed through his grandmother's sin. The interpretation shows that Brand's God is the God of the Old Testament. Brand can convince himself intellectually of the rightness of this savage law and can argue that the only redemption for man lies in willing sacrifice, but his arguments again come into bitter conflict with his feelings. Brand can expound his belief, but he finds he cannot pray to this God. He cannot reconcile himself, as he once scornfully insisted all mankind must, to the utter darkness of his fate. Brand shows again how much the need for warmth and gentleness and love possesses him in spite of his attempts to separate them from his will. His cry of desolation is a cry of dependence:

> Light, Agnes – light, if you've the strength!

And Agnes meets the need – not, again, through her words, but through the image that defines her quality in comparison with Brand's. For she brings on the Christmas candles and '*a bright glow fills the room*'. The image reminds us of her great warmth of character and of the coldness that Brand imposes upon his own. Agnes is defined in this moving way just as Brand sets in train the relentless demand that destroys her.

As the scene develops, the poem constantly opposes the two sets of imagery: light, warmth against coldness and darkness:

AGNES   Oh, how cold you are;
      you must be frozen –
BRAND   No!
AGNES   You're proud!
      won't feel the need for light and warmth.
BRAND Hm, 'won't', you say!

Agnes, in contrast, sets the candlestick so that 'the full gleam of the candle' falls on her son's grave outside; she opens the curtains so that her son may look in on the 'sparkle', the 'glitter and gleam' of the festive room. Brand orders her to close the shutters until Agnes feels that everything is 'closed and barred' and she is driven to despair. This is Agnes and this is Brand. His will is great but these are its effects. This man who sometimes seems to see himself as Christ will not suffer his own little child to come unto him.

The Gipsy-woman enters to permit the screw to be given its last turn. Agnes must give up every relic of her dead baby to the gipsy child. But the intruder also helps to strengthen a little the obscure affinity between Brand and this sort of creature. Gipsies, like Brand, seem not to tolerate light and warmth; their natural abode is the wild outdoors.

Brand's final demand on Agnes, that she surrender all or nothing is a repetition of the demand he made on his mother. Brand has not been changed by his earlier experience. But Agnes is different from his mother. She accepts his demand and this leads to one of the most impressive and mysterious moments in the poem. For Agnes passes through her total despair into joy. She becomes radiant, she feels free at last.

For an instant it looks as though Brand has been proved right –

after will has been pressed to victory, then comes the turn of love. But this is not so. Agnes has lost the will to live. She has not come through to a brighter vision but to Brand's repressive vision; it is Jehovah whom she has looked upon. She rejoices that Brand's way brings light while her way leads through darkness – but we have seen the contrary. Brand has not been proved right. The end is not what he expected. Agnes tells him that she will die unless he revokes his demands and restores her sacrifices. At the end of Act III, Brand pleaded for the cup of choice to be taken from him. At the end of this Act an even more terrible choice is forced upon him, with Agnes now making the demand of him, not him of her. When he stands firm, and Agnes goes off, already, we feel, doomed, we are not left with any sense of a dawn beyond night and death but of oppressive night and death alone. A splendid, warm human life has been sacrificed, not to pure principle, but to the exigencies of a will that is at once magnificent yet contorted and unaware of its own deformity.

And yet the setting of Act v seems to confirm something which Brand said near the end of the previous Act:

> Total loss brings wealth in train: –
> only loss brings timeless gain.

– for out of the devastating losses of Act IV a new church has been created. It stands completed and decorated for the consecration. Eighteen months after Brand chose to let Agnes die, the church she inspired is ready. But only as a travesty of what was intended. Petty officials set the tone – the building is a useful addition to the Establishment. This is the gain.

Brand's crashing discords on the new organ express his anguish; the speech that elaborates on his state of mind does more than simply confirm. It shows that Brand is floundering. He still cannot pray; God still seems remote and terrible. The church is not what he intended. Why? Because it lacks inspiration. It would have been different if Agnes had lived. Brand, it seems, has deprived his will of inspiration and direction by sacrificing Agnes, paradoxically by insisting on the subordination of love to will. And this shows in other ways.

In his dialogues with Dean and Sheriff he lacks force because he no longer knows positively where he stands. He shows a new strain of exaggerated violence as he contemplates the departing Sheriff – not the censorious contempt he showed in Act I towards the peasants, or the more humane regretfulness of Act II towards his dejected petitioners, but a violence that suggests desperation:

> I'd like to crush him with my heel!
> Each time I try to make him rise
> in spirit above tricks and lies,
> he vomits out his rotten soul,
> regardless, in my very eyes! –
> Oh, Agnes, why were you too frail?

How far the travestying of his hopes has driven Brand can be sensed from the different way he now refers to God's dove. In Act III he was confident: once will had triumphed in the fight

> and *then* the turn comes round of love,
> Love *then* descends like a white dove...

Now the same image is used to express despair:

> God's dove of brightness sits concealed;
> alas, it never swooped on me –
> if I met *one* who *did* believe –
> and gained assurance, ceased to grieve!

Yet when his wish is apparently granted by the arrival of Einar, travesty is added to travesty. It is illuminating that Brand does not, in fact, greet him as a true believer. His welcome shows what his needs really are: warmth and human feeling. He welcomes him as a man not made of wood or stone; tries to embrace him; tries to interest him in news of Agnes and the baby; but only to discover that Einar, pale, emaciated, dressed like Brand in black, has become through Brand's influence a travesty of Brand – bigoted, stupidly doctrinaire, inhuman. For the second time Brand is forced to contemplate the grotesque failure of his influence to regenerate. The cumulative effect is to break the last link with the scene of his failures, and at this his eyes brighten. He is glad to be alone.

Brand's new sense of direction shows as he addresses the crowd. He finds he can identify his great mistake: by building the church, he had entered upon the way of compromise, which he now denounces as the arch-enemy, Satan. Brand has become totally dominant again and his voice sounds like that of the old Brand before he floundered. And yet his apparent recovery is marked by two qualities. The first is wildness. Brand recovers his sense of direction in a scene which begins with the crowd bursting in with '*wild disorder*'; it cries out with rising excitement, shouts, screams. The wildness seems to colour the moment; it is more than a mere accompaniment. Brand causes the wildness and he shares in it.

The second is sameness. Brand is repeating himself as he was earlier in the poem. His denunciation of those who call on God for mercy is in the same spirit and tone as his denunciations in Acts I, II and III. Furthermore he is back at his old task of haranguing the folk, fighting weakness in other people; he is planning to return to the wilderness in which we first encountered him. This is the old Brand repeating himself; he seems to have learnt nothing from his experiences.

Indeed he seems positively obtuse of feeling. How else could the man who doomed his wife and child to death in terrible gloom, darkness and constraint summon his flock to obey that same destructive will in these terms:

> Come, men and women, while each face
> still bears roses, childhood's grace,
> congregate in life's great church.

The Agnes we remember was pale, Alf died in infancy. Or the man who forced his wife to shut their dead son off from the Christmas brightness use such words as these?:

> There with daily task shall be
> mingled flights to starry way,
> Christmas tree and children's play,
> David's dance before the Ark.

Brand does not speak in this way because he has changed his doctrine; he does not recognise the gruesome incompatibility. Wild as his flock now, he leads them on the first stage of his journey back into the wilderness, to break their, and his, long truce with compromise.

Brand has recaptured his old vitality but his greatness is even more heavily modified by the setting of the next scene. The crowd has reached the highest mountain hut in the district. Mountains rise up behind. It is the setting for high and stern endeavour, but it is bleak and miserable; the mountains are a wilderness and it is raining. Brand's leadership takes us back into familiar gloom not forward into the life and joy he promised. It seems right that the steep path he has chosen should have led them all close to the ice-church.

Nonetheless Brand succeeds for a while in whipping up the energies of the folk, to the extent that they begin to speak to him as to Christ – hail him as prophet, ask for miracles. And Brand is ready to accept the identification. When he defines man's final reward it is as:

> A crown of thorns for each man's brow –
> lo, that shall prove thy recompense!

The archaic language, the obvious reference, show the familiar direction of Brand's mind: he is once again equating men in general, himself included, with Christ. When the people turn against him, crying 'slay him' as the Jews cried 'crucify', when they drive him out into the wilderness with stones, the self-identification becomes dangerously complete.

With the next scene the sense of repetition is complete. Brand is back in the atmosphere of Act 1: '*On the great mountain plateau. The storm is gathering and drives the clouds in heavy masses over the snowfields; black peaks and summits stand out here and there and are veiled again in the mist.*' Brand is again alone, engaged in his old task of judging the weakness of others as though he himself were not involved in weakness. Even the long, scathing survey of modern Europe, surely a sign of Ibsen's desperate eagerness to bring his poem into direct relationship with the modern world, has some justification through contributing to this sense of self-righteous isolation. Brand has returned to his beginning.

There is, however, a crucial difference. However little Brand acknowledges intellectually the experiences he has undergone, he has been marked by them emotionally. He lacks his old confidence.

His survey ends with his throwing himself down in the snow and covering his face.

Throughout the poem, Brand has exercised his will on other people, fighting the trolls of weakness, frivolity and wildness in them. Now that he is alone, he has to fight the trolls within himself. That at least is what seems to happen in the series of temptations he now undergoes.

First his weakness is tried by the Chorus of invisible voices. The thoughts they express are thoughts that have occurred to Brand but been rejected. Now they come back. At the moment when Brand wonders whether his whole life has not been a sick vision, the Chorus amplifies his doubts about the accessibility of God, about the worth of his sacrifice. Brand seems ready to collapse under the challenge of weakness; he sits in the snow dejected by loneliness, calling on Agnes and Alf.

The first test merges into the second test – by frivolity. An apparition appears who is Agnes. Yet little about her recalls the Agnes who was Brand's wife. The references go back to the Agnes of her first appearance. The apparition coincides, as Agnes's first entry did, with the effect of brightness breaking through the mist. In that early meeting, Brand called out in warning:

> Stop, stop! there's an abyss behind.

Now it is the apparition who calls to Brand:

> Don't cross over!
> Look at the chasm that's between us!

The apparition invokes sun and summer as Einar and Agnes did. Brand is reacting to the attractions of the life of frivolity.

And yet the apparition is also externally Agnes the wife and mother. It repeats, almost exactly, the words Brand used to Agnes at the beginning of Act IV:

> Brand, you've got me here again.

– and it refers to the son and the grandmother. The apparition does not represent the life Brand knew but sacrificed; it reminds him of the life he might have chosen instead, soft, cosy, safe; it stands for the rejected alternative from his past.

Brand is sorely tempted by these appeals from his sense of weakness and his longing for a less rigorous life, but he does not fail. But neither does he change. Again the effect is of repetition as Brand says that he would relive his life in exactly the same way. He has overcome his self-doubts but only to resume the old path that leads to disaster and deadlock. But there remains his third trial.

When Brand reaffirms his mission, the apparition vanishes. The mists close in again – this has been a delusive dawn. There is a 'shrill, piercing shriek' from aloft and Brand glimpses a hawk-like figure which he identifies as his old arch-enemy, compromise. This moment could be taken as a symbolic representation of Brand's victory in this crisis over that which he feared and detested most. But it is much more complex than that. For the hawk has been not only Brand's foe but Gerd's too, and the two are brought together as Gerd comes on with a rifle.

They are brought together to confirm the affinity that has been hinted at before in the poem. When they met in Act I for the first time Brand could not see the hawk:

GERD   Didn't you see the hawk?
BRAND Here? No.

But now it is different and the comparison is invited:

GERD   Did you see the hawk! the hawk?
BRAND Yes, my friend; this time I saw him.

Gerd suggests they hunt it together. Brand and she are more closely identified.

Indeed Gerd turns out to be as much the mouthpiece for Brand's own thoughts as the Chorus and Apparition were. She expresses Brand's own sense of himself as Christ and tempts him into full self-identification. Under her impulse, Brand lets himself fall into a kind of ritualising of his own sufferings:

GERD   Why, you limp, priest, in one foot.
BRAND I was hunted by the people.
GERD   Brow as red as blood from heart-root.
BRAND I was smitten by the people.

GERD   Once your voice sang, loud and clear
          – now it crackles, withered, sere.
BRAND   All the people –
GERD   What?
BRAND   Betrayed me.

Gerd sees Brand as the greatest of mankind; Brand confesses to the same thought:

> Like a fool I almost thought so.

Brand has come close to self-pity, self-dramatisation and worst of all, spiritual arrogance. Not for the first time in the poem, but most strongly now, he is tempted to identify himself with Christ.

This I take to be the reason why Ibsen's imagination fused together the figures of Gerd and Brand. His spiritual arrogance, his certainty of being God's messenger, redeemer, physician to mankind is his peculiar form of wildness, the hardest temptation to overcome. The climax of the poem is his overcoming it.

For when Gerd tempts him too hard to make the blasphemous identification Brand suddenly becomes, not with part of his being but with the whole, a different man. He sets aside the tempting thoughts in language that still suggests his self-image – 'Get thee hence' he says – but after that he becomes totally humble:

> I am the meanest worm that crawls.

The significance of the moment is marked by the imagery that accompanies it: the clouds begin to thin, and his progressive transformation is reflected in elaborations of natural images of cloud and sun, cold and warmth. Through the clearing mists he discovers where his mission has led him: to the ice-church. The promise of identity with Gerd that was offered in Act 1:

> That was a church-goer, like the rest

is confirmed here by Gerd's:

> Church-goer you became at last!

His spiritual arrogance has led him to this church, this dreadful end; but now Brand can acknowledge how terrible it seems to him:

Rather a thousand miles from here! –

Now he longs, openly and without reservation or subordination, for what he once repressed, and he calls upon Jesus in a new tone of humble supplication:

> Oh, how utterly I hunger
> after light and sun and mildness,
> after peace and sabbath-stillness,
> after life's warm realms of summer! (*bursts into tears*)
> Jesus, I have often called thee;
> Never once dids't thou enfold me;
> thou camest near, but like vain diction
> gliding off the tongue, slipped past;
> of thy mantle of redemption,
> dipped in wine of true contrition,
> let me touch the hem at last!

As he speaks, he weeps. Brand has wept before but never so significantly. His weeping marks his release, at last, through humility and acknowledgement of love, from the icy sterility of his life. Through the imagery this becomes the turning-point of the whole poem. His movement of spirit becomes large, magnified by the movement of nature.

GERD   What's this? You are crying, man,
          warm tears, and your moist cheek steams –
          warm, and now the ice-shroud streams
          dripping from each peak and crest –
          warm, and frost-bound memory
          thaws to weeping inwardly –
          warm, and down the vestment glides
          from the glacier-priest's chill sides – ! (*trembling*)
          Man, why no tears shed before?
BRAND (*in a clear voice, radiant and as though rejuvenated*)
          Hold to law's grim, icy way –
          Heaven sends summer to repay!
          Till this day I had to be
          tablet for my God's decree; –
          from this day life shall transform
          to a poem, rich and warm.
          Now the crust breaks. I can cry,
          I can kneel down, – I can pray!

'Man, why no tears shed before' – tears of this gentle, humble, cleansing sort are what we have missed in Brand. By weeping he liberates himself – a magnificent liberation – into complete humanity at last, and into communion with his God such as he never achieved before.

Brand seems to have come through as he foretold and as he still believes. His mission was to follow the icy path of God's law to the bitter end and then the moment of love could descend. Brand still sees his life in the old terms as justified even though he has passed out of involvement with them. Yet that in itself is enough; because he has passed beyond the need for obsessive will, Brand need no longer be haunted by his arch-enemy, compromise. The killing of the hawk is for Gerd the hour of redemption, the time when she will no longer fear. Her wildness drops away as Brand's arrogance drops away. For neither does their demon hold any further terrors; Brand need not be haunted any longer by fear of compromise now that he has thrown himself upon the love of God.

And yet this is not quite enough. Brand cannot simply escape from his past life. The white dove of God does descend on Brand and Gerd together. The hawk is shot; the ice-church shatters into avalanche and buries them.

Brand still cannot understand why God's love should show itself in his destruction. Brand's transformation is still not total. He still believes that his death proves that every child is doomed by parental guilt. He dies on his knees yet still looking upwards, still arguing. But he no longer speaks with his old dogmatic certainty. His last words are, uncharacteristically, in the form of a question, and, by recalling the words spoken years earlier by the humane Doctor, they show that his mind now entertains, at least as a possibility, that alternative philosophy of love:

> Though I die, God, answer still; –
> does large store of human will
> count for nothing there above
> towards redemption – ?

Brand dies a changed man but not changed out of all recognition. No man can be; the past cannot be undone. He does not hear the answer for the avalanche buries him, but we do. A voice calls through the thunderous din a message that proves the Doctor right after all:

A VOICE   God is love.

We hear and understand better than Brand himself the mystery of his ending. Brand is destroyed because no man can re-make his life. No man can grow up in coldness, dedicate his life to the icy fulfilment of his will, subordinate and sacrifice love, and then emerge transformed into warmth and humanity and love. Brand can change, but the change is such that it can only destroy the man. Brand is destroyed because he served God in the wrong way, suppressing love. Brand was no Christ. If any doubt remains, consider the ending in relation to Matthew III. 16–17, IV. 1; I have italicised the common terms:

III. 16.   And Jesus, when he was baptised, went up
             straightway out of the water: and *lo, the*
             heavens were opened unto him, and he saw the
             Spirit of God *descending like a dove*, and
             lighting upon him;
III. 17.   And lo, *a voice* from heaven, *saying*, This
             is my beloved Son, in whom I am well pleased.
IV. 1.   Then was Jesus led up of the spirit into
             the wilderness, to be tempted of the devil.

Ibsen follows the sequence closely:

GERD   *Heaven's tent expanded* wide,
         ten-fold wider, as he died!
         Look, he's tumbling...
         White indeed, just *like a dove...*
A VOICE (*calls* through the thunderous din)...

There seems undeniably to be a parallel. Yet every parallel involves distance between, and the distance here between Jesus and Brand is manifest. Jesus knew he had the love of God before he was tempted in the wilderness; his baptism inaugurated his mission to men. Brand is forced to undergo his temptation in the wilderness without that certainty, and his baptism is the termination of his mission. Instead of acceptance, destruction. And the reason lies in the greatest discrepancy between the texts. Instead of 'This is my beloved Son', the Voice says 'God is love', and says it as that God seems to destroy a man still arguing for will against love. Ibsen seems to invoke the parallel to stress the distance between them. God kills Brand because Brand has not lived by love.

And yet the ending does not feel like a simple rejection. Brand's end is, after all, magnificent. He matters, he involves the whole of nature about him, he prompts not the indifference but the intervention of God. His ending comes after that astonishing moment of liberation which proved what richness lay locked up within this man. And his ending seems to be caused by a God of love, of heavenly love and charity. It seems possible that his death may also be an acceptance by a God capable of recognising the greatness with which Brand has tried, mistakenly, to serve him. Rejection and acceptance, judgment and love. A difficult fusion, yet how right at the termination of Brand's great career. For Brand has emerged as a magnificent imperfection; a great inspiration in a world of mediocrity, a great seeker for perfection in a world complacent with imperfection. Set Brand against his fellow-men and his greatness is clear. Yet he is himself imperfect. Because of his past the temper of his idealism has been loveless and cold and hard; he has done terrible things. Our judgment must encompass both the magnificence and the imperfection; the ending of the poem is a superb fusion of both.

Brand, like its protagonist, is a magnificent imperfection; imperfect largely because it fails to accommodate together three different modes of writing: the modes of social comment, symbolism and realism.

Approximately one third of the work is given over to social comment expressed mainly through confrontations between Brand and petty officials, most of them occurring in the last two Acts. It is reasonably easy to guess at Ibsen's purpose. In choosing an isolated rustic community in a remote dale as the setting for the action, he had lost that immediate reference to the world of his audience that *Love's Comedy* provided. He gains in concentration and intensity, but loses in immediacy and in breadth of social

71

reference. *Brand* is an emblem of modern society. Ibsen's indulgence in discursive social comment looks like an attempt to restore to the emblem that immediacy and that breadth, but it does not fully succeed. These confrontations, for all the emphasis implied by their sheer extent, are not impressive; symptomatically, Brand seems less involved in them than he is in less obviously challenging circumstances. The writing is pointed and amusing but there is little or no pressure behind it, and it is too long. Ibsen seems to feel the need to insist that his work relates to modern life by throwing in every reference that occurs to him, without regard to balance or due emphasis or relevance. He has made *Brand* a modern play but at the price of flaccidity.

The jolts are painful as one moves from the mode of social comment to the mode of symbolism. The work is congested with symbols – snow, mountains, mist, hawk, ice-church, sun, dove, Gerd. It is not that they are chaotically organised, but that they compete for attention. It is as though Ibsen, having chosen a small-scale emblem, wished to emphasise the significance behind the smallness and chose to do so by wealth of symbolism as he chose sheer wealth of social reference. And this causes problems. One is that with so many symbols competing for his attention, he does not always secure the right emphasis between them. The most striking example is the symbol of the hawk. Ibsen reserves the word 'hawk' with almost total consistency for the purpose of symbolising what is gradually revealed to be not only Gerd's but Brand's particular enemy, namely compromise. The moment when compromise ceases to haunt Brand is the crisis of his life. But the work seems to invite us to relate his haunting by compromise to the fact that he learnt to hate and fear it from the example of his mother who compromised fatally by sacrificing love to wealth. The point is made in other terms, but only dubiously through the symbolism. For although Ibsen comes close to establishing the connection between son and mother in this regard, there remains a faintly disturbing fuzziness. Brand likens his mother to an eagle and to a falcon, not to a hawk; and although these birds of prey might seem adequately to suggest the link, they are not used with the same consistency elsewhere in the play, and in any case are made to seem different in significance by the symbolic consistency of 'hawk'. Ibsen has not quite satisfactorily defined one of his most important symbolic connections.

Furthermore the symbols are of a kind to invite straight translation into other terms; we feel that each has an equivalent meaning which it is its function to represent. This induces what might be called an intellectual curiosity which, in my own experience, sometimes inhibits emotional response to a crisis: the problem is especially acute in Act v where Ibsen brings together the various strands of symbolism and thus makes demands so heavy as to be confusing on our understanding.

On the other hand, Ibsen uses symbolism far more impressively in *Brand* than in *Love's Comedy*. It is no longer repetitive. Symbols recur but now with a slightly different charge of significance; they register change and development in the essential progress of the poem, and in consequence Brand emerges as a man involved in a constantly varying two-way relationship between himself and his environment, each constantly changing and being changed by the other.

If we cannot help but notice the disconcerting discontinuity, in terms of intensity and quality, between the social and the symbolic modes, then the discrepancy between both of these and the mode of realism is even greater. The most effective part of the poem is apparently the most narrow in social reference and the least obviously elevated in significance; it is Act iv, where Brand confronts Agnes within the walls of their home. This Act comes closer to substantiating them as individuals than any other part of the poem; and because of this the thin typicality of the Sheriff (for instance) and the exclusively symbolic identity of Gerd seem in comparison forced, almost didactic in their narrowness of purpose.

This discontinuity between three different modes gives the poem the appearance of trying to cope separately with three aspects of one complex problem. To explore the possibilities of heroism within modern circumstances, Ibsen needs to create the social circumstances in an idiom related in scale to the society he portrays; to express the nature of a modern hero's experience within those circumstances in the idiom of personal experience; and to convey his sense of the inherent significance generated within the small scale of his chosen material, in the idiom of symbolism. Ibsen achieves at least partial success in each endeavour, but he does not succeed in fusing them together artistically. There is not enough pressure of imagination at work yet to play equally over the whole range of his problem. He does not quite fully understand what modern heroism in terms of actual living would amount to. But *Brand* is, nonetheless, a tremendous advance in the direction I surmise Ibsen to be travelling.

Brand, being an emblem of social reality rather than a portrait, could be said to be more remote from the world of Ibsen's audience than *Love's Comedy* and to this extent not an advance but a retreat. This is true only superficially, for *Brand* grasps the essential that *Love's Comedy* lets slip. In *Brand* Ibsen shows that he is beginning to understand what involvement in modern society means. Falk was involved intellectually but was not located in any real relationship. Brand is much more fully located; he has a job, parents, wife, child, a place of work, obligations and responsibilities. His present is related to his past so that we feel the constant tension between his conscious aims at any one moment and his unconscious responses to past experience. He is placed in situations where words are not sufficient; unlike Falk he has to choose and act, and Ibsen can see now how, in so tight a web of relationships, such a man as Brand cannot move a finger without consequence.

Ibsen may not be able to give a fully satisfactory artistic form to this sense of intricacy, this inevitable and complex involvement of an individual in modern society, but his poem shows that he has at least begun to enter into imaginative possession of the theme. It is this that makes the poem so much more impressive than the earlier plays.

One thing *Love's Comedy* and *Brand* share in common: articulateness. Falk and Brand can both reasonably be described as poets of living. Falk is important less as a poet in the technical sense than as a young man with a vision of how life should be lived. Brand, different though his kind of vision is, is in the same sense a poet. And both are able to articulate their poetry. Each has a clear vision, not necessarily of the full intricacy of their situation, but of what it is they strive for. They are able to express this in words and sometimes in deeds. They are able to recognise moments of crisis in their lives, and to give an account of what those moments mean to them. Ibsen seems to envisage that his modern hero, whether lightly or tightly involved in his social circumstances, is able to preserve what may be called his essential self, that part of him which generates the idiosyncratic sense of mission, not merely uncontaminated by circumstances but within reach of the intellect and within the possibility of definition through words.

To say this is to praise or blame neither play; but this confidence that a poetry of living can be articulated by and through the modern hero is a crucial point of contrast with the later plays.

4

'GHOSTS'

The play opens by creating something like the atmosphere in which *Brand* begins: a gloomy fjord landscape, shrouded in steady rain. But here the landscape is framed and distanced by being seen through the large glass walls of the conservatory at the back of the stage; it is no longer the whole setting, but only part, and out of this the distinct character of *Ghosts* begins to emerge. The landscape stands in contrast to a domestic setting that is very different.

Ibsen himself has indicated, in a letter, what the main stage should look like: Mrs Alving's garden room would have a plain, wooden ceiling and wainscotting, sombre wall-coverings and furniture in First Empire style but with covers of a darker hue. But dark though it might be, it is also attractive: spacious, we know it to be; tidy and well-appointed we may assume; books, periodicals and newspapers suggest intellectual liveliness, and there are the flowers in the conservatory to lend a touch of brightness.

It is these that help, unobtrusively, to suggest the relationship that exists, imaginatively speaking, between exterior and interior. With all that rain outside, the maid, Regine, has been watering the plants. This little touch helps to focus the impression that this room is a protected, artificial haven from the awful weather; a haven which, from rise of curtain, is under threat of invasion. Regine, garden-spray in hand, is trying to repel Engstrand the carpenter, and he is presented as a creature of the outdoors. He is dripping wet, yet wears no protection against the steady rain; the first words proclaim his acclimatisation: 'It's God's own rain, my child.' His deformed left leg and thick-soled boot add a faintly distasteful touch to his intrusion. The outdoors is his element and he seems to threaten to bring it into the house with him.

The scene between the two serves the obvious purpose of exposition – Mrs Alving's son has arrived home for the dedication of her memorial to her dead husband, Regine has an interest in Oswald, Engstrand is a bully, a drunkard, and prospectively the owner of a bawdy-house – but it also begins to define the social situation to which we are being introduced. For Regine and Engstrand share the habit of using two distinct languages.

Regine's natural idiom, which she demonstrates freely in what is clearly only the latest skirmish in an unending family row, is coarse and common. It suits her sentiments towards her 'father', and it indicates her social standing. But from time to time she shows evidence of aspiring to a more 'respectable' kind of language, that of the class for which she works. Her pathetic scraps of French are part of the evidence but her 'second' language comes into play more evidently when Pastor Manders comes on, and its nature is prepared for by the way she reacts to him. One moment Regine is threatening to clout Engstrand; the next, she is busy at the mirror, restoring her appearance to the right kind of demureness; she returns to the decorous task of tending the flowers; she, who was callous towards her 'father' – and however false that relationship, Engstrand is the nearest she has to a relative – fusses over and pampers the Pastor. She is putting on a show of manners, and it extends to her language. She hastens to correct a mild colloquialism in her speech: 'He did the whole trip from Paris in one go – I mean, he travelled the whole way by one and the same train'; where she uses not merely a more formal run of language but an uncommon word for 'train' to emphasise the difference in idiom. She begins to use an 'educated' catch-word, 'awfully': Oswald is, she says, 'awfully tired', and she herself will be 'awfully necessary' at the Orphanage. Not only does she put this on for Manders, but he seems to be the source of her verbal habit, for he has his own polysyllabic catch-word: 'positively'.

For the most part, the pains that Regine takes in language and in manner to present an ingratiating front to her social superior are amusing, but something more is hinted at behind the comedy. It is amusing to watch Manders struggle vainly against the spate of entreaty Regine directs upon him when she tries to enlist his help to find a new position – until we register that in all seriousness Regine is alone in the world, that she is very lonely in this isolated household, and that pleading for the interest of someone like

Manders is her only hope. It is possible to see her concern for propriety of language and manner as an indication of the sort of society she lives in: to get on, one has to behave, look and speak as society expects one to.

Engstrand also uses two languages. His first is a coarser version of Regine's: 'out on a binge', 'half-seas over', 'what the hell' are characteristic. His second, high-lighted by being jammed into close juxtaposition with his first, is larded, not with directly social clichés as Regine's is, but with clichés of a moral or religious kind. 'I was out on a binge last night. Yes, for we humans are weak, my child'; and '...when I was half-seas over...Temptations are manifold in this world' are sequences of this sort. There are other clichés: 'God's own rain', 'a father's guiding hand', 'what a child owes its father' etc.

This interplay of languages serves first of all, and obviously, to characterise Engstrand as a gross hypocrite; indeed by the time he leaves the stage his crippled leg is likely to have established itself as a visual image of his undoubted moral depravity. But the fact that he so consistently uses moral clichés to skin over the ugly reality combines with Regine's use of her second language to suggest that here we are listening to something other than mere personal idiosyncrasies of speech. They both use language as a means to presenting a socially acceptable appearance to those that matter in society. Their use of language is a comment on them, but also an oblique comment on the society they live in. It likes demure appearances, demure language, demure social and moral clichés. Meanwhile the opening scene has presented a very ugly situation to which demureness bears only an ironically inadequate relationship.

And Manders is again the source of Engstrand's verbal habits. He talks and thinks in clichés similar to those invoked by the carpenter. If Engstrand represents himself hypocritically as a weak but repentant sinner, Manders seems to accept the stereotype without question; if Engstrand invokes, hypocritically again, the natural bond between parent and child, Manders invokes it ingenuously. He even uses some of the phrases that Engstrand has used, or ones very similar: 'guiding hand', 'instances are manifold in life', 'weak humanity'. Engstrand, like Regine, seems to have learnt his habits from Manders, and Manders, as clergyman, is spokesman for his society. He is innocent of hypocrisy, yet he promotes this concern for seemliness. He believes in the validity of appearances and platitudes that Regine and Engstrand exploit to hide unseemly realities. He is an innocent, yet strangely he belongs to the same world as Engstrand, the world of moral clichés. It is not too early to feel that the setting of steady rain and gloomy landscape is by no means an inappropriate image of the society in which the action is to take place, and that Manders' entrance, in from the filthy weather, well protected against it (unlike Engstrand) by overcoat and umbrella, is an image of his relationship to that society. It is his element too, or so the vague impression suggests.

When Mrs Alving comes on to greet her visitor she seems indifferent to the gloom. She is the first character not to comment on the weather. She seems to accept it, to take it for granted. And this suits the person she at first seems to be: apart from an unexpected spark of mischief (when she twits Manders on his absurd reluctance to spend a night in her house) she seems to be a sedate and conventional matron, never more so than when she, in her turn, declares her assumptions about the natural bond between her son and herself – the cliché already drawn upon by Engstrand and Manders in their different ways. Mrs Alving believes in it passionately. Whether justifiably, we may begin to question, since Engstrand has already shown that clichés can sometimes hide ugly realities.

But unlike Manders, Mrs Alving has a second side to her personality. To the disgust of the Pastor, she reads 'advanced' books and is fully prepared to defend her freedom to do so. The conventional matron is also an intellectual radical of sorts; but only of sorts and only intellectual. For once again, and in this new sphere, we are made to feel the pressures exerted by this society to procure a seemliness of conventional appearance. When Manders argues that at least she should keep her new ideas to herself, within the four walls of her own room, she makes no resistance. It seems never to have occurred to her to do otherwise. This form of what may be called obscurantism in her may be different from Eng-strand's cynical hypocrisy and Manders' naive innocence, but it marks her as another product, or part-product, of this society. Of course one keeps one's radical ideas quiet; society expects it of one.

As she and Manders settle down to the business affairs of the Orphanage it becomes plain that more is being covered up than radical ideas. Mrs Alving's behaviour is, in a variety of small instances, odd. When Manders, with revealing relish, produces his documents and becomes the committee man, this should be the climax of her life. The papers mark the completion of her memorial to her husband. That they signify a great deal to her is obvious from the way she gazes at them for a long time, but then she shows indifference. To all requests for instructions, her reply to Manders is, in effect: 'do as you please'. Something must lie behind this puzzling lack of interest, but Mrs Alving keeps it concealed.

The interview develops into the broad and obvious comedy of the question of insurance, but it contributes more to the play than that. It helps to define both the nature of the society within which they live, and Mrs Alving's own relationship to it. We sense the weight of public opinion from Manders' abject fear of it. Mrs Alving can see the total absurdity of the prejudice against insuring, but if public opinion is against it, then she is perfectly willing to accept. It is that sort of society; she is that sort of radical, willing to think for herself, but not to act.

Oswald's long-delayed entrance is likely to have generated some tension, but not much. We have heard only of a beloved son visiting his affectionate mother to share in this moment of celebration in honour of his father. When he appears the stereotype gives way to a much more interesting person, one under strain. Oswald is less well adapted to his surroundings than either Engstrand or Manders: he wears only a light overcoat. There is a touch of aggression in the way he introduces himself to the clergyman as 'the prodigal son', and of impatience when he cuts through Manders' pompous formalities over the use of his first name; he is restive when the Pastor speaks of great achievements to come.

Mrs Alving becomes edgy too. When Manders remarks that,

with Alving's pipe in his mouth, Oswald is the spitting image of his father, she objects. And yet she is honouring the memory of her beloved husband. It is puzzling, but Mrs Alving does not explain.

Then comes the extraordinary story that lies behind the pipe, of Alving forcing his young son to smoke himself sick. Both Manders and Oswald put it down to his cheerful, happy disposition but this clearly is not explanation for an ugly, distasteful episode. Mrs Alving knows all the facts; she reacts uneasily, but she will not explain.

The atmosphere of the play has become heavy with the presence of facts concealed; there is acute tension between the surface appearance, of propriety, regularity, success and the sense that underneath things might be different. Oswald's outburst against Manders does not so much clear the air as define the fundamental discrepancies. Their squabble is ostensibly confined to the question of marriage amongst poor artists, but Oswald expands into his definition of two different moral and social climates. Most of his energy goes into a denunciation of Norway as a hypocritically corrupt society where 'respectable' men indulge their taste for depravity beneath a disguise of outraged decency. Paris he describes as a place where people can live by a true, natural morality; a life suitable for 'young, warmblooded people in love', that is 'beautiful, glorious, free'. By the time he has finished Oswald has, by positive and negative definition, confirmed the impression that has slowly been built up in Act I, that the gloom beyond the windows is a fitting image of the social and moral climate of Norway. There is enough truth in what he says.

Not that Oswald can be accepted as an objective judge. His argument, which moves wildly from the particular to the universal (all Norwegians are corrupt because some are corrupt, all artists are decent because some are decent) is not impressive. His language which, at moments of emphasis, clots into clusters of emotive words, denotes not merely the man of feeling, the artist responding emotionally to life, but a man under acute pressure of emotion. There is a touch of hysteria by the end. He seems to speak less from simple enthusiasm than from anguish at the defilement of the life he extols. And there is a faint but sinister connection between his clasping of his head and that recent and ugly story of the pipe-smoking episode when his father caused beads of sweat to break out on his forehead. There is enough evidence in the play to support the general tendency of Oswald's characterisation of Norway and Paris, but he cannot be taken as an objective judge. He is obviously involved.

At this point in the play, which concerns Mrs Alving as well as the two men, since she acknowledges Oswald as the spokesman for her own views, modes of speech become distinctive and emphatic; characters begin to reveal themselves by the way they speak under emotional pressure. Oswald's rhetorical style has already made its mark – emotional and unstructured.

Manders' style is very different. His rhetoric is highly patterned; so much so, indeed, that some of his characteristic speeches, when set out as sequences of natural rhetorical units, reveal themselves as constituting a kind of pseudo-verse. The versions which are offered here follow very closely the symmetries of the original Norwegian even though this involves at times a certain stiffness of idiom beyond even Manders' habitual stiffness; sections which do not contribute to the 'verse' structure are printed as prose; sections which do are aligned to bring out visually the patterns referred to:

(*a*) I shall begin by refreshing your memory, madam. The moment is well chosen.
>To-morrow is the tenth anniversary of your husband's death;
>to-morrow the memorial will be unveiled in honour of the departed;
>to-morrow I shall address the whole assembled flock; –
but to-day I wish to address you alone

(*b*) Do you remember that after barely a year of marriage you stood on the uttermost brink of disaster?
>that you left your house and home, –
>that you fled from your husband; yes, Mrs Alving,
>>fled, fled and refused to return to him,
however much he begged and besought you to?

(*c*) I was merely a weak weapon in a higher hand. –
>And surely my making you submit to duty and obedience,
>>surely that grew into a mighty blessing in your life that followed,
>>>throughout all your days.

Did it not happen as I predicted?
Did not Alving turn his back on his profligacy, as befits a man?
Did he not live with you from that time forth in love and blamelessness
all his days?
Did he not become a benefactor to this district?
and did he not raise you up to him, so that gradually you became a fellow-
worker in all his undertakings?...
(d) You have been governed by a fatal spirit of self-will throughout all your
days.
All your bent has been turned towards recklessness and lawlessness.
Always you have refused to acknowledge any tie upon you.
All encumbrances on your life you have thrown off with heedlessness and
unscrupulousness,
like a burden that could be disposed of by you yourself at will.
It did not suit you any longer to be a wife
and you parted from your husband.
It became irksome to you to be a mother,
and you put your child forth amongst strangers.

There is nothing subtle about this rhetoric; Manders' habits are
blatant enough to register on first hearing. But they deserve
analysis. One of his predilections is for a sort of rhyme effect.
Several of his 'lines' have identical or similar beginnings; in an
idiomatic translation the fact is likely to be obscured that his prose
abounds in terminal 'rhymes' too. Three 'lines' (two in (c) and
one in (d)) end in variations on the phrase 'all your days', and a
fourth ends in a phrase of similar shape, 'all his undertakings'
(in (c)). Two (in (d)) create a 'rhyme' effect through the use of
identical word-terminations: 'recklessness and lawlessness'
'rhymes' with 'heedlessness and unscrupulousness'. The effect
here is reinforced by the internal 'rhyme' within each doublet.
There is a strange, because apparently pointless and contrived,
'rhyme' (in (d)) between the noun 'self-will' and the reappearance
of its constituents a few 'lines' later in the sequence 'yourself at
will'.

Manders has a fondness for the doublet that is not satisfied by
the two sets used for 'rhyme'. He also uses 'house and home',
'begged and besought', 'duty and obedience', 'love and blamelessness'. He enjoys facile alliteration: 'weak weapon...higher
hand'. Several of his 'lines' come to their point in a resounding

stock phrase: 'the whole assembled flock', 'uttermost brink of disaster', 'house and home', 'a higher hand', 'as befits a man'. Manders' idea of a climax is a cliché.

His rhetoric is so permeated by formality, seems so to relish formality for its own sake, that he gives the impression not of creating his own speeches but of following patterns already established as suitable for an occasion such as this. He is not thinking for himself or speaking directly from his own feelings. These have been subdued to a convention, to a pattern. And the rhetorical patterning seems to reflect a pattern of conventional, formal, moral thinking.

This does not make Manders a hypocrite. He seems to be deeply and sincerely moved, but in conventional ways. Still less does this detract from the weight of his speeches. Formal and conventional it may be, but his rebuke is massive and in its way impressive. Listening to him we recognise a demonstration of society's power to coerce and it is not negligible. It is against the force of this kind of rhetoric that we then gauge Mrs Alving's replies.

For the most part Mrs Alving has spoken in a simple and direct fashion. Where she has departed from this style it has usually been when she has echoed, often with amusement, some portentous phrase of Manders'. It is typical of her that she should preface her deeply serious response to his censures by playing with the word he made pompous use of in (a): 'You've finished your address now, Pastor; and tomorrow you will make a public address in memory of my husband. I shan't address anybody tomorrow. But now I shall address you for a while just as you have addressed me.' But as her feelings increase in warmth, her speeches too develop into patterns.

a)   I had endured a great deal in this house.
    To keep him at home in the evenings –
         and at night –
            I had to turn myself into a drinking-companion in the secret sessions
                   up in his room.
    There I had to sit all alone with him,
       had to touch glasses and drink with him,
          listen to his obscene, mindless chatter,

   had to use my fists and fight with him
   to get him dragged into bed.
b) I would never have survived if I hadn't had my work.
   Yes, I think I can say that I have worked.
     All those extensions to the estate,
     all the improvements,
     all the useful developments Alving got the praise and credit for...
     I was the one who drove him on
       when he had his more lucid intervals;
     I was the one who had to carry the full load
       when he relapsed into debauchery
         or sank into whimpering spinelessness.

What is remarkable is that a woman so unlike Manders in personality should speak in forms so similar. Her heightened prose too falls naturally into 'lines' marked by identical or similar beginnings. She gets an effect of 'rhyme' from the repeated line-ending 'with him' (in (*a*)) and 'work...worked' (in (*b*)). The similarity in patterning shows most clearly in a comparison of her speech (*b*) with Manders' (*d*). In both a triple repetition ('All...Always... All' in Manders, 'All...all...all' in Mrs Alving) develops into a kind of stanza, a form of quatrain of alternately balanced lines ('It did not suit you...and you parted...It became irksome...and you put' in Manders, '*I* was the one...when he had...*I* was the one...when he relapsed' in Mrs Alving). There is no mistaking the similarity of rhetoric between these two educated people. Indeed, since their habits are shared, it suggests here as it did in the case of Regine and Engstrand that more is involved than personal idiosyncrasy. They speak as society has educated them to speak. They have been trained to form their speech, and, we may gauge from the simple forthrightness with which they put their points of view, their thoughts into neat, clear and above all shapely, well-defined patterns.

   And yet Mrs Alving's language helps define a person who, for all the similarity, is also very different from Manders. For with her it is at least her own direct, personal experience which is expressed in these formal patterns. The clauses of (*a*) are not balanced for a mere conventionally rhetorical effect; they are balanced because they take us step by equal step through the stages of an actual

evening spent with Alving, all of them distasteful. Her 'rhymes'
are not flourishes but registers of emotional preoccupation; the
repetitions of 'had to' register her living sense of compulsion, of
'all', a vivid indignation; and '*I*' is repeated to express her strong
sense of personal injustice. Mrs Alving has no time for the trappings
of purely formal rhetoric; she uses no word-play, no doublets, no
alliteration; her 'rhymes' and 'lines' serve to express her own
feelings; and her climaxes are not clichés. Hers is the rhetoric of a
woman expressing her own responses to her own experience, who
has been forced to see the ugliness that underlies the smug façade of
marriage, but who is sufficiently under the domination of society
still to control her thoughts and her language into conformity with
the social demand for a neat shape to things. She has reduced
painful confusion to tidy order.

Mrs Alving's rhetoric helps to emphasise the essential ambiguity
of this woman. She thinks of herself as an intellectual radical, but
the story of her past reveals a woman who, in spite of that
intellectual independence, has accepted much of that social
discipline that has produced a Manders. She seems now to believe
that she is free from mental coercion: she has seen through the
social shams of marriage and she has at last spoken out. Moreover
she feels that by her long and careful plotting she has managed to
seal off the consequences of the initial disaster, her marriage. It is
impossible not to marvel at the selfless devotion, the sacrifice and
the sheer determination towards a good, clean, decent life for her
son. Mrs Alving is a wonderful woman. We can understand her
sense of relief and recognise her satisfaction at having brought the
long, hateful comedy to a successful conclusion, but we cannot
share that confidence of hers. Mrs Alving may, with half her mind,
be a radical, but with the other half she has chosen to act by the
social standards she sees to be false. She has worked by shams, she
had played society at its own game by its own rules.

The final scene of Act I brings an abrupt and shocking revelation
that she has failed to seal off the past. The ghost of Alving walks in
his son when we hear sounds of furtive sex-play from the dining-
room. The episode further implies that Mrs Alving's attempts to
seal off the past have only made the present more dangerously

complicated; because of the way she has kept the family scandal secret to preserve the appearances society demands, she has made it possible for half-brother to make overtures to half-sister in ignorance of their relationship. History is not merely repeating itself. But the scene also contains, in brief, a further indication of just how deeply Mrs Alving is still imbued with the convention-ality she despises. In a situation that cries out for frankness, that shakes her so badly that she can hardly walk, Mrs Alving shows how far she is from being able to break free from the pall of conventionality, of hypocrisy, of sheer moral deadness that by now hangs over the play. Her last words 'Yes, come. Not a word!' show that she is as committed as ever to working through concealment, through the preservation of appearances. No wonder the setting is as obstinately murky at the end as at the beginning of Act I.

Act II opens on the same note. The setting is as gloomy as ever, and Mrs Alving still desperately tries to keep up appearances. Her first words are a social formula, the formal reply of a hostess to formal compliments from a guest on the meal. She is concealing what she and Manders know behind social propriety.

And her attempt to do so is not confined to this brief phrase. The solutions she goes on to propose point in the same direction. Whatever happens, the truth must somehow be kept hidden. But immediately difficulties begin to arise. Regine must be sent pack-ing. But where? The conventional place would be home to her father; yet Mrs Alving's careful plotting has made that home and that relationship a lie. Regine cannot be sent home to Engstrand because he is not her father. The original attempt to rectify through concealment makes rectification now more difficult. And yet Mrs Alving does not seem to grasp this fact. She goes on to propose remedies that have already been tried and have already proved disastrous. Regine's mother was sent packing and we know the outcome of that. Joanna was given money so that she, a fallen woman, could buy herself a husband; and Mrs Alving, who married a fallen man for money, knows only too well what comes of that sort of arrangement; and yet she proposes the same sort of solution to the Regine problem – she must be financed and married

87

off. The radical woman can still see only one way of acting, and that is in conformity with the appearances that society wishes to be presented with. She has learnt nothing. And it may be added that there is something else that she has not recognised, namely that in the pursuit of her intricate plans, she treats people as objects to be manipulated. She proposes to treat Regine as such, not as a person.

Strong as these tendencies are in her, Mrs Alving does not cease to be ambiguous. Side by side with the conformist in action there lives the radical. As the discussion continues the radical shows herself. Mrs Alving becomes restive. She proposes to go on playing the social game, but simultaneously she feels the need, as she says, to work her way out to freedom. She wishes she had told the truth about Alving to his son; wishes she could tell it now, wishes she could advise Regine and Oswald to disregard their blood relationship and come to any arrangement they please, so long as it is an open one. Her radicalism is extraordinary.

And yet she is restricted to mere wishing. The radical collides with and submits to the social. However much she may wish to bring things out into the open and permit free, uninhibited decisions, she dare not for fear of what people will say. In the event her impulse towards freedom emerges as nothing more than verbal aspiration, and nervous, impotent impatience with the enveloping gloom. Her only action is to stare out of the window and tap on the window-frame. Her speeches are caught in the sad, insistent refrain: 'I am such a coward'. Mrs Alving recognises that society is haunted by the ghosts of dead ideas; she includes herself when she says that everybody is 'so horribly afraid of the light'; but for all her radicalism she does not seem to recognise how many of those ghosts haunt her.

One sign of this is her lack of real concern for the truth – a point which is made during the scene with Engstrand, but many other points are made first. Indeed this scene, for all its broad and obvious comedy, is one of remarkable complexity and importance. To begin with, Engstrand's physical appearance presents a strong and striking image not just of the man, but of the society he exploits. The depraved man with the ugly deformity is dressed in his Sunday best. He knows the surest means by which society can be deceived, by the neat and seemly appearances it likes to see.

Beyond that, a verbal process takes place which is difficult to define adequately, though perhaps the term 'contamination' will serve. Repeatedly Engstrand's language is made to refer outwards to several of the leading issues in the play. When he says, for instance, 'We menfolk mustn't judge a poor woman too hardly, pastor', he echoes the words and sentiments of Manders when he rebuked Mrs Alving: 'But a wife is not set up to be her husband's judge.' When Engstrand asks 'Isn't it right and proper for a man to restore the fallen?' he uses a term already employed between Manders and Mrs Alving:

MANDERS Yes, just think of it – for a miserable three hundred dollars to go and let himself marry a fallen woman.

MRS ALVING What about me, then, for going and letting myself marry a fallen man?

When Engstrand defends his duplicity on the grounds that he concealed the truth about his wife 'so that people shouldn't know how flighty she had been', he echoes Manders who described Alving's early dissoluteness as 'youthful flightiness' and also Mrs Alving who explained that she had kept the truth hidden 'so that no-one should know'. When Engstrand refers to his bawdy-house as 'a sort of institution for sailors...a sort of home' there is an obvious cross-reference of sorts to that other institution, the Orphanage.

The echoes are too frequent to be fortuitous; their effect is difficult to describe. It seems not to be a case of deliberate echoing on Engstrand's part; he has not been present on the occasions when Manders and Mrs Alving originally employed the key words and phrases. In every instance Engstrand uses fine phrases with hypo-critical intent, but the effect is not to suggest that Manders and Mrs Alving are equally hypocritical; clearly they are not. What seems to be happening is that the neat moral assumptions by which Manders and Mrs Alving work are made to seem danger-ously naive; the main characters seem to rely upon them, but Engstrand proves that they can be used to conceal very ugly realities. Manders' assumption that Alving was no more than

conventionally and innocently 'flighty', Mrs Alving's assumption
that she can judge her husband, the shared assumption that there
can be no debate about what is meant by 'fallen', Mrs Alving's
assumption that people must not know, and that a respectable
institution is a right way of concealing a depraved life – all of
these are contaminated by the way they are drawn on by the
reprobate Engstrand. Through him we recognise that fine phrases
can conceal ugliness, and that Manders and Mrs Alving rely upon
those same phrases. He contaminates the certainties by which they
live. They think in neat patterns but the reality can be quite other.

Neither of the educated pair recognises this. The episode demonstrates their readiness to be taken in by the fine phrase – it is that
sort of society. Not that Manders and Mrs Alving react identically.
Engstrand's clichés are accepted with eagerness by Manders. Mrs
Alving is not hoodwinked; and yet she is prepared to allow
Engstrand to get away with his outrageous lies. She knows the
truth and yet it does not seem important to her to insist upon the
truth. She is still conditioned to believe that seemly appearances
matter more. Thus she does not intervene; she merely smiles and
calls Manders a great baby. She shows little sign of restiveness: a
last glance out of the window to remind of her longing to work
her way out to freedom, a sigh – those are the only reactions she
permits herself against the atmosphere both inside and outside the
house. Truth, as an absolute, does not seem to matter to her.

For the next episode the gloom grows worse; such light as there
is begins to fade. Appropriately, in view of what transpires. Mrs
Alving discovers that Oswald has been sitting at table alone,
drinking. He is being his father's son, again; he is slightly tipsy –
he needs to be told twice that the Pastor has left – but the main
impression is of unease in the presence of his mother. Given
permission to smoke, he holds the cigar behind his back, like a
schoolboy; his display of affection is too elaborate to be convincing: he strokes and pats his mother and makes a fulsome refrain
out of her name: 'Imagine, – for me, to have come back home,
to sit at Mother's own table, in Mother's room, and eat Mother's
lovely food.' But in another moment his true feelings show
themselves: 'And what else can I do with myself here? I can't

settle to anything...In this gloom? Without a glimpse of the sun the whole day long? Oh, and then – not to be able to work – !' and with this, something less tangible but strong: resentment against his mother for having left him abroad for so long, resentment strong enough to make him crumple up a newspaper at the moment of expressing it; a desire to get close to her now, stiffened and formalised into the stilted: 'Mother, have I permission to sit by you on the sofa?' It strikes hard that he should be able to break through the inhibitions he suffers under, and cast himself into his mother's lap, only through disaster, when he breaks into sobbing for the ruin of his mind and his ambitions. The relationship between parent and child looks vastly different in reality from what it sounded like in Mrs Alving's unquestioning assumptions in Act I.

She listens with truly maternal restraint as Oswald describes the symptoms but then the doctor's diagnosis, as Oswald reports it, hits her hard. 'The sins of the fathers' makes her rise slowly to her feet and repeat the words. Yet astonishingly she retains self-control; that movement, and a brief pacing of the room while she repeats yet again are her only reactions. And when Oswald goes on to reveal not only that he is ill by inheritance but that, because of his mother's creation of a false image, he cannot believe that his father is indeed the cause, her reaction is even more remarkable for its restraint: Mrs Alving wrings her hands and walks to and fro, but in silence. And this at the moment when she must have perceived two terrible things; first, that the 'hateful comedy' is, in a far worse sense than she expected, not over, the baleful influence of the husband not sterilised; and second, that her very remedy has caused additional pain to the beloved son who, thanks to her careful, well-intentioned plotting, can only blame himself for his breakdown. Even at this moment, she covers up, even from her own son.

But in part she is herself blind. Something, perhaps sheer maternal instinct, perhaps an inability to accept the situation in all its virulence, leads her simply to deny that the situation is as disastrous as it clearly is. She cuts short Oswald's despair with 'No, no, my dear, beloved boy; it isn't possible;...It isn't as

desperate with you as you think.' She seems, as usual, to be trying
to reduce a problem to a manageable shape, here by ignoring the
fact of illness and of its origins, and by concentrating on one
tractable aspect of the whole affair, Oswald's anguish. At least she
believes it to be tractable, but her actions show up as painfully,
pathetically inadequate to the situation. When Oswald complains
of the gloom, we know how much more he means than the physical darkness, and the physical image itself is strong enough to
engulf the whole set; yet Mrs Alving's reaction is to have a lighted
lamp brought in. A little later, when he breaks down in horror,
Mrs Alving orders champagne: 'I want my boy to be happy.' The
single table lamp and the bottle of wine stand as evidence of their
own pathetic inadequacy against the huge darkness of the night
and all that it suggests, and against the torment that is driving her
son near-mad.

Her estimate of what can make her boy happy is made to seem
even less adequate because Oswald has just defined what happiness
means to him. To his description of life in Paris that he began to
offer in Act I, he now adds 'that joyful, blissful life of young
people amongst friends'. The characteristics of Oswald's rhetoric
have not changed; he still heaps emotive words together without
structure; the headlong vehemence again suggests not merely the
artist but the strain of near-hysteria. Oswald is so passionate about
joy and bliss because they are lost to him. It is no clear definition;
but it has substance, and it indicates if it does not define.

It is the pressures of his sense of loss that make him suddenly and
surprisingly project on to Regine the highest of significances:
'Mother, Regine is my only salvation.' Surprisingly because
Regine is, after all, a commonplace girl. But the terms of his
praise indicate the reasons for his estimate: she is 'magnificent to
look at', 'nicely built', 'wholesome', 'pretty' – physically
inviting. He values her for the health that he has lost, not as a true
embodiment of his ideals. Thus she constitutes no full definition
of the key term that is now attached to her – she is his only
salvation 'because I saw she had the gift of happiness'.

Translation presents an insoluble problem here. The normal
rendering of 'livsglede' is 'joy of living', but the phrase remains

alien to English; it is inflated in a way that the Norwegian word is not. The prefix 'livs-' is much used, without any sense of pomposity; and '-glad' is the common word for 'happy', '-glede' for 'happiness'. Alving was described as 'livsglad' by Manders in Act I; Mrs Alving has just wished her son to be 'glad'. 'The gift of happiness' is longwinded, but it may serve.

Oswald's use of 'gift of happiness' after his purely physical admiration of Regine suggests that he is using the term too in a limited way, but Mrs Alving seizes upon the combination of ideas: 'The gift of happiness – ? Can there be salvation in *that*?' This begins to force upon her a complete revision of her ideas.

For the first time in the play, Mrs Alving shows signs of being ready to learn at last, to try to expose herself to a new point of view. For a few moments she ceases to give the impression of knowing all the rules of the game, and thereby of being in control of events. Instead of giving, as she has habitually done, clear and confident explanations of how things were and how they will be, she now asks questions, humbly. She listens carefully as Oswald completes his definition of the life he knew in Paris, where work was happiness, where merely to be alive was glorious and blissful, where his paintings always represented the gift of happiness, always showed light and sunshine and holiday atmosphere and happy, beaming faces. She listens as he expresses his fear that to live at home would be to have all this reduced to ugliness. The imagery relates to the setting of the play. Oswald seems to define more fully, by negative means, what the enveloping murk stands for, and by contrast the life in Paris that he describes seems to define the significance of the excluded sun.

After her careful listening, Mrs Alving suddenly resumes her customary role. The critical utterance is: 'Now I see how things connect. . . Now I can see it for the first time. And now I can speak out.' The brief sentences bring her sharply into focus, as a woman who has to discover the connections, to perceive a shape and a pattern that she can grasp, before she can speak out. It is a woman that her patterned rhetoric has in part prepared us for, educated to project that mode of thought on to experience. The basis of her life has, it seems, changed, but, now that she has regained it, not her confidence that, on whatever basis, she can proceed to plan life in this new direction as she planned it in the old. She resumes command; she appears to know what must be done. She requests Regine to stay and listen to her speaking out.

Just for an instant or two it is possible to feel that good may come out of all this. We can see on stage this family of mother, son and half-sister united as it should always have been, as Mrs Alving prepares to tell them all that they need to know to come to a free decision.

Progress in this direction is immediately blocked. Not by Manders, for his obtuse intrusion is easily brushed aside, and Mrs Alving can continue with her plan. It is blocked partly by the revelation that Mrs Alving is still thinking in terms of the ideal image, that is to say the social image, of a father that she has instilled in her son. This conventional ideal she does not intend to abandon; quite the contrary, its preservation remains one of her essential aims: 'And what's more no ideal will suffer.' The statement sits oddly in company with what immediately precedes it: 'because now I can speak right out'. And then there is a more radical blockage that is only intimated. Mrs Alving has again reduced experience, even this new experience, to a pattern and a plan. She seems to know exactly what is to be done; but what that is is defined by her continued attachment to the old ideals. She has restored order out of confusion, but it seems not to be an adequate order. The grasping for a pattern precludes her from really facing all the facts of the case. For that is the impression that emerges; that the crucial fact, the fact of Oswald's inherited disease, is not amenable to the kind of clarification she proposes. This does not fit the pattern which enables her to feel that she can control events; she seems to leave it out of consideration.

But before she can expose the implied inadequacy of her new grasp on things it is denied by events. The Orphanage is on fire. This is an external disaster, beyond the reach of Mrs Alving's capacity to control and organise. The physical fact implies an end, a disastrous end to her attempt to control experience in that way; the pious institution that was to bury for ever the depravity of Alving's life and bring a long, hateful comedy to its conclusion is burning down. The sham adopted to placate society has failed. And the failure is in physical terms threatening.

There is no specific stage indication, but Oswald refers to the light from the fire. Light, at last, to penetrate the persistent gloom; but a sinister because destructive light. And simultaneously the momentary grouping together of the family is destroyed too; the characters dash off in disorder. The room is left empty, open to the night. Mrs Alving has not, after all, restored things to a new shape; she is not, as she thought, in control; the room, once a haven, has been invaded by something more sinister than a jobbing carpenter.

Act III begins on the same note. The doors still stand open; the lamp still does its puny best against the darkness; the only other light, a faint glow from the gutted Orphanage, is hardly reassuring. There is a restless feeling as the company comes back indoors, no longer a group but a number of variously agitated individuals. Even the language, brief, shocked, banal, manages to insinuate an obscure and unintentional threat: Mrs Alving's great discovery in Act II was that in the gift of happiness lay the possibility of 'salvation'. Now that possibility seems to be called in question by Mrs Alving's use of the same root word: 'There's absolutely nothing to be salvaged.'

Her preoccupation is entirely with Oswald. What the disaster means to her we cannot know from her brief initial appearance, but she says enough to suggest that she is directly confronting the experience. Her sentences are very brief and direct; they match her action in going off herself to fetch her son. In contrast Manders and Regine cling, at this of all moments, to their social catch-words. 'Isn't it an awfully bad piece of work, pastor?' asks Regine; 'But I positively can not remember. . . ' says the pastor. The level of their concern is as shallow as their language.

So much is obvious from the way the scene develops between cleric and carpenter; Manders is terrified for his reputation. The episode is broadly comic; it is disconcertingly more than that because of Engstrand. He serves to give final definition to the kind of society that he shares with Manders. His use of sanctimonious cliché becomes outrageous; bad enough when he claims to be 'a sort of angel of salvation', almost blasphemous when he says, 'I know someone who has taken the sins of others upon himself once before, I do.' He describes Christ; he means himself.

Engstrand, of course, unlike Manders, uses language in this way for a purpose, and he defines Manders, and society, by succeeding. The more flagrant his mimicry, the more readily Manders is able to persuade himself of its genuineness. He persuades himself because he needs to believe, not so much in Engstrand as in the sanction for what he feels driven to do. He cannot face public disgrace; he needs Engstrand's help to save him; he needs the pious clichés to make it easy for him to justify to himself his own cowardice.

As Manders clutches at the stock phrases fed back to him by Engstrand, the feeling of real identity between this unlikely pair grows stronger and stronger. Different though they may be, they are both products of a society to which the right appearance or the right phrase matters more than the truth. A genuinely coercive society – Manders is truly terrified; a society that nonetheless breeds the deft hypocrisy of Engstrand who exploits it with such ease. It is the final comment that Manders and Engstrand should leave the play together and that they should go off to become co-founders of a bawdy-house with a respectable name.

There is another strand to the scene. Engstrand has become the living proof of the way real depravity can conceal itself in such a society. Seeing him succeed we can understand how Alving succeeded – the man on whose reputation no rumours would take hold because of his social charm. He epitomises the man Mrs Alving has had to deal with, and, by proposing to use the name she chose for the Orphanage to adorn his institution, he also epitomises the radical dishonesty of her well-meaning attempts. There is truth as well as humour in Engstrand's last words: 'And if I can run the place according to my own notion, I dare swear it'll be worthy of the poor Chamberlain.' Engstrand is again contaminating the main issues. Even 'salvation' becomes suspect when he uses it as he does.

By the time they leave the stage, Manders and Engstrand have defined the reality of the social situation. The company is narrowed by their departure. The family, Oswald, Regine and Mrs Alving, come together again but no longer in an atmosphere that holds promise of true intimacy. The doors are shut, but there is no sense of cosiness: Oswald is desperate to shut out his feeling of dread. The house is beleaguered, invaded – Oswald cannot separate himself from the destruction of the Orphanage: 'Everything will burn. There will be nothing left to remember father by. I'm beginning to burn up too.' In his agony of dread he turns to Regine for a 'helping hand'. He will not explain what he means by this but the term, innocent enough in itself, is another of those contaminated by Engstrand who, in Act II, had longed to be given 'a helping hand by some kind person'. He wanted the help to set up his establishment; as usual the fine phrase hides an ugly possibility. When Oswald uses the phrase, there is the vague threat that there too it should not be taken at its face value.

Mrs Alving is not sensitive to the implications of what has been going on. She seems to feel that she has regained control of the situation; she has faced her experiences and is confident that she can reduce them to a comprehensible shape and a tidy plan: 'And now, my poor, suffering boy, now I'm going to take the load off your mind...everything you call resentment and remorse and self-reproach – .' She believes that she has digested what Oswald had had to say about the 'gift of happiness'. It is an indication of how radical a truth she thinks she has discovered that she expresses it in imagery antithetical to the pervasive gloom in which she has always elected to live: 'it was as though a new light had dawned for me over everything in the whole of my life'. In this mood of confidence in the new truth and in the control its possession still gives her she goes on to re-assess her life with Alving.

Her crucial speeches are fascinating. Like the earlier speeches, they fall gradually into neat symmetries:

You should have known your father in his really young days when he was a lieutenant. He certainly had the gift of happiness, my dear...
It was like a holiday just to look at him. And then that incredible energy and abundance there was in him.
And then a child of happiness like that
had to – because he was like a child in those days –
he had to exist home here in a half-sized town that had no happiness to offer,

only diversions.
Had to exist here without any vocation;
he only had an official position.
Couldn't see any work he could throw himself into, heart and soul;
he only had business
Didn't possess one single friend capable of feeling what a gift for happiness was
all about;
only lay-abouts and drinking-pals.

The speeches develop into a beautifully organised contrast between two different ways of life – the rhetorical patterns reflect patterns in the mode of thought. Mrs Alving has digested her new experience until it has taken on a shape that she can easily grasp and thereby, or so her confidence of definition suggests, control. The symmetries of speech set antithetically alongside each other what can be called her new vision of the full life and her sense of the inadequacies of what society had to offer Alving – happiness/diversions, vocation/official position, work/business, and so forth. The speeches create no impression of stiffness; the refrain 'had to [exist]' modulates into the different structure and rhythm of 'Couldn't see...', 'Didn't possess...'; yet the passage is unobtrusively held together as a unit, as one shaped thought, by the recurrent 'only' that is common to all the variations. The language is patterned but alive. Still less does it suggest insincerity. And yet it does suggest strongly that Mrs Alving has thought long to perceive this pattern before she could give expression to it. At no point does she hesitate or grope for the terms of her antitheses; they are not stock terms, but they are already, it seems, present in due relationship in her mind as she speaks. She is declaring the connections between things that she saw as long ago as Act II. There is no real spontaneity.

The rhetoric is therefore typical of Mrs Alving, and a typical indication of the mode of thought that she has been educated to apply to experience. She has analysed, until she has recognised a clear and simple pattern, and now she intends to act upon that in order to control events.

But what makes her speeches fascinating is the tension between form and matter. Mrs Alving's definition of the full life is easily extractable: it involves youth ('in his really young days'), the gift

98

of happiness, holiday spirit, vocation, work, friends. These are terms taken over directly by Mrs Alving from Oswald, who rejoiced in 'the life of young people amongst friends' in Paris, who described the 'holiday atmosphere' in his own paintings, who admired the 'gift of happiness' and the energy to 'work' that went with it. 'Vocation' is a word that he has not used but the concept has been implicit in all his definitions of the full life.

Mrs Alving has taken over Oswald's ideas but not his form of rhetoric. His instinctive philosophy emerged in impetuous language, spontaneously and shapelessly used. Mrs Alving believes that she has made his values her own, but the way in which she has subdued the spontaneity of his language to the careful neatness of her own suggests that she has possessed his ideas only intellectually, only insofar as she can fit them into her own mode of thought. She uses the words, but the spontaneous vitality is missing.

Consequently the speech does not quite convincingly register as a critical turning-point in Mrs Alving's life. Apart from its rhetoric, its content leaves too much unaccounted for. It is not enough for her to say that Alving had the gift of happiness when he was young; we also know that he was a broken-down man before marriage. It is not enough to be told of his incredible energy and exuberance when we have also heard of his self-pitying indolence. It is generous of Mrs Alving to exonerate her husband by reference to the social limitations he had to exist with, but she, a woman, coped differently; far too generous of her to take much of the blame on herself – how much 'holiday atmosphere' did Alving bring into the home? And what of Alving's responsibility for the one fact that Mrs Alving never seems quite able to face, Oswald's inherited disease?

Mrs Alving has met a crisis and is trying to cope, as usual. But her need to cope in a certain, inculcated fashion, by producing neat and clear patterns and plans out of difficult material, here leads her into a sure demonstration that the neatness can only be achieved by oversimplifying the difficulty. She believes that she has digested Oswald's new ideas, had reassessed her life by them and can now reassert control of events as she sees them. What follows is terrible disproof.

It is not simply that her plans fail; indeed one succeeds. It is that the mere attempt to implement them opens up dimensions of failure stretching back over the whole protracted endeavour of Mrs Alving to make sense of her life. She plans to end the dangerous liaison between Oswald and Regine by revealing their blood relationship. She has always used people as pawns in her campaign. She has created Regine's role as servant without regard to Regine; she seems now to assume that the girl will accept without question her newly revealed role as sister. What she discovers is that she has, by her past actions, destroyed all possibility of real relationship between the pair. How can Regine suddenly feel as a sister towards a sick brother when Mrs Alving has ensured that this relationship has had no substantial fulfilment? She has sacrificed a real relationship to the false ideal of relationship demanded by society; Regine has been sacrificed to Alving's reputation and the damage cannot be undone. She has also allowed to come into being a simple attraction between two young people and this too has been destroyed so that Regine is left with nothing beyond a burning resentment and a determination at least to throw off the restraints she has accepted so long as she could hope. Regine wants to gratify her gift of happiness, superficial though it may be; and one of the shortest and saddest speeches in the play, 'Yes – unfortunately' is Mrs Alving's recognition that she has done nothing, for all her freedom of thinking, to make true happiness a possibility for this misused young girl. It is too late to try to adopt Oswald's philosophy; the damage has been done.

The irony of it all is pointed by Regine's exit. With her typical ambiguity Mrs Alving mitigated her sacrifice of Regine to social propriety by extending personal and private benevolence; Regine has been brought up in the moral safety of the Alving home. The final outcome of Mrs Alving's plan is that Regine hurries off after Engstrand to claim her place in 'Chamberlain Alving's Home' – the bawdy-house for sailors. There is the further implication that Mrs Alving's attempt to bury Alving's evil influence under a monument of hypocrisy has merely diverted its power. She has unwittingly ensured that the ghost of Alving shall walk in his second child too. And there is nothing to be done now.

Her chief plan concerns Oswald. She expects to be able to relieve him of his burden of self-blame and yet keep unharmed the ideals she has fostered in him about his father. Her discovery is even more painful; for the son, the ideal is just one of the ghosts Mrs Alving thought she could identify. Again she finds that for the sake of the semblance of relationship she has destroyed a reality. If Oswald had known his father, that would have been something at this juncture; but his mother has made certain that that relationship too has been kept devoid of substance. Oswald does not care about his father, one way or the other.

Mrs Alving anticipates the most painful reversal to her confident expectations:

MRS ALVING Oswald – then you don't love me either.
OSWALD   At any rate I do at least know you.

In this brief but fierce series of shocks, she is being faced with consequences she never suspected could follow from actions performed with the best of intentions, and is recognising that it is too late to try to change them by exchanging one pattern of thought for another. People, she has discovered, are facts and not pawns; relationships must be real and substantial or they are nothing. Speaking out now cannot cancel the effects of not speaking out earlier.

Even so, Mrs Alving remains buoyed up by confidence explainable only in terms of maternal instinct. Something in her still prevents her from fully registering the fact of Oswald's disease. It still seems important that she might succeed in at least part of her plan. All the years of frustrated maternal longing show in her pathetic gratitude at having her beloved boy home with her again; she could almost bless the illness that brought him back. She will win back his love; she will be good and patient, yes, happy too, as Oswald pathetically asks her to be. That, surely, must take away his resentment and self-reproach.

Even when Oswald reminds her that what seems all-important to her simply does not touch the real problem that she cannot or will not see: 'But who is going to take the anguish away now?' she shows her feeling that after all, and in spite of everything, the vital part of her neat plan has worked. The mood comes across as she goes to the large windows in the conservatory and says, 'The day's beginning to dawn already on the mountains. And it's going to be a fine day, Oswald! You'll soon be able to see the sun.' There is a devastating wrongness in her response. At the most superficial level she has no sanction to be so optimistic. At a deeper level, images of light and dark have gradually become loaded with implication, and what the series of shocks has demonstrated beyond question is that there can be no simple emergence out of the murk that surrounds the whole action into a bright future.

Mrs Alving is oversimplifying again, reducing the complex to neat proportions. The image of sun-rise may suggest a happy ending to her, but in itself it carries intimations vastly different.

The dawn injects a new tempo into the play. Something manifest, objective; something that will, in some sense, dispel the darkness; something, moreover, that will be beyond Mrs Alving's power to control and organise, is about to break. Oswald gives a first hint of what the dawn may really mean as distinct from what his mother imagines it means; he begs her to sit down for a talk: '– and then in the mean time the sun's coming up. And then you will know.' Through his words, dawn becomes associated with knowing the real facts. The rest of the play is the process of Mrs Alving's relentless education in knowing.

Oswald tells her more about his illness. He points to his forehead and says, 'This illness I've got as an inheritance, it – it's lurking inside here.' His words imply more than he means. By echoing the terms 'inheritance' and 'lurks' that Mrs Alving herself used to describe what she meant by 'ghosts' in Act II, he gives a wider reference to his disease; it is no longer a single, individual fact, but a fact related to, produced by, those ghosts of dead ideas by which society and, as has been abundantly revealed, even Mrs Alving, have always been haunted. He does not himself see the connection but it is clear: Mrs Alving has helped produce this horror by her partial, ambiguous subservience to that dead morality. Here is a 'ghost' she has not recognised.

It is the ambiguity that is now harshly identified by the compressed ironies that attend the progressive revelations. Mrs Alving observed the dictates of that dead morality so that her son might grow up morally healthy; the result is disease and the impossibility of health of any kind. She conformed in action so that Oswald might preserve his ideals; he has none. She postponed the real relationship of mother to child in order to preserve the ideals, in expectation that eventually it would be hers to enjoy. She has her beloved child home again, all to herself, as she planned; but her subservience to form has brought back to her a grown man who will indeed be a child but only through disease. She bore a son as an act of social duty and then sent him away to become an artist. The artist is crippled. The only real demonstration Oswald makes in the whole play of his aesthetic sensibility comes in the blood-chilling description of softening of the brain: 'I think that expression sounds so beautiful. It always makes me think of cherry-coloured hangings – something delicious to stroke.' Everything that Mrs Alving has done for the best has, because of her partial surrender to a dead morality, emerged in disaster.

The ironies are for the audience, not for Oswald or even for Mrs Alving yet. Even the facts keep meeting in her the astounding instinct she has for reducing complexity to comforting shapeliness. It is almost unbelievable, and in its way affecting, that when Oswald speaks of his horror of being turned into a helpless child, Mrs Alving can actually find comfort in the cliché she drew upon with such confidence in Act 1: 'The child has his mother to look after him.' The meanings of words have changed, changed terribly. 'Child' now means horror, yet Mrs Alving still tries to see in the situation the kind of relationship she has been brought up to accept as good without question – after all the questions that have been asked in the course of the play.

Even so, she can no longer obliterate from her mind all the facts. Oswald asks her for 'a helping hand'. The obscure contamination of that phrase by Engstrand turns out, in the event, to be justified. For Oswald uses the seemly phrase with a terrible significance. He means a helping hand to kill him when the next attack comes. As this, the ugliest of facts, emerges from behind the bland surface of an acceptable phrase, Mrs Alving for once loses control of herself. It is a shock to see this dignified, courageous woman suddenly try to run, physically run from the facts that she has for so long, so staunchly though so misguidedly tried to control.

Mrs Alving tries to escape from the room that she imagined she had created as a private haven. What it has in fact been all the time is emphasised when Oswald brings her back and locks the door. The haven has always been a prison and its very seemliness not only increases the shock of discovery but indicates what kind of prison it is. Mrs Alving has confined herself within the appearances and the decorum of a society which she despised but dared not break with. And part of her torment is that the consequences are locked in with her.

Mrs Alving has at last been made to know the consequences of her past compromises. It takes great courage, but she possesses it, not to simply collapse. She pulls herself together and gives her promise to help her son die when need arises. And yet, almost beyond belief, her mind is still at work shaping and forming her terrible circumstances into patterns she can grasp and control. To persuade herself that perhaps the morphine may never have to be used is natural optimism. For her to say: 'Home with your own mother, my darling boy. You shall have everything you point to just like when you were a little child,' shows how appallingly insensitive she still remains to the fact that by now some stock words and stock relationships have been redefined out of recognition. She relies upon a mother/child relationship that is horribly at variance with the foul reality – she can actually find comfort in being mother to a son reduced to childlike imbecility.

In keeping with this failure, even at this late stage, to fully comprehend the facts that she is slowly having to recognise, is Mrs Alving's reversion to the imagery of day-break. After all that has happened, she can look out of the windows and say 'And do you see, Oswald, what a lovely day we shall have? Bright sunshine. Now you can really see your home.' For her, a happy omen; she seems to feel that somehow she has come through, that she has brought off her plan in spite of everything. There is just a touch of this in the purely physical action of her turning out the table-lamp – it was meant to dispel the gloom and it has served its turn.

For the audience the dawn is a mighty force that simply takes over control from Mrs Alving. Her attempts to direct and shape events are swamped by the sudden, last demonstration of the full truth. The sun rises and she does finally, as Oswald promised, know. Her son collapses into idiocy; he babbles, 'mother, give me the sun'.

He is beyond meaning anything by his words, but they condense the whole of Mrs Alving's life into one brief phrase. She has never been able to give him the sun; but the image means much more than the superficial 'happiness' that Alving wanted and Regine has gone off to seek; more than the happiness of life and work in Paris. The sun subsumes all these into something greater and more comprehensive. Mrs Alving has never been able to be true to truth – true to her feelings, to her instincts, to her conscious knowledge that her morality was superior to the dead morality imposed by society. She has accepted, under protest and in full awareness, the murk of social hypocrisy. From that betrayal of truth all the other betrayals flow.

There is no evidence that Mrs Alving comprehends the pattern in events that has now been revealed. Like Lear she can only concentrate upon the awful human fact that confronts her. But one thing is quite clear; she has been forced out of her inculcated habit of trying to control events by projecting patterns upon circumstances. At this ultimate crisis no clichés, no assumptions, no agreed pattern of behaviour, can serve to shape this horror into something graspable and controllable. At last there is nothing left to intervene between Mrs Alving and her full exposure to the grim ugliness that she had thought she could conceal. Her personal decorum, which has always been part of her subservience to the decorum of appearances, breaks down: '*she jumps to her feet in desperation, tears at her hair with both hands and screams.*' So too does her language. She cannot organise this experience into patterned rhetoric:

'It's intolerable! (*whispers as though petrified*)
It's intolerable! Never! (*suddenly*) Where has he
put them? (*gropes hastily at his breast*) Here!

recoils a step or two and screams) No; no; no! –
Yes! No; no!'

At long last she has been forced out from behind the defences she accepted from the society she despised yet conformed to. The pattern-making on which that society depended has time and time again short-circuited her understanding; now it can no longer operate. Mrs Alving faces the real fact and responds to it with language that has become naked.

What she will decide to do about her son, whether she will eventually be able to piece together a true pattern out of events are matters that Ibsen is not concerned with. He leaves us at the moment when Mrs Alving is seeing the worst piece of the truth for the first time; it is a terrible moment, and yet it has its beauty. For the sun has risen; it dispels the gloom; it shines brightly upon the glacier and the mountain-peaks. For all the pain and disaster, the existence, the beauty and majesty, and the irrepressibility of truth have been affirmed.

The ironies compressed into that final scene are likely to be almost as unendurable for the audience as for Mrs Alving. She worked so hard to create for her son a corner of health and sanity in a corrupt world; that son is mentally diseased. She planned to clear the house of all other but herself and her beloved child; she has succeeded, but only in this appalling travesty. She thought that she could bring the long, hateful comedy to a neat end, sealing off all consequences, but she has unwittingly written a final act which is tragic. She worked to preserve a life and must now decide whether to destroy it.

The sum of these reversals to her expectations amounts to a condemnation of Mrs Alving; not for her trying, but for the mode of her trying. The essential quality in her is ambiguity, that strangely constant mingling within the one woman of radical and conformist; she is strong enough to try to think for herself, but too cowardly to act in any other way than that required by the society she has, in part, seen through. Her radicalism itself is never complete; it may, under Oswald's influence, expand, but at no point can she fully liberate herself from the influence upon her, acknowledged or unacknowledged, of dead social habits. All that can be said of her at the end of the play is that at least at that moment she is being forced to face facts as they really are; what she will make of the experience we cannot know.

Thus the play could be taken as the trial and condemnation of a misguided, inadequate woman. If Mrs Alving had been true to her own feelings she would not have married Alving, or remained with him once married; had she been true to her own sense of the genuine, she would not have decided to rectify the disaster of her life by preserving appearances, whose falsity she recognised, in order to appease society. It is a strong indictment and the play undoubtedly levels it at her; and yet an account that stopped there would seem to me not to acknowledge much else that is offered.

For all her misguidedness, Mrs Alving remains in the imagination as a splendid woman. This impression comes partly from her personality and character taken by and for themselves. She has been so strong, to have coped with a life like that without weakness and to have coped alone. She must have had nerves and a will of steel to have conceived and carried out a plan of such complexity and long duration without losing heart. She always fights to control and shape events, never allowing herself to be passively overwhelmed. She is indeed a strong woman. And we can only admire the direction in which her strength is constantly directed. Misguided or not, blinkered though she may be in ways unsuspected by herself, she is always trying to see through pretence and hypocrisy to the truth behind it. She often fails to get through, and she initially fails to act on the truth that she has discovered, but that is the direction her bent of mind leads her in. And out of her private understanding she hopes for one single thing: to create the possibility of a decent life.

There is an element of selfishness in all this, yet even that is forgiveable in a mother. She wants her boy to herself. But she is no child-devourer; Oswald has always been free to come and go; but for his illness he could return to Paris; Mrs Alving relishes the thought of his staying but she has never suggested it, still less demanded or engineered it. The element of maternal selfishness is minor compared with the selflessness that has made her sacrifice her own happiness to her son's well-being. Everything that she has done has been directed towards that.

Thus even on a narrow view of Mrs Alving as a character in isolation she seems to merit deep respect and not mere blame. For the full assessment we need to see her in her context.

In simple terms, Mrs Alving has always been at war with society. Her stature, and her achievements, must be gauged in relation to her antagonist. And here the play creates a force of peculiar horror. Society is presented as an openly coercive force, but that is not its chief characteristic. We see it in action upon Manders and through him upon Mrs Alving. The coercion is strong, certainly not negligible, but it is not remarkable.

Society's real power lies in its unobtrusiveness. The trap it lays for Mrs Alving is one into which she and millions of other women have slipped without recognising that it was a trap. There is nothing openly coercive about the advice of relations when it comes to choosing a husband. Mrs Alving was not aware of facing a great crisis in her life when she decided that Alving was the best catch in social terms; and yet in that choice she subdued her own feelings to the criteria created by society. The essential falsification occurred then, yet who could have identified such a crisis in so commonplace a decision? Part of the power of society in *Ghosts* is that it works through small-scale events which do not proclaim their real significance at the moment of occurrence. Brand could identify his crises; Mrs Alving could not.

Yet once in, the consequences are fatal and inescapable. From the initial falsification all others flow; and these too hide their significance in unobtrusiveness. When Mrs Alving sent Oswald away from home and made arrangements for Regine and so on, she was being false to her knowledge of the truth, but she was conditioned by society to accept without question that this was the reasonable way to act. Her plans were reasonable submissions to society that followed from her first reasonable submission. And she has gone on living for years without having much reason to recognise that such submission of personal integrity to social demands could be critical and fatal.

And yet in the end the magnitude of crisis must become clear. To submit, to the extent that Mrs Alving has, to society is to cause terrible corruption to set in. Oswald's disease is the outward and spectacular sign of the corruption, of its secretiveness and of its fatal inevitability, but it is not the only form of corruption. There is corruption of will, corruption of courage, corruption of integrity, of relationships – indeed a creeping invasion through many different veins and arteries of the play simultaneously. In *Brand* the sequence of events was linear; Brand moved on from one crisis and its consequences to the next. In *Ghosts* the various streams of corruption move apparently independently and in unsuspected ways towards the one moment of dissolution.

Perhaps Ibsen's greatest discovery in *Ghosts* was the way in which his protagonist must necessarily be involved in modern society. Falk, in *Love's Comedy*, by virtue of his favoured status as student, was allowed to stand outside the social structure he condemned. Though affected by his antagonism to his surroundings, he was not contaminated by them. Nor was Brand; even though he was woven into his community far more intimately than Falk, his small parish can serve only as an emblem of real modern social existence; and he too, Ibsen seemed to imagine, could preserve his spiritual integrity.

Mrs Alving cannot preserve hers entirely from the corruption she later comes to identify. However clearly she may, by the time the play begins, recognise that she married for the wrong reason, may have acted wrongly since, may need to revise and enlarge her sense of truth and honesty, she constantly reveals that society continues to influence her ways of thought and action. Ibsen can see now that no individual, not even one with the basic integrity of a Mrs Alving, can escape permeation by the very corruption by society that their integrity makes them identify and oppose. Significantly one of the images of that permeation is the gloom which envelops, as an all-pervasive natural force, the action of so much of the play.

This is Mrs Alving's antagonist, and it is in its peculiar fashion powerful enough to explain and justify total submissiveness in all the individuals who compose it. Mrs Alving is conditioned;

she is partly submissive, deliberately and unconsciously; but she is never totally subdued. And this refusal to give up trying to discover what is the truth and the right way to respond to it is again significantly defined through the image of a great natural force, the sun. Notwithstanding her wounds and blemishes, indeed because of them, Mrs Alving emerges as a great fighter against a terrible opponent.

In *Ghosts*, then, Ibsen has entered more deeply into the nature of modern society and its relationship to the heroic individual; he has also created a dramatic form for embodying his vision. Whatever else it may be, *Ghosts* cannot reasonably be assessed as a mere surrender on Ibsen's part to theatrical expediency or as a betrayal of the poetic copiousness of *Love's Comedy*, *Brand* and *Peer Gynt* to the seductions of naturalism. Its form is essential to the vision.

The language, for instance, is limited in range because this is one of the effects society has on its members. It educates them to think decorously and to express themselves with conventional neatness. Anyone who tries to break these limitations must create his own language and in Oswald's shapeless rhetoric the impression of overemphasis, of straining after effects not to hand in the common use of language, is indicative not of Ibsen's verbal impoverishment but of the spiritual impoverishment of the society that cannot accommodate Oswald; and, as we have seen, Mrs Alving's reduction of his vision to the careful patterning that she has been educated in illuminates the same point from a different angle. Ibsen can no longer imagine for his modern hero that degree of mental and spiritual autonomy that allowed Falk and Brand to be fully articulate poets. Their significance lies in their being poets of living, men with a vision of a finer life than society offers, but their ability to be poets in words, to speak out with full-blooded rhetoric to expound, explore, define their visions, is one way of asserting that they are spiritually free men. But they were so only because Ibsen had not, at that time, really sensed the power of modern society: Falk can stand outside it, Brand encounters a simplified version, an emblem. Nobody, not even Mrs Alving, can preserve his autonomy in the face of the complexity of power that society now represents for Ibsen, and the language is one means of expressing this fact.

The same is true of the setting. Mrs Alving's handsome room may be less spectacular than Brand's mountains and ice-church but it is not to be despised for its ordinariness. The set mirrors Ibsen's conviction that it is by its unobtrusiveness, by its very reasonableness and seemliness, that society is able to exercise its power; the very decency of appearances helps him emphasise the horror of discovering that the attractive setting is a monstrous snare, and the limiting of the action to one room takes away the illusion, still preserved in *Love's Comedy* and *Brand*, that there is somewhere else to go. In modern society, as Ibsen sees it, there is nowhere else; the great battles must be fought out amongst comfortable furniture in a handsome house; the mountains offer no escape to Mrs Alving: they are remote images of ultimate truth, not to be trodden as they were by Falk and Brand. The setting is an essential part of Ibsen's harsher vision.

The setting is created partly by verbal, partly by visual imagery. Both kinds indicate further advances beyond the artistry and vision of his earlier works. The extremity of imagery in *Brand*, those blatant and massive symbols of opposition – storm, mountains, ice-church, narrow dale, sunshine and so forth – help create what amounts to an almost comforting sense of clarity. The opposed values are identified for us; the crises that arise out of the opposition are made manifest not merely to us but to the protagonist. In *Ghosts* everything is made less precise. Instead of storm, steady drizzle and mist, not a challenge so much as an enervating atmosphere; instead of miserable dale, Mrs Alving's country house, outwardly a haven. There are no sharp indices of crisis; we have to discover them as Ibsen now sees them, as latent and lurking. Out of this lack of clarity comes a further virtue. Instead of establishing his imagery *ab initio*, as he does in *Love's Comedy* and in *Brand*, and then working by repetition, Ibsen allows his imagery to grow organically, establishing itself and its significance progressively. He works not by massive and blatant groupings but by small affinities gradually discovered. Yet he holds all this together, more successfully than in *Brand*, by creating a feeling of tempo, of inevitable movement towards a climax. All of the imagery is ultimately controlled by the image of Oswald's disease and by the image of day dispersing night. Thus Ibsen can represent deviousness and cryptic consequence without losing his sense of the essential unity of the action or of the pace in which the action moves. There is little feeling of development or progression in *Love's Comedy*; in *Brand* there is progression of a relatively simple linear kind, with little feeling of tempo; *Ghosts* moves much more impressively.

In *Ghosts* the vision is enriched and the form for its expression brought almost to perfection. Not quite to perfection because there are signs, here and there, that the effort to elucidate for himself the pattern that underlies the seemingly petty detail of modern living led him into oversimplification, both of vision and form, in the interests of clarity. Some of the cross-weaving of images into patterns is of this kind – the equation of the drizzle with the spiritual climate, or of Oswald with the Orphanage, does not need the kind of emphasis it is given. Manders need not be as inadequate as he is to give a reasonable representation of society's inadequacies.

Ghosts has its imperfections but it is a great play for all that. Though different in kind it is arguably a finer dramatic poem than *Brand*, if by poem we mean an imaginatively organised structure of imagery constituting a profound and unified vision. Less debatably, Mrs Alving is a more convincing kind of hero than Brand, by virtue of her fuller involvement in a society more fully understood and represented. From *Love's Comedy* and *Brand* we gain insight into the issues that govern the quality of living; in *Ghosts* the issues are played out upon our nerves and feelings as we experience, with Mrs Alving, what it feels like to be a woman like that condemned to live in such a world. *Ghosts* is, above all, an experience, immediate and immensely painful. And yet, for all its greatness, it marks only Ibsen's entry into artistic maturity; the greatest works are amongst those that follow.

5

'THE WILD DUCK'

The lighting of the first set draws attention. The scene is prosaic enough: an upper-class study on the main stage, with a big, elegant music-room visible through open doors at the back; servants getting the rooms ready for the company as a formal meal ends with toasts in the dining-room off-stage. The effect that is striking is the contrast between the brilliance of the room at the back and the subdued, green-shaded lights of the main stage. The contrast is still being established as the first words are spoken: servants light still more candles in the bright room, while Pettersen, the butler, puts a green shade over the lamp he has just lit in the study.

He is being kept busy fending off the curiosity of the hired waiters (though he is ready to give the straightforward information that the son is home on a rare visit from the Høydal works), when he is upset by the unexpected entry of old Ekdal. He has the trappings of respectability – hat, gloves, stick – but he is seedy. The little grey moustache mocks the reddish-brown wig; the pretence is blatant and pathetic.

Old Ekdal sounds pathetic too, at first. He is mildly slipshod in speech; he does not take trouble to complete his sentences, which come out staccato, lacking the personal pronoun – 'Must get into the office...Heard it at the door, old chap...Been this way before'; though there is a flash of resilience in his muttered 'Clot!' when Pettersen lets him through at last.

The butler shows no reluctance to talk about him: a fine chap in his day, a lieutenant, but ruined and sent to jail over some timber-business that nearly involved Mr Werle; or so people say; Pettersen is not very sure of the facts behind the obvious fact that old Werle has come down in the world. Then he is interrupted by the emergence into the study of the company.

Mrs Sørby's position in the Werle household seems to be that of hostess rather than housekeeper; she leads the way and the host follows up amongst the others. Before they pass into the brilliantly lit music-room there is time to respond to the unprepossessing appearance of some of the guests; one is fat, another is thin on top, another short-sighted. Their chatter is brief but enough to show their triviality and a certain knowing familiarity of tone when Mrs Sørby – Berta to them – is mentioned. If the host (and hostess) are to be judged by their company the verdict can hardly be entirely favourable. Two people seem to hold a little aloof: Gregers Werle and Hjalmar Ekdal come last in the procession and remain in the dim light of the study rather than follow the socialites into the brightness – which seems appropriate to them – of the music-room. But not before Gregers' father, Werle, has made the extra guest uncomfortable by his reference to their having been thirteen at table. He seems also to show a genuine uneasiness at the unlucky circumstance, which is left to depress a little the apparently convivial atmosphere.

Thirteen at table, unprepossessing guests, an ill-defined but perceptible tang of rakishness, a ruined old lieutenant once a friend and partner of the host, a son who rarely visits his father – there is already enough to inspire curiosity about what really lies behind the sparkling appearance of social success; there is already this justification for the shaded light, the something-less-than-full clarity, of the main stage.

There seems a chance that everything will emerge from the conversation between Gregers and Hjalmar. As two old school-friends, one the son of Werle, the other of old Ekdal, they must have plenty to reveal. Especially since Hjalmar, according to Gregers, is his only and best friend. In fact little emerges that can be relied upon as substantial fact. Not even the friendship, for they have not met for sixteen or seventeen years, or corresponded.

It is clear that Hjalmar, like his father though less spectacularly, has come down in the world; he is not normally invited to the house; once a university student, he has become a photographer. It is also obvious, from the frequency with which he refers to Gregers' father, that the old man occupies a prominent place in his thoughts. No wonder, since he set Hjalmar up in business, in spite of the way he was almost involved in old Ekdal's ruin and in spite of the financial debt owed to him.

That is one possible version of events – Werle the generous family benefactor. It is a stereotype of charity but it is created out of a verbal style that in itself would be enough to call in question the truth, or rather the perceptiveness, of the account. For Hjalmar's style is florid and stereotyped in its own way. He has a weakness for the intensive adjective or adverb – 'you know how dreadfully everything has turned out', 'my poor, unhappy father', 'shatteringly heavy', 'fate's shattering blow', 'the great misfortune', 'this frightful business' – and for the ready-made emotive phrase – 'he has absolutely nothing else in the whole world to hold on to', 'for inviting me to your father's table'.

Gregers' style is different. He settles down to a kind of brief, sceptical cross-questioning. He too responds to the repeated 'your father' and it is obviously of importance to him to establish what his father's role has been. He is more and more astonished at what he is told about his generosity; he is on the point of accepting Hjalmar's account, obviously against his previous inclination. But there is something in his style too which helps to indicate that these otherwise dissimilar men indeed share at least one important characteristic; for from time to time Gregers' close cross-questioning burgeons forth into the same sort of emotional cliché as Hjalmar uses: 'my best and only friend', 'we two old schoolfriends', 'this certainly shows a kind heart. It is a sort of conscience –'. But when Hjalmar mentions his marriage to Gina Hansen as having been furthered by Werle the flow of emotional approval towards his father ceases abruptly and he reverts to being the sharp questioner.

Nothing emerges to settle the matter. Hjalmar continues to demonstrate his simple trust and gratitude; Gregers is clearly inclined to set a different construction on events; but there is no clarity. What is interesting is not so much the pattern of events as Gregers' lively suspicion of anything concerning his own father. The facts remain obscure but the attitude becomes clearer, of filial hostility and mistrust.

When Mrs Sørby invites the rest of the company into the study

for drinks, we discover that Werle's eyes cause him trouble; but
the scene contributes more than that. The faintly rakish atmosphere is re-asserted as the guests exchange mild innuendoes with
Mrs Sørby, and we can gauge her ability to more than hold her
own. Hjalmar's position of social inferiority is established as the
guests patronise him and Mrs Sørby tries, unsuccessfully, to draw
him out. His worst gaffe is over the wine. Mrs Sørby skilfully
diverts attention from him but he does not recover – he drops out
of the conversation entirely. His demoralisation is completed by
the apparition of his father cringing his way out of the office
through the crowded study. He dare not acknowledge him. The
guests try once again to be kind, in terms even more offensively
patronising than before; Gregers turns on him with a sentence that
has echoes of Peter's betrayal: 'And you actually stood there and
denied that you knew him!' (cf. Matthew XXVI. 7, 'And again he
denied with an oath, I do not know the man'; Luke XXII. 57,
'And again he denied, saying, Woman, I know him not').
Hjalmar salvages such self-respect as he can by spouting words:
'When a man has felt fate's shattering blow upon his head...',
but he can only retreat, and Mrs Sørby is wise enough not to
try to persuade him to stay.

By bringing the figure of the ruined old man into the scene of
social success the episode has demanded an answer to the question,
how has this spectacular degradation of the Ekdals, once a family
in Werle's social ambit, come about? Father meets son unwillingly
to have it out in the shaded light of the study. Gregers implies that
his father was more guilty than old Ekdal in the timber-poaching
affair; Werle denies it and blames old Ekdal. Gregers blames his
father for the family's degradation; Werle blames old Ekdal's
spinelessness: 'You come across people in life who dive to the
bottom just because they stop a couple of pellets in the body, and
then they never come up again.' Werle claims that he has been
generous to Hjalmar, Gregers imputes the base motive of provid-
ing for an ex-mistress. Werle blames his late wife's neurotic
jealousy, Gregers blames his father for making her unstable. And
so it goes on – revealing not facts but dark, concealed possibilities,
except for the one blatant fact of gross mistrust – the adjective is

deserved now – of father by son, and the deplorable family situation out of which it has grown.

The mistrust may or may not be justified – we cannot take sides – but it is extraordinarily intense. It shows in two highly characteristic statements by Gregers that are entirely different in tone and thus demonstrate the essential division in his personality. In one of them the old emotional clichés well up again:

> – and now there he sits, with his great, trusting child-soul, surrounded by deceit...lives under the same roof as a woman like that, and doesn't know that what he calls his home is built upon a lie... When I look back over the whole of your career, it's as though I looked out over a battlefield with shattered human fates all over the place.

Interestingly Gregers manages not merely to sound like his earlier self ('my best and only friend' etc.) and like Hjalmar, but he actually re-uses one of Hjalmar's more emotive clusters of words: the Norwegian for 'battlefield with shattered human fates' is 'en slagmark med knuste menneskeskjebner'; for Hjalmar's 'fate's shattering blow' it is 'skjebnens knusende slag'. One side of him, as he tries to express his sense of human morality, employs the grandiose vagueness and generality of Hjalmar.

The other side is even more disturbing. His final words to his father, who he knows is going blind and who intends to marry Mrs Sørby, are full of compressed nastiness. There is a cruel jibe at the blindness, and an unpleasant innuendo at what is likely to happen when blindness comes in his: 'Look, father, your guests are playing blindman's buff with Mrs Sørby.' This seems to be the true motive-power behind Gregers, this hatred for his father. It sits uneasily with the facile idealistic phrases but the connection is obvious: Gregers projects on to his friend the qualities he has not found in his father. Obvious enough, but disturbing. His behaviour seems to merit the implications of Werle's concluding line: 'and he says he isn't hysterical!' But *is* Werle right? The Act ends, in more ways than one, in less than total clarity; except that Gregers emotional history has been sketched in.

In Act II the change in social grade is obvious: the top-floor studio flat in which the Ekdals live is furnished poorly, though it is comfortable and neat. Instead of the handsome appointments of the business-man's study, here is the combined living-and-working room of a professional photographer. Gina Ekdal is sewing, Hedvig is in the posture of any child who has no private place to read in – hands shading her eyes, thumbs in her ears.

Gina tells her to stop reading, as many a mother in a non-bookish household has and will, for no better reason than that her father doesn't like it; but there's a touch of anxiety, and a suggestion of possible significance since Act i ended on Werle's encroaching blindness. But nothing immediately to disturb the impression of a very homely, prosaic, family setting.

The petty business of totting up the household account for the day tells as much about Hjalmar as it does about the economy. They use a lot of butter – against Gina's inclinations, it seems – smoked sausage, cheese, ham, beer. And it all *has* to be bought; but not for mother and child. If father is out for lunch, they go without a warm meal. And it was Gina who took the money for some photographs. All of this, together with a strong sense of relationship between mother and daughter, comes out of this brief and in its minor fashion fascinating little scene, which develops with the arrival of old Ekdal.

It is a nice indication of the difference in relationships of daughter-in-law and grandaughter to old Ekdal that while Hedvig addresses the old man directly in the familiar second person, Gina addresses him in the third person:

GINA   Grandfather's late coming home today.
HEDVIG Did they give you some new stuff to copy, grandfather?

The old man, still in the pathetic subterfuge of his reddish wig, indulges in more pretence as he tries, transparently, to pass off as devotion to work what we, and the womenfolk, know to be addiction to brandy. But before he gets fully involved in his pathetic manoeuvres he pulls back a little way one of the two big sliding doors in the back wall. They – whatever they may be – are all asleep; and she – whatever she may be – has bedded down in the basket. The old man is pleased; Hedvig is as interested in 'her' as he is; Gina gives the impression of being long-suffering and forbearing. The womenfolk do not begrudge the old man his brandy.

Nor the father his party at Werle's, though the reason for this comes disconcertingly from a child as young as Hedvig; she knows the value of having her father cheerful when he comes home; otherwise things aren't so pleasant. Hedvig obviously lives closely involved with her parents and their moods; very much an only child in that respect. And with her grandfather's weakness for drink. The family seems if anything the more tightly intimate for this experience unselfconsciously, naturally shared between the generations. But behind the forbearance there is again subterfuge; they know what old Ekdal is up to, but neither would dream of breaking his illusion of secrecy. They let him lie to keep his self-respect.

Hjalmar's entry causes more of a stir than his father's did; Gina tosses her sewing aside and rises, Hedvig jumps to her feet. The master is greeted with fuss and attention which he seems to take for granted; wife and daughter help him off with his overcoat, Hjalmar does not condescend to thank them. And his first words are a lie, the first of a series, about the party. He is shifty and uneasy until he receives his cue for a characteristic bit of rhetoric 'My God – my poor, old whitehaired father...' Then, when old Ekdal comes out to join the group, the lies grow in number and confidence as Hjalmar realises that he has successfully skipped over the dangerous ground of not acknowledging his father at the party. It is not merely that he builds up the importance of the function, and thus of himself, or transforms his humiliating awkwardness into an insolently superior performance, but that he borrows the very witticisms directed against himself. There is not a single touch of firsthandedness, even of creative lying, in his account. He is a borrower, a toucher-up, of other people's ideas, and he manages to coarsen by his manner the originals. And in the midst of this inauthenticity, there comes a discreet, rather pathetic indication of what has happened to this family. The son recounts the story about wine as though it were a piece of recondite knowledge – he is a stranger to the luxury; the father shows that he knows about Tokay and vintages – once he was no stranger.

Hjalmar's vanity and his general character show again when Hedvig flatters him on his smart appearance. He accepts unblushingly; but it seems now to fit his character, not merely his social position, that his formal jacket was borrowed, like his witticisms. Gina helps him on with a loose and comfortable coat of his own (again unthanked); he loosens his tie to make a pair of flowing ends; squabbles mildly with Hedvig about the right description for his hair – wavy or curly – and there we have him, visually defined – a seedy little pseudo-bohemian: vain, silly, derivative, a petty tyrant. His unpleasantness comes out when Hedvig discovers that he has forgotten to bring home something nice for her to eat; the scale of behaviour is tiny, but that is the scale of family life and by that measurement he is obtuse, even cruel. He works off such shame as he feels on his wife, bullying her for not getting more orders and for not letting the spare room. It is a very unpleasant display, not improved by the way in which Hedvig instinctively uses wheedling and flattery to bring him round. He is that sort of man; and the reason for the expensive luxuries that meant the womenfolk going without a hot meal; Hedvig tempts him back to good humour with the offer of some beer and his flute. He clinches his self-portrait by a display of gross sentimentality in words and in music.

And yet, incredibly, this is a family. However spurious and shoddy the father may be, there is a feeling of warm intimacy. The basis may be wrong, but it supports the little group of accommodating wife and adoring child as they watch Hjalmar perform.

The mood, and the picture, are shattered by a knock at the door. Gregers comes as a friend but acts as an intruder. Gina is for some reason shaken; Hedvig fades into the background; Hjalmar the seedy bohemian sits down to talk with a Gregers who wears a simple, grey suit of countrified cut; out of the social uniform they both wore at the party, the men show their differences in their respective exteriors; and this effect colours the whole of their discussion.

Hjalmar speaks in character – that is, sentimentally – about Hedvig and her inevitable blindness. Gregers starts at the information that the trouble is hereditary, but Gina hastens to mention that there was similar trouble on Hjalmar's side of the family and the possibility of some connection with Werle's eyesight seems to recede for the moment. Hjalmar feeds his feelings with the beer and some well-buttered bread – we remember the household bills again, and the fact that Hedvig is, and for all her father cares, will remain, hungry – and meanwhile Gregers begins to reveal himself in a way that emphasises his lack of real connection with this family. He is the outsider who intrudes with questions – insistently with questions. They are not motivated by a genuine personal interest. He seems to be doing what he tried to do in Act I, get at some facts to fit a theory: how old is Hedvig? she looks big for her age; how long have you been married? – really! He makes his hosts very uneasy, disrupts the mood.

His reaction to old Ekdal expands this impression of insensitivity to people in pursuit of theory. The old man comes on looking unmistakably what he is, the wreck of what he once was. The old army cap reminds us of the days when he was Lieutenant Ekdal, friend and partner to Werle; the seedy appearance, the unsteady gait, the wig, the sheer decrepitude prove what he has become, a pathetic old drunk. The old man seems almost frightened by a visit from one of the Werles. Gregers blunders into a conversation by reminding this old wreck of his younger days as a famous hunter in the forests. It is a stupid question to ask: 'have you given up hunting now?' but he asks it. He is talking to a man ruined for poaching timber from the forest; old Ekdal shows his agitation by his inarticulate brooding over the word: 'Because you see the forest – the forest, the forest –!' It is something too deep for him to come out with, but Gregers doesn't respect or even notice the pressure of feeling. He plunges on to talk about the very process that caused old Ekdal's downfall; the forest is: 'Not as fine as it was in your day. There's been a tremendous amount of thinning out.' 'In your day' is especially insensitive. This reference to the past is enough to drive old Ekdal into a kind of frightened, private nightmare: 'Thinned out? (*more softly as if afraid*) That's a dangerous thing to do, that is. That has consequences. There's vengeance in the forest.' And yet even that demonstration is not sufficient for Gregers. He seems incapable of seeing old Ekdal as he is; he continues to harp on what he thinks of him as, still the open-air hunter, not inquisitively now, but expressing that other side of his character, the emotional idealist; the pressure shows in the rhetoric: 'But [what about] all those things your mind has grown up amongst? That cool, brisk breeze, that open-air life in the forest and on the moors, amongst the beasts and the birds?' Gregers seems to need to hark back to an idea of perfection, an ideal; he does not recognize what is actually in front of him. Absurdly he even tries to persuade the old man to return with him to the Høydal works in the forest – this physical and, it sometimes seems, mental wreck whom he insists on calling by his old rank, now wildly inappropriate, of Lieutenant.

In the end his clumsiness provokes reactions. Old Ekdal insists on proving that life in the flat is not so dull as he seems to think. It contains something that draws three members of the family together – the old man, Hjalmar and Hedvig help each other open the big double doors at the back. Gina is not interested.

The something, the place where 'they' and 'she' live, is the attic, a large, long, irregularly shaped space with nooks and corners and a couple of free-standing stove-pipes; bright moonlight shines through some skylights into some parts of the room, while others lie in deep shadow. The effect is astonishing. Here is a mysterious kind of beauty, richly evocative yet made out of an attic and stove-pipes and moonlight and deep shadows, created out of ordinariness, out of waste roof-space that lies just beyond the door of this commonplace family-room. It is an image that challenges the poetical imagination yet it is presented as a familiar component in the life of this shabby household.

The characters, not only Gregers but all of them, begin to define themselves by reference to this attic and its inhabitants. Gina fills out the impression we have already of her by proving totally indifferent to them – soon she complains of the draught. The old man and the young girl share a simple enthusiasm; Hjalmar hasn't the courage to admit to any – he attributes all this nonsense to his father but this is typical cowardice. Gregers is as totally out of touch with the attic as he is with people. He stands at the door peering in, asking prosaic questions, always reducing the inherent poetry of the situation to prose: 'Then you keep poultry, Lieutenant Ekdal!'; 'And I can see a bird lying in the basket';

'Isn't it a duck?' etc. Even when he learns that the bird is a wild duck, he is quite unable to enter into the spirit that moves old Ekdal and Hedvig who are so proud of this rare possession. Instead, he asks, 'And can it live up here in the attic? And thrive here?'; when old Ekdal prepares to expound on the remarkableness of wild ducks, Gregers asks him how he caught it. His mind is not on the thing itself that he has just seen any more than it was on old Ekdal when he spoke to him. He remains outside the mystery and the beauty and the enthusiasm, outside and peering in inquisitively as though looking for evidence rather than for experience.

In fact he soon begins to probe in a way that shows his old obsession to be driving him on; suspicion of his father seems to formulate some of his questions for him, not personal interest. He 'guesses' that it was his own father who caught the duck, and from that moment begins to create for himself a symbol. It is a deliberate creation; he quotes the words his father had used of old Ekdal and similar weak creatures in Act I. He is obviously delighted at finding this physical analogue; and old Ekdal, unconsciously on his part, gives the simple image just that expansion that perfects it for Gregers' moral purposes. He mumbles about the strangely heroic instinct of the bird that makes it drown itself amongst the weed when shot; he tells how this bird was rescued by a clever dog; Hjalmar adds that it thrives in the attic and has forgotten what real wild life is.

For Hedvig and Hjalmar and Ekdal the bird is a bird; for Gregers it has grown beautifully into the ideal symbol of the situation as he sees it. He does not immediately expound his vision in these terms; he seems to hug his discovery to himself; but the idealistic pressure suddenly manifests itself in his grandiose language again, as a kind of emotional hunger for the absolute: 'You are absolutely right there, Hjalmar. Only never let it catch sight of heaven and sea –.' He does not complete that sentence; he breaks off to ask if he may rent the spare room; but the emotion returns in its obverse shape, as a sudden, startling, unmotivated burst of hatred or disgust. Gregers is saying that he hopes he will be like the wild duck – the image obviously fascinates him – and that now (a significant word) he thinks he will remain in town, when he erupts. It is almost as though he were vomiting:

HJALMAR ...What do you intend doing, then?

GREGERS Yes, my dear chap, if only I knew that – I shouldn't be doing so badly after all. But when one's burdened with the name 'Gregers' – 'Gregers' – and then 'Werle' to follow; have you ever heard anything so disgusting, Hjalmar?...Ugh! Pah! I should want to spit on the fellow with a name like that. But once you're burdened with being Gregers – Werle in this life as I am –

There is no provocation for this; the disgust wells up unbidden. And its cause is obviously not the mere names but the fact of having been named by his father and with his father's family name. Disgust with parentage, together with self-disgust, disgust with things as they are in contrast to the ideal and absolute, provides the violence of feeling here. This is the other side of Gregers again, the hysterical, suspicious hater, product of a miserable family history.

The Act ends with this side of him being put directly alongside the emotional idealist; Gregers recovers from his fit with remarkable rapidity to say that if he had the choice he would like to be a clever dog, the sort that rescues wild ducks. He is again quoting. He has formed together in his own mind all that he has heard about wild ducks from his father and old Ekdal to create for himself a symbol that defines both the situation and now his own role in it. He has shaped the symbol, discovered that the duck is the perfect representation of the human situation. The discovery seems to give him energy and decisiveness as he arranges to move in next day.

Three things nag at the mind. Gregers has, throughout the Act, behaved towards Hjalmar as towards a man potentially of the same character as himself; the actual difference, kept before the audience by the dissimilarity of dress, apparently escapes him. Then the Gregers who casts himself in the role of rescuer is the same man who erupted into violent disgust a moment before; hardly the soundest of recommendations for the part. The third dissatisfaction is with the patness of the symbolism. For Gregers it runs easily, but, in view of what we have seen and heard, it seems glib, too much the conscious creation of a bludgeoning mind. But for the moment an assessment of this symbolising is less important than the effect it has on the other characters. Hjalmar treats it as an incomprehensible joke; Gina does not understand but she is uneasy. The most significant and the most sensitive reaction comes from Hedvig. First of all in her involuntary ejaculation when Gregers says he would like to be a clever dog. 'Oh, no!', she says. Which shows that while Gregers is thinking in symbols, she is thinking in terms of real live creatures; for her a dog is a dog, and an unwelcome creature to have near her wild duck. Her cry is a sensitive indication of the void between the adult symboliser and the adolescent rooted in fact. And yet she also shows that she, more than her elders, nonetheless senses that Gregers is trying to communicate something other than fact: 'I'll tell you one thing, mother, – I think he meant something else when he said that. . . I don't know; but it was as though he meant something different from what he was saying – all the time.' She cannot understand this symbolic mode, but she shows that she is sensitive to its use.

And that, so far, is the extent of Gregers' intrusion into this slightly shabby, but comfortable and intimate family circle. He has generated a mild stir, made Gina uneasy, reinforced Hjalmar in his self-conceit, puzzled the understanding of Hedvig – but the family group is unshaken as the final tableau shows. The Act ends with Gina and Hjalmar carefully taking old Ekdal off to bed, watched by the child.

The opening mood of Act III is totally prosaic. The studio is filled with daylight; Hjalmar is occupied with his trade – it seems right that we should see him touching-up rather than taking photographs – and Gina is busy with household chores; she has been shopping. And she is in a bad temper: Gregers has made a filthy mess in his room; he insisted on lighting his own fire, couldn't manage it and tried to put matters right by pouring a jug of water into the stove. The story seems to translate into physical terms the persistent, clumsy obstinacy of Gregers and his incapacity to deal with actual facts. He is made to seem hopelessly and, in these minor terms, disastrously theoretical.

Gina obviously knows that she has a couple of idlers on her hands, and they show some fear of her, however mildly she hints at work to be done. But the moment her back is turned Hjalmar and old Ekdal turn to what really interests them: they open up the attic. It looks different now, with the morning sun shining in, the pigeons flying and the hens cackling. It looks all fact. But it suddenly becomes a trap when they let down a piece of fishing-net skirted with sail-cloth to block the doorway. Old Ekdal enters it immediately; Hjalmar has to wait until Hedvig relieves him of his job. It is comical when he refuses to be responsible for the damage Hedvig may do to her eyes, but in its way deplorable too. Then he too goes off to waste his time, into the trap. Gregers' symbolism seems to be in process of vindication.

When Gregers comes on, there is a brief exchange of trivialities between him and Hedvig, a brief pause, and then he takes charge of the conversation. His first sentence shows where his mind rests: 'Did the wild duck sleep well last night?' and then he turns to the attic – it looks different in daylight, he says. That gets Hedvig talking and they chat about the attic. Hedvig and he seem to find quite a lot in common. She too is sensitive to the changes in mood that the attic can generate in different conditions. He suggests that the attic must be like a world of its own: that is how it strikes Hedvig too. They come close together; but there is a reminder of the void between them too. When Hedvig describes the clutter of strange objects in there she mentions the big clock that doesn't work any more. Gregers immediately turns that into a symbol: 'So time has come to a dead stop in there – with the wild duck.' And the dragging in of the duck makes it seem that Gregers is alert, throughout this conversation, to add to and enrich the symbol which preoccupies him. For all his apparent sympathy of intent, he is not so much responding to the young girl and her imagination-stirring playground as using the occasion for his own abstracting purposes. Hedvig's reply shows that she simply does not register his symbolism. She says 'Yes' and goes straight on to talk about the old books left behind by the old sea-captain. The assent means nothing.

The suspicion that all of Gregers' apparently undirected questions have an intention behind them, an intention that seems to grow out of the symbol he has created for himself, is confirmed when he suddenly applies it to Hedvig. She loves to spend her time in the attic where the wild duck lives; wouldn't she like to get out and see the big, real world? Hedvig doesn't agree; she is happy; but it is evident that Gregers is piecing together in his mind the picture of her as another human being cut off in a world of make-belief and limitation from the real world. And not just Hedvig – he hears that Hjalmar and Ekdal are almost as deeply involved. And yet, although he gives the impression of remaining outside the imaginative world of Hedvig, he manages to keep contact. Perhaps it is by mere chance, but when she lets herself go in a rush of imagination about the mysterious loneliness of the duck, he chimes in with a phrase that sparks off a kind of electric arc of sympathy between them. When he says that the duck has been down to 'the sea-deeps', instead of the normal and prosaic 'bottom of the sea', he discovers that Hedvig herself, fascinated by the strange marine character of the attic, thinks of it in the same phrase. It is a surprising point of contact.

Gregers manages, or almost manages, to break it in his next words, by thrusting forward again with his obtuse symbolising. Hedvig ends her embarrassed admission about her flights of fancy – all of them set off from actual things – by saying that of course it's only an attic that she has been describing. Whereupon Gregers leaps in, heavy-footed:

(*stares at her*) Are you sure of that?
HEDVIG (*dumbfounded*) That it's an attic?
GREGERS Yes, are you so certain?
HEDVIG (*says nothing and looks at him openmouthed*)

He is trying to force her to see it in his way, symbolically; the imaginative girl is too firmly rooted in fact to have any notion of what he is getting at.

With Gina, who comes on to get the table laid, he reverts to his probing, faintly hostile questioning, always with, it seems, some sort of purpose. He is angling to find out what part Hjalmar plays in the bread-winning when he gets his answer – a shot from the attic and the emergence of the hilarious, faintly mad fact that the Ekdals actually hunt their rabbits with pistols and live ammunition.

It is mad and yet it is obviously a very normal activity in this household, a way of getting some fun and satisfaction out of daily life. The attic, and all that goes on there, is fully integrated in that life. And it is into the attic, obviously, that most of Hjalmar's energy goes.

The episode completes the introduction of the wild duck; before, the talk has been of the species; now it is of the individual. It is typical of Gregers (significantly he stands outside the netting looking in at Hjalmar who appears inside the trap) that he notices what he wants for his symbol, namely the blemishes: the duck droops one of its wings, and drags one foot – damaged by the dog that retrieved it from 'the sea-deeps' – Gregers repeats the phrase with intent, glancing at Hedvig as he does so; and with a highly significant addition: 'who has been in the sea-deeps – for so long'. He seems to be completing his symbolic identification of the bird; his observations suddenly become, in retrospect, projections upon the duck of his symbolic expectations; the wing and the foot fit in well; the 'sea-deeps – for so long' proves that he is looking at the attic in the symbolic terms that habitually hold for him. He has developed his analogue a little further – the attic *is* the sea-deeps for him. And Hjalmar is, for him, the duck.

This identification by Gregers develops out of his long conversation with Hjalmar. Gregers adds little to it except persistence; and does not need to. Hjalmar hardly needs the stimulus of questions to talk about himself, and he need say little to manifest the idle pointlessness and flaccidity of his life. Gregers draws him out and then, after one of Hjalmar's more outrageous pieces of complacency, formulates his conclusion: 'My dear Hjalmar, I almost believe you've got something of the wild duck in you...You have dived under and bitten fast in the bottom-weed.' At this point Hjalmar himself tries his hand at the symbol-ising game: 'Perhaps you refer to the almost fatal shot that has hit father in the wing – and me too?' – but Gregers insists on his interpretation:

I wouldn't say that you are wounded really; but you have ended up in a poisoned swamp, Hjalmar; you have caught an insidious disease in the body, and you've gone to the bottom to die in the dark...But don't worry; I shall be sure to have you brought up again. Because I've got a mission in life too, now, you see; I got it yesterday.

The key vocabulary has all been used before – the echoes are even stronger in the Norwegian – 'dived under' 'bitten fast' 'wounded' 'caught (same word as 'stopped' in Werle's disquisition on ducks in Act I). . . in the body' 'to the bottom' 'bring up again'. They were introduced by Werle, old Ekdal, Hjalmar to describe ducks; they have been seized upon by Gregers and pieced together into a single pattern as the final statement of his symbolic interpretation. His words run out so glibly, with so little questioning of their real validity, that the effusion helps to clinch our emergent conception of Gregers. He is a man who seeks to abstract patterns from life, who thinks naturally in terms of ideals and absolutes translated into symbols; and it can be added, with even greater confidence now, that his abstracting zeal makes him blind to the individual people and situations he faces. What he seems to call a poisoned swamp we have seen to be, for all its failings, a closeknit, warm, family life; the man he likens to the beautiful wild bird that prefers death in the dark to the outrage of wounding and capture, whom he admires for great qualities of mind and soul, is a selfish, callous, stupid idler. Indeed, so wrong does Gregers' symbolism seem to be that it begins to challenge each reader or spectator to see if the attic and its inhabitants could not be symbolised more sensitively. And this is possible; indeed an alternative interpretation is so obviously to hand that it is hard to resist: Hjalmar is not to be thought of as the free creature who might still be rescued and restored, as Gregers thinks of him; he is the rescued wild duck as it actually is: plump, contented, slightly damaged, totally domesticated and never restorable to its freedom and beauty. Gregers' symbolism ignores the obvious implications of the facts revealed.

The episode has displayed Hjalmar but, more important, Gregers too. His character as arch-simplifier, arch-idealist, arch-symboliser is clinched by his confrontation with his opposite, Dr Relling. The introductions go smoothly enough. Molvik, the alcoholic ordinand, has nothing to say; Relling and Gregers have met before. Relling opens with a bluff piece of sub-humour; but then Gregers says something strange in reply:

RELLING And Molvik and I live underneath, so you won't have far to go for a doctor or priest, if you should need anyone of the sort.

GREGERS Thank you, that is possible; because we were thirteen at table yesterday.

Gregers has not forgotten his father's phrase in Act 1; his mind moves on that plane of understanding where superstition counts. And it seems to be implied that he sees himself as the possible victim of that ill-omened circumstance: 'If you should need...' 'Thank you, it is possible.' But this is only a fleeting preliminary.

Relling quickly demonstrates his peculiar style of medicine when he bolsters Molvik against his weakness by calling him 'daemonic' – he keeps people going by finding the pretence suitable to their particular weakness; he is no healer (and no believer in absolutes). The evident tension between the men is more than Relling can disguise; he suddenly provokes Gregers. What he says amplifies and confirms rather than changes our estimate: Gregers has always been an idealist, has always tried to impose a set of absolute 'claims of the ideal' on people not strong enough to meet them. Gregers replies that he has still not abated his claims so long as he is dealing with a man who is a real man. Conflict is headed off only by the intervention of old Ekdal with a freshly killed rabbit.

Relling's response to this cranky absurdity is characteristically to accept it and dignify it as he dignified Molvik's drunkenness: 'Let us empty a glass for the old hunter.' – yet it is clear that he does so not out of conviction nor, as Hjalmar does, sentimentality. He fosters the illusion but shows that he is aware of the facts: 'To the grey-haired (*drinks*). By the way, is it grey hair or is it white that he's got?' His philosophy seems to be epitomised in his next sentence: 'Well, one can get through life just as well with borrowed [hair].' A philosophy, this, which fits not only Molvik and Ekdal but retrospectively Hjalmar too and the whole ethos of the Ekdal family; by covering up, by pretending and imagining, they have managed to impart some semblance of happiness to their deeply imperfect lives. Relling's philosophy is not a fine one, but it fits better than Gregers'.

Relling distributes a few more placebos by flattering Hjalmar to

Hedvig, Gina to Hjalmar, Hedvig to Hjalmar until he has provoked a demonstration of family affection; and that in turn provokes Gregers. He disrupts the happy mood; he and Relling begin to argue furiously for and against his idealism. When Gina reminds him of the filthy mess he made of his room, that trivial incident seems to become truly indicative of his role in the play; but the uproar is silenced by the arrival of Gregers' father.

Father and son meet again in prosaic surroundings and broad daylight now that the issue, if not the facts, has been clarified. Gregers has indeed, as he has indicated earlier in different ways, found his vocation, to open the eyes of Hjalmar Ekdal. But more is revealed than that. There is a reminder of the reason why Gregers pursues the ideal and the absolute with such myopic determination. It is not merely a reaction against his father; it is his only bolster against total self-mistrust and disgust. His conscience tortures him for not having warned Lieutenant Ekdal of what he was pretty sure was a trap. He must, if he is to go on living, find a cure for his sick conscience; the only way is to rescue Hjalmar from the lies and deceit that are ruining him.

That is how Gregers sees it. His father sees him as his neurotic mother's son. There's a touch of substantiation for Werle when Gregers throws out the accusation that Werle never got over the fact that his wife's fortune wasn't all that he expected – it seems a faintly vulgar jibe, as though Gregers were prepared to use anything to hand to hurt his father. Werle breaks off the squabble before it can develop and gets down to essentials of their situation.

He finds his son determined to sever all connection. There is, too, a faint, disturbing hint that builds up on the hint about 'thirteen at table' – Gregers does not need much money: what he has will last out his time. Gregers seems to feel that he himself, whatever he may hope to do for Hjalmar, is doomed. But he refuses to answer any more questions.

The Werles have wrecked the cosy family lunch. Gregers moves into action at once, again disruptively – he virtually orders Hjalmar to go out for a long walk with him, away from the rest. Relling obviously sees the danger but he cannot prevent it – the danger of 'inflamed rectitude' that Gregers suffers from. They all disperse, leaving Gina walking restlessly about the room. But the most important person is Hedvig who has been quietly observing. She looks searchingly at her mother and says: 'I think this strange.' For the second time, the adolescent girl has been forced to realise that grown-ups can mean more than they seem to say. What it is she does not understand, but that it is so, she does. She has this last, important word. Or perhaps, metaphorically, Gregers has it; for the family that could resist his intrusion at the end of Act II has broken up at the end of Act III.

Act IV seems to reflect the change of mood following on these events. The paraphernalia of studio photography reminds us not merely of the Ekdal profession (and of Gina's greater energy in pursuit of it) but, as an image, of that recurrent strain of make-believe that runs through this family's life. The light – late afternoon, very close to sunset, verging on darkness which soon sets in – dictates the tone. Something has gone out of life for these people.

Physically it is Hjalmar, but the real loss is peace and contentment. Gina obviously expects no good to have come of his walk and talk with Gregers and she is right. Though she and Hedvig try their usual cajolements on him, this time they are firmly rebuffed. He takes off his coat himself; refuses food; brushes aside his 'invention'; the new man obviously intends to take life seriously from now on. His most violent reaction is against what once gave him pleasure: the attic and the duck – he would like to wring its neck.

It is obvious where all this has come from. It is interesting to see that Hjalmar has found no difficulty in absorbing Gregers' abstract, symbolising callousness, and that Hedvig is still totally unprepared for this kind of symbolising; she takes his threat literally as her scream and her physical protest (she shakes her father) show. For him the duck has become a symbol, Gregers' symbol, of disgrace and degradation; for her it is a pet bird. Not that we need take his change of heart seriously; his version of Gregers' ideals comes out, unconsciously, as broad parody; yet it is parody of a kind that demonstrates that its object lends itself to that treatment. Hjalmar's laborious elaborations are not much worse than Gregers'.

Hjalmar has taken over, besides the clumsy symbolism, the probing manner of Gregers. It is successful, after its fashion. It brings to light some interesting facts – that Werle has not only been maintaining old Ekdal but that he was once Gina's lover before marriage – and an interesting person. Hjalmar's commonplace responses are far less impressive than the rock-like commonsense of Gina. Yes, she went wrong, but of course she kept quiet otherwise they couldn't have married and that would have been very bad for both of them. In these terms duplicity and pretence sound very sensible. Certainly the blunt, factual simplicity of her language shows his up for mere posturing. It is unfortunately impossible to quite preserve in translation the polysyllabic pomposity of his self-pitying phrase describing his dream that she should be left 'som den hedengangne oppfinners velhavende enke', 'the departed inventor's well-provided widow'. And his borrowed pomposities do him no good; the final result of his applying Gregers' ideals is collapse. Everything is over.

Gregers never looks so ridiculous as he does at the moment he cautiously enters to find out how his ideals have worked, face beaming with joy. Gina doesn't mean to mock his chronic symbolism when she removes the shade from the light, but that is the effect. He tries hard with Hjalmar. It is interesting to hear both men fall readily into the same kind of religiose cliché, as a reminder that they have something in common:

GREGERS For there can surely be nothing in life that can compare with the joy of feeling forgiveness for a sinner and of raising her up in love.

HJALMAR Do you imagine a man can so easily recover from the bitter draught I have just drained?

But Gregers fails in this attempt to rescue his friend and has to acknowledge the fact, in his obsessive imagery: 'You have a great deal of the wild duck in you, Hjalmar.'

It looks as though this is to be the cue for renewed battle with Relling, who comes on at this moment, but instead he contents himself with biting scorn before imparting a new emphasis to the play. He swings attention towards Hedvig. Let the grown-ups do as they please, but be careful of the pubescent girl. Mrs Sørby reinforces the swing.

She comes as another counterblast to Gregers. Her simple, uncondescending friendliness towards Gina is a reproach to his politely disdainful manner, for one thing. For another, her relationship with Relling, whatever it amounted to at the time, makes her, and him, seem people more to be relied on for mature judgment than Gregers; they have experienced life even if it has been rather sordid experience; perhaps that is why Relling is such a good doctor in his limited way. For a third, the forthrightness of the woman. Gregers has preached full honesty but he has been oddly devious; he has always tried to work on and through other people and here he tries to head off Mrs Sørby's reference to his father's blindness. Mrs Sørby takes the wind out of his sails by saying that she and Werle have no secrets.

She offers this to Gina as a sovereign recipe for happiness, but by now we have seen, in these characters, a sufficient diversity of personality and circumstance to feel that Gina's protest against this absolute, as against Gregers', is sane and sound: 'Oh, we women-folk are so different, we are. Some have one way and others have another.' It is Relling's philosophy in simpler terms.

Gregers does not recognise Mrs Sørby's virtues. He sees her as the messenger of his arch-enemy, sent to tempt the noble soul he is determined to rescue. He shows a comical lack of faith in Hjalmar when he replies for him to the offer of financial help from Werle but his inflated style is not needed; in this respect at least Hjalmar is fully capable of matching Gregers. He spews out a stream of absurdly inflated stuff, to which Gregers' response is highly illuminating: 'You are the man I have always taken you for.' Gregers is taken in because this is the kind of emotional pomposity he himself is from time to time capable of. And once started, Hjalmar flows along in turgid parody of Gregers, embarrassing his master by the basic meanness of his responses, the basest being that Hjalmar is happy because he can see some kind of justice at work: Werle is going blind.

Returning from her lonely walk in the dusk, Hedvig runs straight into another situation where adults puzzle her. Her father cuts her off when she mentions meeting Mrs Sørby; he hopes she has seen her for the last time. In the silence, Hedvig looks round at their faces for enlightenment. Her innocent glee at receiving a letter at the hands of Mrs Sørby is something she cannot repress, but Hjalmar does it for her. He connects, at last, the deed of gift with Hedvig's poor eyes – whether rightly or wrongly is left uncertain.

Gina, insulted by his lack of trust, answers him with the most torturing of answers – she doesn't know who is Hedvig's father. And at that Hjalmar breaks from his master's control. The ideal course of action is abandoned. Hjalmar behaves with abominable cruelty. There is no need, now, to minimise it as one could on earlier, trivial occasions. There is nothing crueller than the sudden rejection of a loving child, and Hjalmar rejects Hedvig: 'Don't come near me, Hedvig! Go right away. I can't bear the sight of you.' The callousness is different from Gregers' but it is similar. Hjalmar is so obsessed with his vision of her as the emblem of his shame that he does not see her as a suffering child. Gina soars above him with her response: 'Look at the child, Ekdal! Look at the child!' But it is no use.

Hedvig is in utter despair; even Gregers is reduced to pleading that he meant well. Yet it is to him that Hedvig turns for guidance. He is the only grown-up with whom she has experienced that flash of poetic sympathy; the only one who, however strangely he may have spoken in the past, seems to know what is to be done. She delivers herself to him: '(*sits upright and wipes away her tears*) Now you must tell me what's wrong. Why won't Daddy have anything more to do with me?'

Gregers' uneasiness as she comes close to what he believes is the truth about her parentage is interesting; in this case at least he is unwilling that there should be total frankness; we are perhaps witnessing his only concession to the thought that, if he is right, this child is his half-sister.

Talking to this man who has turned the duck into a symbol, Hedvig herself begins, in her acute despair, to try to make sense of her confusion in something like his way. Perhaps, she guesses, she is like the wild duck in some ways. She never achieves the fatal fluency of Gregers' symbolising; it is always recognisably a childish imagination rather than an adult theoretical intelligence that is at work, yet it is clear that Gregers has begun to have his effect on this mind too.

He first seizes upon her reference to the duck as a simple diversion away from her grief, but he cannot resist his own obsession with it as a symbol. When Hedvig speaks of praying for her father and for the bird and uses the evocative phrase, 'he would spare it for my sake', he seems suddenly to perceive an extra, religious dimension to the symbolic possibilities: 'But would you make a willing sacrifice of the wild duck for *his* sake.' In her deep anguish Hedvig is now prepared to enter into his way of seeing things. She does not reject the idea of sacrificing her duck; it has become a significance rather than a pet: 'Yes, I will try that.'

The intense moment, terrifying in its way, as the child's mind succumbs to the adult's, is undercut by the ending. Gregers tries to dignify Hjalmar's distress as a wrestling-match for his soul; the prosaic fact is that he has gone out with Relling and Molvik. Gregers ends on a high note of expectation of good, but he leaves the family not merely dispersed but shattered now, with Hedvig sobbing her heart out. Gina's last speech may not be grammatical but it is sound: Relling was right about Gregers.

The lighting of Act v sets the emotional tone of the play now that Gregers has had his effect on events. Cold grey morning light; wet snow lies on the large panes of the skylight. A dreary scene.

Gina takes a resolutely sensible view of the hullabaloo of the previous night but Hedvig shows her need for her father. It is not his master, Gregers, who brings news of Hjalmar, but Relling. Hjalmar has not lived up to Gregers' image of the spiritual gladiator; he has been very drunk. In the analysis of his personality, Relling has far more evidence on his side than Gregers; he provides information about Hjalmar's upbringing that we have to take on trust, but we are prepared to do so because of Relling's deadly accuracy when he describes details that can be checked: Hjalmar's skill in declaiming other people's ideas, for example. And we accept his estimate of Gregers too, as a sufferer not merely from 'rectitudinal fever' but from the need to worship something that doesn't concern him.

And yet Relling is not a distinguished person, not a distinguished doctor. His regimen has made neither him nor his patients into specimens of radiant health. Gregers may be absurd in his obstinate search for the absolute but Relling is depressing in his estimate that just about everybody is sick and that the only thing to do is keep each going with his own life-lie. In Relling's analysis, Hjalmar and old Ekdal are at best the equivalents of the actual crippled wild duck, damaged beyond repair and contented with captivity, saved as much as they can ever be saved – his nostrum is the antithesis to Gregers'. And yet his method works; illusion can make people happy. And Relling will not allow that ideals are any better than lies. The opposition between the two men is absolute and irreconcilable. They stand for two antithetical views of life, the ideal and the pragmatic; each has some virtue and many vices. Their discussion ends, as it must, in a declaration of war from Gregers: 'Doctor Relling, I shall not give up until I have rescued Hjalmar out of your clutches!' So much the worse for Hjalmar, is Relling's reply and he immediately begins to exercise his kind of therapy on Hedvig when she comes on: 'Well, little wild-duck mother, I'm going down now to see if your dad is still lying and pondering on that marvellous invention.' Those few words are carefully chosen to cheer and reassure.

Gregers sets to work in his own way. He thrusts himself at Hedvig physically and mentally. His first words to her are portentous: '(*draws close to Hedvig*) I can see from your face that it is not finished.' 'It is [not] finished' is the phrase from St John – 'when Jesus therefore had received the vinegar, he said It is finished'. The emphasis, the intensity, are quite frightening; it seems a let-down to be reminded of what is involved – that business with the wild duck, as Hedvig calls it.

She has slipped away from him. Last night she had accepted his symbolism; in the light of day her sense of fact has reasserted itself. Gregers takes this as evidence that she too has been ruined by her environment; like her grandfather and her father, she has lost her courage at the critical moment. He implies that she is yet another version of the wild duck, but again it is a resistible interpretation; it follows from his theory but it does not match up to the impression Hedvig has made.

Gregers makes a last, emotional appeal to win her back to his way of thinking: 'Oh, if only you'd had your eyes opened to what makes life really worth-while, – had the genuine, joyful, courageous spirit of self-sacrifice, then you would soon see how he would come up to you – But I still have faith in you, Hedvig.' Those insistently rhetorical words, those accumulated, loaded terms, are the last words that Hedvig hears from him, the final message to remember.

They are enough to make her return to the plan she accepted under Gregers' domination the night before. When old Ekdal comes out of the attic – where, incidentally, he has virtually lived since the beginning of Act III so far as his stage existence is concerned; and where Hedvig has never yet been seen to enter in behind the net – she coaxes out of him the best way to shoot a duck and seems about to do so when she is interrupted by the return of Hjalmar.

The comic scene takes a stomach-turning lurch into agony. It is quite extraordinary. There are five brief lines of conversation between husband and wife; Hedvig runs in and cries out with joy 'Oh, Daddy, Daddy!', Hjalmar waves her off with 'Go away, go away, go away. Take her away from me, I tell you', and Hedvig goes in silence. That is all, and yet a child's agony (the word will stand repetition) is compressed into that moment of rejection. It is not obliterated, indeed its painfulness for us is sharpened by the comic egocentricity that Hjalmar goes on to display. He thinks only of himself and his self is worthless. And yet Hedvig loves him. She has to endure his callousness again in a scene of even greater pain when Hjalmar hounds her out of the kitchen. His words about 'intruders' reduce her to frightened confusion. She cannot respond with words; all she can say is 'The wild duck', but that is enough to show that she is determined now to put Gregers' precepts into action. But as she enters the attic for the first time, wounded, bitterly wounded by these terrible events, the symbol seems to expand. This wild duck is plunging to the sea-deeps in a totally different way.

She is not forgotten while she is in there behind closed doors. The dialogue sets up an acute tension between the girl who has been revealed and the girl who is described so wrongly by Hjalmar luxuriating in self-pitying cynicism. It is not as though he can be taken seriously. His fury seems no more substantial than his other emotions and resolutions. He is not the man Gregers took him for. But Gregers can gain some hope when at last Hjalmar turns his mind away from his piddling affairs to his child; he is able to say that perhaps from that quarter Hjalmar will receive proof of genuine love. Then the shot is heard. Gregers is ecstatic; when it is all explained to him, Hjalmar is filled with the appropriate emotion. They look for the girl in her room.

Old Ekdal's appearance on stage does more than heighten the tension – after all it was assumed that it was he who shot the duck, yet here he is, coming from his room. He makes a striking spectacle. He is more fully clad in his past, so to speak, than ever before. In Act II he wore his uniform cap; now he wears full uniform, with sword. It looks like a grotesque fancy-dress on this old wreck, a faintly mad obsession with the past.

The discovery of Hedvig dead in the attic drives him further back. He repeats the strange phrase he let fall in Act II denoting the effect his ruin has had on his mind. It is an idea that obsesses him, and it is this which comes to the surface, not any direct response to the immediate situation, under the shock: 'The forest avenges.' On this wild duck at least Gregers has had an effect opposite to what he intended. Instead of bringing him up out of the swamp he has driven him deeper. What has he done to Hedvig, that other wild duck? Here the play leaves an open doubt except insofar it is certain that this is not what Gregers meant to happen.

Did she die by accident, fumbling for the bird she intended to shoot? Relling's evidence seems to dispose of that; it was no accident. Did she, as some have thought, shoot herself in despair when she heard Hjalmar say: 'If I asked her then: Hedvig, are you willing to give up your life for me (*laughs scornfully*). Yes, thank you, – you'd soon hear what answer I got! (*a pistol shot is heard. . .*)' The balance of evidence is against this. All through the play the attic doors seem thick enough to prevent overhearing. And in any case, the timing is wrong. This interpretation demands that Hedvig should hear Hjalmar, register what he says, decide on her action and perform it in an instant.

There is a more probable reconstruction that makes her death not the reaction of a moment but the culmination of a process in keeping with her character. Hedvig is a thoughtful child. She has listened to her elders and has understood that they, and especially Gregers, mean something different from what they say. She trusts Gregers because he shares part of her imaginative world and because he knows what should be done. She starts by thinking that she understands what he intends her to do – shoot a bird – but when she finally enters the attic after the second terrible assault on her feelings she is no longer sure. All she has to go on are those final words of his. Is the willing sacrifice the bird, or she herself who is like the bird? She accepts the latter; it is her final surrender to an adult symbolism that she does not fully comprehend.

Uncomprehending or not, and even though for an ignoble father, Hedvig dies for love. Her entry into the attic and her death there suddenly makes her seem the one and only person in the play for whom a wild duck is an apt symbol. Not the damaged, contented creature in the attic, but the wild duck in nature, wounded and choosing death rather than accept the outrage. The wild duck in the play is a travesty of nature; the wild duck Hedvig becomes is nature itself.

Gregers seems to sense this when he repeats that poetic phrase that equates the attic with the 'sea-deeps'. She has gone wounded to the bottom to die. But he cannot feel proud of this outcome; she has coined her own symbol, not followed his. He has rescued nobody, but caused another and fatal casualty. Old Ekdal he has driven deeper into a fantasy world. 'The forest avenges. But I'm not afraid.' he says, and we see him go back into the attic, for him a world of fantasy that has suddenly become terribly real. Hjalmar he has driven to a sickening display of facile emotion. Gina, thank God, he has not been able to change. She stands as a rebuke to his idealistic inhumanity, thinking all the time, as he has never thought, of the dignity of the dead child.

Hedvig is carried off by her parents, but she is not forgotten during the bitter scene that ends the play. Nothing can obliterate the impact of the past few minutes. Her death and its conjectured reasons hover in the air as the unspoken alternative to Relling and Gregers. Each puts his case. Relling has fact on his side, but what his philosophy leads to is merely the preservation of Hjalmar as he is; Gregers has idealism, but his philosophy leads to death. They speak from their fixed positions, each seeing himself as spokesman, the one of empiricism, the other of idealism. Neither is justified in this assumption. Ibsen has not created spokesmen but individuals. Relling is an empirical whose rough and lax experience has led him to conclude that all men are sick; Gregers is an idealist whose vision and drive have been distorted by the peculiar deprivations of his own youth. It is not a matter of choosing between them, but of recognising how different men, and women, can be as a result of their previous lives. If we had to choose, and choose one of these, then the play would be dismal. Hedvig supplies the alternative. Her act of love, for however unworthy an object and performed in whatever confusion of spirit, is one that Relling's philosophy cannot account for. Nor Gregers'. She provides the human dignity that Relling cannot understand, and the deep, untheoretical integrity of emotion that is lacking in Gregers. Gregers goes off, probably to suffer, as he always felt he would, the fate of being the unlucky thirteenth at table; Relling stays to curse. Neither has changed. But Hedvig has; and with her has changed our conception of what it is possible for a human being to become.

The Wild Duck has often enough been praised for its amplitude. Love's Comedy and Brand were thronged with characters but they, like the symbolism, were made primarily to serve as components in the controlling pattern rather than to be in their own right. In The Wild Duck it is different. Each of its many characters has a fully distinctive life of its own; the play presents a marvellous range of habits acutely observed – habits of mind, feeling, language, behaviour. This praise is deserved but sometimes mis-applied; the diversity is commended as though it were an absolute dramatic virtue that Ibsen would have done well to display in all of his works, as though diversity were something separable from a play's concept.

The theme of *The Wild Duck* requires diversity. It has as its ostensible protagonist a Brand-figure reduced in stature. Everything in the play is smaller in scale in comparison with *Brand*, but Gregers is subjected to a special kind of diminution. It is not that he speaks prose instead of verse, but that he can fall into sentimental and inflated prose; not that his actions are necessarily small in scale but that he does not choose to act himself – he characteristically attempts to get other people to face the crisis he has provoked; above all his propensity for symbolising armours him in an insensitivity which was certainly not Brand's and which amounts at times to comic obtuseness. The diversity of characterisation is essential to that identification of Gregers. Relling may argue intellectually against his monomaniacal insistence on one absolute set of ideals for all people, but the strongest disproof is provided by the sheer variety in the people who surround him. No single set of values or course of action could possibly be appropriate to them all. Amplitude is a virtue inseparable from the theme.

Because of this placing of Gregers, it becomes impossible to take him, as he often has been, as Ibsen's rejection of the idealist. Ibsen does not work in such general terms. He is fascinated by the spectacle of this or that individual, each in his own set of highly particularised circumstances, responding to an inner need to achieve what seems to him a supreme end. Brand was a study in the enormous strength that can be generated in that person by those circumstances; Gregers, by contrast, demonstrates the spurious strength that comes of hysterical over-compensation for circumstances. The play does not demolish idealism, it demolishes this particular individual's claim to be an idealist.

Peer Gynt can be brought into comparison too. One of the most telling pieces of evidence for Ibsen's fascination with heroism is that he wrote two great works, the one devoted to exploring the positive, the other the negative side of the concept. And there is significance in the fact that each, Brand the hero and Peer the anti-hero, is explored with equal conviction and yet is kept apart from the other in a separate poem. It is as though Ibsen were exploring and assessing equal and opposite tendencies in human nature but could not yet see how they could co-exist in one set of circumstances or one person.

The Wild Duck is the first play in which Brand and Peer live together in the same world, in Gregers and Hjalmar respectively; but Peer has undergone the same kind of diminution as Brand. Peer's marvellous vitality, the sheer imaginativeness of his role-playing, have dwindled away into Hjalmar's petty posing. This reduction affects our estimate of Gregers. Brought into contact with Hjalmar he reveals in himself something similar enough to Hjalmar's inauthenticity to make it impossible for him to judge clearly what sort of man it is that he has to deal with. One of the severest criticisms made by the play of Gregers' kind of idealism is that it lets him be taken in by blatant shoddiness.

Ibsen seems to have reached an understanding of what must happen to Brand and Peer when they are translated out of the large-scale, emblematic structures in which they originated into the dense and intricate limitations of modern social conditions. That Peer in real life would be no better than a Hjalmar is the secondary conclusion; the primary is that Brand would be no more than a Gregers. What is implied, though, is not a rejection of idealism so much as a recognition that a narrowly ethical or moral idealism is no longer adequate to the task of challenging the quality of modern life. It is too restricted, and by reason of what it excludes, does more harm than good. What the play does is offer an alternative version of idealism and with it the renewed possibility of heroism. The statement requires some elaboration.

One of the most remarkable features of the play's amplitude is its symbolism. In the earlier plays this works powerfully but pointedly; perhaps because Ibsen was at that stage struggling to define for himself the patterns he felt to underlie the complexity of the hero's position in modern life, he created symbolism which tended towards a one-for-one equivalence, powerful but simple, sometimes single, in its effect, amounting at times to little more than an underlining of what had been conveyed in other terms. In *Ghosts* the same kind of single-strand symbolism co-exists with

and, it has been argued, may at times obscure, a more organic and evocative symbolism; the older form is still potent: in *Enemy of the People* it is fully to the fore again.

In *The Wild Duck* Ibsen seems to attain a sudden confidence in his insight into the modern predicament and in his ability to convey it. There is less evidence of a desire to concentrate on and emphasise the underlying pattern; the result is a symbolism that is constantly expanding into new significances. Pointedness is a strong feature of it, but one-for-one equivalence is now used to identify a certain kind of mind. Symbolism has become one of the issues in the play. Gregers' wrong-headed schematising serves as a stimulus to find a more sensitive response to the rich potentiality of the image of the bird, and it proves capable of satisfying the need his deficiencies generate. Gregers' application of the symbol cannot stand. It is easily adjusted: Hjalmar is no wild duck that can be restored to perfect beauty in freedom; he is the irremediable casualty for whom contented captivity is the only life, the wild duck in the attic; but what is more impressive is the symbol's capacity for positive growth. Out of the action of the play, and inseparable in development from that, emerges the most poignant and poetic implication as the full potency of the image is developed. The latent idea of the wild duck in nature, the bird that, by some deep instinct, will not tolerate the outrage of wounding or capture, is released by the death of the one truly sensitive, genuine and unspoilt character. The symbolism does not substantiate a pattern, it creates one in its own delicate way, without imposition or blatancy.

Another feature that can be connected with the new symbolism is insight into character, for the symbolism goes beyond the representation of externals, but, significantly, only when a character has something besides externals to be expressed. It helps define the unshakeable factuality of Gina, Werle's callousness, Hjalmar's irredeemable spuriousness; but it also helps to illuminate in two characters a level of experience hardly communicable by them in other terms. When old Ekdal mutters 'The forest avenges' and shuts himself in the attic the old wounds open in his soul; the experience he is reminded of lies too deep for words to explain; but his words indicate its obscure potency. When Hedvig dies she dies in silence. There is no explanation from her in words because words cannot encompass the kind of logic that makes a girl kill herself to win back her father's love. What the symbolism does is give us the quality of two personalities in other terms. In both instances Ibsen denotes a quality that is heroic – minor heroism in Ekdal's case, major in Hedvig's – and in both he senses that the drive towards the heroic (which is, of course, unintentional and unselfconscious as presented in the play) comes from this inner, hidden area of the personality. Mrs Alving, Brand, Svanhild and Falk affirmed with their intellects, coloured or not as the case may be by emotion but not dictated to by it; each was capable, at moments of crisis, of identifying them and describing their own intellectual response – 'Within, within, that is the word', 'Now I see the connections'. Ekdal and Hedvig can only say 'The forest avenges', 'The wild duck'.

The play does not have this as its main preoccupation; Hedvig is not the protagonist though she is a vital contributor to the final effect. Ibsen seems only to be beginning to understand the importance of this subterranean life of the individual, but that in itself marks a decisive advance over his earlier work. It can be defined as a broadening of Ibsen's concept of idealism. In all of the earlier plays, even in *Love's Comedy*, idealism is conceived of as heavy with ethical and moral content, and for that reason accessible to discussion, debate and explanation. Gregers' idealism is of this sort and it is now presented for condemnation; what Hedvig offers is more elusive yet more comprehensive. It is difficult to define in terms of morality and yet it seems to deserve that description more than does Gregers' systematising. It amounts to a passionate conviction of feeling rather than of intellect about one essential value upon which depends the quality of life as a whole. Love is, for Hedvig, the value without which her life would be intolerable. Through it she demonstrates a beauty of character, not a mere mental strength or rigidity, an intuitive fineness that leads her to make essential rather than superficial discriminations. Ibsen has begun to see that moral choice of this kind can only be conducted from the centre of feeling and must necessarily, in a society that places so many impediments in the way of self-expression, be less readily accessible to any formal kind of articulation than he had earlier conceived. Hedvig is the first of Ibsen's inarticulate poets of living. She is handicapped by her social circumstances: by her immaturity, blindness, lack of education, of intellectual challenge and stimulus. She could never express her poetry. Yet the play convinces us that the impulse towards a poetry of living, though frustrated of utterance, is not killed in her. In one person at least there is an integrity of purpose towards a finer morality that is, in the crisis, invincible.

That is all that Ibsen chooses to set against the defeat and despair and scepticism generated by the rest of the play. That little is further diminished by the circumstance that only an adolescent girl is capable of this integrity; all the adults have, in one way or another, suffered corruption of the spirit. Had Hedvig lived on. . . but the play does not invite this surmise. It is enough that the small affirmation has been made. Ibsen has lost his old type of hero, the moral stalwart; he has not fully developed the new kind, but the intimations are there, affirming the persistent faith that in some rare persons at least, heroism is possible even in the modern world.

6

'HEDDA GABLER'

Hedda Gabler is perhaps the severest challenge offered by Ibsen. It is so ironical in its presentation of characters and events that it may seem to permit almost any partial and contradictory interpretation; until we recognise that irony is not the final or rather the dominating temper. The play makes great demands above all on our sympathies and our understanding; it requires in us a capacity for recognising malice and absurdity, but also that more difficult faculty of appreciating that such defects may still co-exist with other, more positive qualities; we are called upon to respond to the tragedy of this tension. No play by Ibsen is more fully dramatic than this. To penetrate beneath the levels of irony to the heart calls for careful attention to it as a dramatic poem.

The play begins by building up unobtrusively a feeling of expectation. It is named after Hedda but we do not immediately make her acquaintance. Instead we are introduced to two rooms and a couple of old women. The rooms have a character of their own. The drawing-room and the inner room through the wide doorway at the back of the stage are handsome and tasteful in their appointments, but dark in colour and, since they are thickly carpeted, quiet. In the centre of the view, framed by its own frame, by the wide doorway and by the proscenium arch, a portrait of an elderly man in general's uniform hangs on the wall of the inner room. A milky-white lampshade with a matt finish adds a touch of pallor. Hedda's new home.

So much for the rooms themselves; but there is brightness in the set too. Morning sunshine streams in through the french window to the side of the main room. Several bunches of flowers stand around the room in vases and there are more still lying on the table. They do not seem part of the normal decoration of the room.

Miss Tesman and Bertha the maid seem to bring a touch of the fresh outdoors with them. Miss Tesman, neatly but simply dressed in outdoor clothes, brings (in Bertha's hands) yet another bunch of flowers. She goes to the french window and throws it wide open with the words: 'But I'll see that there is plenty of fresh morning air for them when they come down.' And yet this heartiness seems to be subdued by the surroundings. Both Miss Tesman and Bertha speak in hushed voices. Perhaps only because Hedda and George are still a-bed, but we notice the implied deference.

The conversation between the women supports first impressions. Miss Tesman is as nice as she looks. Kindly in her manner towards her servant – her language is direct and homely as of equal to equal – generous in giving up Bertha's services so that George may be looked after, and self-sacrificing in her devotion to her invalid sister. She seems an attractive old lady; attractive without artifice, in a natural, simple way.

And yet she shows signs, as does Bertha, of being in some degree awed by Hedda. It is more than a matter of hushed voices. Throughout their conversation, neither of them manages to utter Hedda's name. Bertha gets no closer than 'the young mistress'; Miss Tesman refers to 'General Gabler's daughter'. Several little touches help to explain this. Miss Tesman is very conscious of Hedda's social superiority. She shows herself to be impressed not merely by the fact of her parentage and style of living in the past, but by the intended style of living already indicated by the fact that the chintzes have been removed from the furniture in the drawing room which will now be in daily use – not kept, as Miss Tesman seems to expect, for special occasions. But beyond this there is an element of fear which seems, from the scraps of evidence, to be justified. The old ladies expect to find Hedda difficult to get on with. With some reason. As soon as she set foot in the door last night, Hedda told Bertha to call her husband 'Doctor'. She ordered the chintzes to be removed; and it was she who gave the orders – George said nothing. Hedda, though she has been back so short a time, has set her mark on these rooms.

What is being built up, apart from the essential basis of information, is a kind of tension – what sort of woman will Hedda prove to be when she appears? The vague hints sharpen the appetite. They continue when George comes on to greet his old aunt.

He does not suit the dark elegance of the room very well. He is untidy in appearance, manner and speech. He also seems weak. He is obviously very fond of Miss Tesman, yet we hear that he left her to find her own way back from the quayside last night – because Hedda's pile of cases had to take priority. Another hint about Hedda; and another is added when he advises Bertha not to go and offer her services: 'No thanks, Bertha – you'd better not. If she wants you for anything, she'll ring, she said.' And again when he explains to his aunt – with only the merest gesture of protest against the financial sacrifices she has made – that Hedda *had* to go on this extended honeymoon tour – emphatically *had* to; and had to live in this particular house. For his own part he appears amiable but lacking in fibre.

By now a considerable interest has been generated in the absent Hedda; she enters to begin to satisfy our curiosity. The room fits her like a glove – elegant, tasteful, handsome but... the reservation is hard to define but its nature is indicated by the cold expression, the steel-grey eyes, the attractive but not very abundant hair and by her dull pallor of complexion. It is interesting to note, in the printed text, that Ibsen used three terms from his description of the room for his description of Hedda – 'tasteful', 'handsome' and 'matt' (of the milk-white lampshade and of her complexion). Hedda, like the room, has style but not exuberance.

Her behaviour immediately begins to confirm the intimations of the previous scenes. The impetuous, natural warmth of Miss Tesman's greeting, 'Good morning, my dear Hedda! A very good morning to you!' is instantly rebuffed by the chill formality of Hedda's reply, 'Good morning, dear Miss Tesman', and the implied rebuke that goes with it, 'Calling on us so early? That was very kind.' There's nothing openly rude about this but it has its effect on Miss Tesman. She seems a little disconcerted; having made her attempt, against the grain as we have seen, to be warm and friendly, she is immediately driven back to a more distant formality, to, in fact, the formally subservient term used by Bertha: 'Well, – has the young mistress slept well in her new home, then?' And clearly Hedda has no desire to undo the damage that she has done – she wants to keep Miss Tesman at a distance. She goes on to complain about the two elements that brighten the set – the sun streaming in through the windows and 'all these blessed flowers'; she has the curtains drawn against the sun, darkening the set. She insults Miss Tesman cruelly over her new hat. Her appearance, her behaviour, her reactions begin to suggest a woman who is unable, for some reason, to accept and enjoy what seems naturally enjoyable, whether it be the warm affection offered by Miss Tesman, the kind thought behind the bouquets of welcome, or the flowers themselves and the bright sunlight.

And yet, aggressively malicious and superior as she already seems to be, Hedda is not immune. She turns away impatiently when George draws attention to her figure. When Miss Tesman, all hostility charmed away by the thought that Hedda may be pregnant, kisses her head reverently and blesses her, Hedda frees herself 'gently' – but it is the gentleness of acute self-restraint as her words show: 'Oh – ! let me go.' Her revulsion from this kind of intimacy provides the first dramatic shock in the play. When she is left alone on stage, and only while she is alone, this cold, domineering woman shows that she is painfully vulnerable after all. She crosses the room, raises her arms and clenches her fists as if in a frenzy. It seems a kind of sudden, aggressive reaction when she throws back the curtains she has just ordered to be closed. She does not do it to enjoy the sun; she stares out into the garden and sees only signs that the leaves are withering, the months are passing.

This brief episode shows that Hedda's distaste for what is naturally attractive is more than superficial. To hate pregnancy, as she seems to, suggests a radical abnormality; and the violence of her reaction shows that it is an abnormality that can place her under acute stress. Hedda may speedily resume control of herself but this has been revealed and cannot be forgotten.

Hedda hides it, and the fact of her pregnancy, from George. She seems to need to keep herself aloof. When George asks her to address Miss Tesman in the familiar form customary amongst members of a family, Hedda fights off this suggestion of intimacy with undue violence: 'No, no, Tesman – don't ask me to do that, for God's sake. I've told you that once before. I'll try and call her Aunt. And that will have to do.' And here her words are as it were coloured by her movements. For when George remonstrates feebly that she is after all one of the family now, she not only queries the assumption but she moves physically towards the doorway that leads to the inner room. That is to say, we see her move away from her husband towards the room dominated by the portrait of her father; we then hear her suggest that *her* piano be moved into that room. Small indications, but they suggest that Hedda's need to avoid warmth and intimacy, her inability to accept what is normally attractive, may stem from her old social position as General Gabler's daughter, may be an expression of an aristocratic fastidiousness that demands privacy from the intrusions of a vulgar world. It fits with this impression that she should explain her snub to Miss Tesman over her hat in terms of social propriety: 'People don't do such things.' It may stem from this, but more than straightforward social snobbery is involved. Hedda's strange hostility towards sun and flowers and pregnancy is expanded by the kind of welcome she gives to Mrs Elvsted. There is at least an implication of jealousy in Hedda's words: 'That woman with the irritating hair she used to go around attracting attention with.' The sentiment doesn't carry its full weight until Mrs Elvsted enters the stage. She seems in every way less impressive than Hedda – slight, soft, vulnerable, scared, not quite fashionable in her dress – save for the one feature that has so oddly stuck in Hedda's mind. It is the one feature in which Hedda, with her agreeable but not particularly abundant hair, is manifestly inferior. Mrs Elvsted's hair is strikingly blonde, unusually rich and wavy. It is beautiful; and yet Hedda dislikes it.

This would be superficial enough if it were allowed to remain simply an additional piece of contrariness on Hedda's part. But just as her irritable rejection of sun and flowers expanded suddenly into her frenzy at the thought of pregnancy, so her jealousy of Mrs Elvsted's hair provides us with another shocking indication of other, deeper levels of feeling in this strange woman.

Mrs Elvsted is not an immediately impressive character. She appears not only nervous but naive. Her speech is jerky and overemphatic in its use of intensive words and phrases – 'so completely confused', 'I don't know a living soul', 'I haven't got the peace and patience that would let me sit down', 'I do so sincerely hope...', 'not in the slightest', 'so terribly afraid for him', 'I beg you so earnestly'. She seems faintly hysterical, faintly silly. And yet from behind the manner emerges a woman of warm emotion, strong loyalty and courage in her attachment to the erratic genius Eilert Løvborg.

We notice the unconvincing friendliness Hedda shows towards her, the satisfaction she seems to derive from divining a delicate situation between this married woman and the family tutor – it is the first time that Hedda has shown an active interest in any other person in the play – but the shock comes, briefly but emphatically, when Hedda tries to insist on schoolgirl intimacy as a bond of confidence between Mrs Elvsted and herself. Mrs Elvsted's replies, 'you always used to pull my hair' and 'and once you said you'd burn it off me', do more than indicate that Hedda was a schoolgirl horror. The lines get the laugh they deserve, but they also refer back to Hedda's mention of 'that irritating hair' and suggest that the jealousy she feels now is of long standing and of a violence, at least originally, that is extraordinary. Hedda may seem cold and restrained, but the woman who was driven to clench her fists in a frenzy, who once made this bizarre threat and who still feels, in some degree, the old jealousy has a hidden capacity for passionate and, we now begin to realise, destructive feeling. But it is still only a hint. In the main Hedda appears to be coolly in command of herself and of the situation.

For a woman who sets store on propriety of behaviour, Hedda is surprisingly active in probing and prying, with evident enjoyment, into what she suspects to be an improper relationship. Her curiosity seems impertinent since it is based upon the mere pretence of friendly concern. What is of greater interest is that from time to time Hedda shows that she is impressed by the woman she despises: impressed and surprised that Mrs Elvsted dared leave home to look for Løvborg, that she acted so openly without regard to public opinion, that she obtained a kind of power over the genius. Hedda is scornful of the way that power has been used:

'So you have reformed him – as the saying goes', but she is obviously concerned to know more about the nature of this power. And at this point she makes a strangely unmotivated contribution to the dialogue in reply to Mrs Elvsted:

MRS ELVSTED Yes! When he wrote something, we always had to do it together.
HEDDA   Like two good friends, then.
MRS ELVSTED (animated) Friends! Yes, fancy, Hedda – that's what he called it too!

Nothing in the dialogue fully explains Hedda's phrase. It emerges as a kind of indefinable knowingness; and when Mrs Elvsted reveals that the phrase was one of Løvborg's, the vaguest of suspicions is aroused that Hedda may be, as it were, quoting. The suspicion, which suggests of course the possibility of a relationship in the past between Hedda herself and Løvborg, is reinforced by what Mrs Elvsted next refers to: the shadow of a woman standing between herself and Løvborg. Hedda's tenseness, her anxiety to discover how much Løvborg has told Mrs Elvsted, and her cold, abrupt rejection of the whole story of the pistol-threat as absurd – using again the phrase of social propriety, 'Of course people don't do such things here' – are sufficient indication that Hedda herself may well be the woman. If so, we have in the threat to shoot Løvborg the second hint of how dangerous and destructive Hedda can be; but also how careful she is to hide this level of behaviour behind a façade of propriety. There is more to Hedda than superficial snobbery and bitchiness; the tension is more acute than that. She is beginning to define herself as a woman of cold, negative restraint, highly sensitive to the social proprieties that go with her status, demanding for herself the freedom to remain private and aloof; yet against that she is vividly interested in another woman's improper affair, may well have been similarly involved herself, and shows that she can be stung, on occasion, into gestures of passionate reaction.

When Brack enters as Mrs Elvsted leaves, Hedda relaxes for the first time in Act I. Brack is entirely different in appearance and in manner from the others. He is more nearly her social equal; he has an air of faintly rakish virility, of bounderishness. It is illuminating to see Hedda's easy intimacy with him and to hear her laugh for the first time. Surprisingly they seem to have something in common.

The final scene repeats Hedda's determination to have nothing in common with her husband. When Brack warns George that his appointment to a professorship must be uncertain now that Løvborg has re-emerged as a competitor, Hedda is unmoved. When George babbles about economies, she shows no understanding or sympathy. Her last act is to signal her desire to remain outside these vulgar considerations and to remind us of the strange destructive possibilities beneath that aloofness. She makes her exit through the inner room where the portrait hangs, to pass the tedious time with General Gabler's pistols. She is what she is because she is her father's daughter.

Act I was in several ways a triumph for Hedda. True, she had to face the fact of the society into which she had married, but all her attempts to snub her husband and his circle succeeded; Hedda managed to ward off all offers of intrusive friendliness or intimacy. Her success, and what it amounts to, is reflected in one aspect of the set at the beginning of Act II – she has seen to it that most of the flowers have been removed: Hedda has made the room a little more to her own liking, and that is less colourful than it was. But her actions do not suggest contentment. In Act I Hedda registered a moment of anguish by throwing open the curtains to stare out at the withered leaves; now she stands by the open french window in an action of much more forthright, reckless exasperation; she shoots her pistol out into the garden. The incident is startling in itself; as it collects to itself the earlier references to the woman who once threatened Løvborg and, less directly, to the other violent threat to burn off Mrs Elvsted's hair, we realise with a shock that Hedda's potential for violence is still active, barely latent now, and extreme. And it is not new – when Brack remonstrates with her he uses a significant 'still' – 'Are you still playing that game?'

The gesture is one of mad, vindictive hostility; she makes it because Hedda, the superior lady, is bored to distraction. There have been no visitors. George is unbearably tedious to Hedda. A peculiar revulsion, something more than mere boredom, shows up in one of Hedda's responses to Brack. When she complains of having to be everlastingly together with the self-same person, there is a faint sexual innuendo in Brack's twist to the idea: 'Both early and late – yes. Think of it. . . at all possible times.' Slight as it is, Hedda will not let pass even this veiled allusion to bed-time: 'I said: everlastingly.' The revulsion comes out more nakedly when Brack, a moment later, suggests that she might love her academic husband – 'Ugh – don't use that sickly word!' – even Brack is startled. But for us her reaction against love connects with her strange, violent dislike of pregnancy. Hedda finds no pleasure in any of the normal relationships. And when Brack suggests, with decorum yet obvious intent, a straightforward affair with him, that too is rejected. Hedda clearly enjoys his company and relishes his 'lively' topics of conversation but she sharply imposes her veto on anything that might expose her to public attention – as Brack, developing the bland image they use of life as a tedious railway-journey, suggests that she move around a little, she refuses 'because there's always someone there who'll . . .'; and when Brack completes her thought for her with a coarse 'who'll look at your legs, you mean?' her rejection is final – 'Don't like it. . . In that case I'd rather stay in my seat.' Her sense of propriety, her fear of exposure, make her incapable of entering even into the relationship Brack offers her, attractive though he is in many ways to her. She will accept his gossip about the lively kind of life he leads; she will not become part of it. She must hold back, it seems, out of a kind of acute fastidiousness.

It is characteristic of the pair that there should be nothing openly improper uttered in their conversation but impropriety certainly lurks beneath the surface of sentences like:

HEDDA . . .I used Tesman as an escort to take me home from evening parties last summer. . .
BRACK Unfortunately, – I was going in quite another direction.
HEDDA True. In fact you were going in other directions last summer.
BRACK (*laughs*) Shame on you, Mrs Hedda!

– where Hedda implies a knowledge of Brack's multiple amorous pursuits; or in Brack's faintly bounderish reply to Hedda's:

HEDDA Yes. My thoughtlessness had consequences, my dear judge.

BRACK Unfortunately – our thoughtlessness has consequences only too often, Mrs Hedda!

HEDDA Thank you!

– where 'have consequences' is the euphemism that can be used of unwelcome pregnancy. Brack is making a heartless joke out of his sexual exploits. For a woman so concerned with decorum, Hedda has a surprising knowledge of the unconventional side of life. And yet she can find no way of committing herself to it or to any other relationship. And that is why she suffers this malaise of boredom. Her explanation is that it is the paltry circumstances in which she finds herself that make life so pitiful and ludicrous, but Brack seems nearer the truth when he suggests: 'You have never had a really stimulating experience to live through.' He hints at motherhood – and Hedda's response again betrays her typical revulsion: 'Be quiet! You'll never see anything of that sort!' – but his words seem to be more generally justified when Hedda stands by the french window in much the same posture and mood as in Act I to say that the only vocation she has in life is to bore herself to death. She has nothing – no respect for husband, no liking for love, no joy in maternity, no relationship, not even such as that offered by Brack, that she can enter into. And her state fills her with the kind of reckless, dangerous exasperation displayed at the beginning of the Act. Hedda is not just bored; she is tortured by the knowledge that she has no vocation.

Løvborg arrives to provide her with an interest. He looks what we know him to be: his face – a little haggard and hectic – bears evidence of past dissipation, while his elegant, sober, brand-new suit suggests the newness of his reclamation. His first meeting with Hedda is significantly hesitant, as though he has reason to think that she may not welcome him – 'Dare I offer you my hand too, Mrs Tesman?' – his uncertainty revives in our minds the hint of a stormy relationship given in Act I. With the men he immediately shows himself to be self-confident both as a man and as a scholar. Here at last a person of some quality enters Hedda's life and she responds to the fact. She hardly tries to conceal her contempt for the poor figure George cuts. When he attempts to involve her in his uncouth glee over Løvborg's refusal to stand in their way,

Hedda insists on her non-involvement: 'Our way? Leave me out of it.' Her words are coloured again by her physical movement at this point – she goes upstage towards the inner room, where the portrait and now her own piano are. She has a prosaic reason for so doing, but the action brings into play again our sense of her need to stay aloof and the origin of that need. Her aristocratic fastidiousness is constantly at work.

The next scene, in which she settles to a *tête-à-tête* with Løvborg is the most important and complex in the play. Løvborg's opening establishes beyond doubt the fact of a past, passionate relationship. He addresses her familiarly, by her maiden name and then her christian name; and immediately runs up against Hedda's sense of propriety when she threatens to end their conversation. Yet characteristically she is ambivalent – she sneers at the idea that she is motivated by love for her husband, yet she is quick to keep clear of the other sort of relationship 'Love? No, that's really good!... No kind of unfaithfulness either. I won't hear of anything of that sort.' And then we move back into the past for illumination. Løvborg asks if there wasn't a trace of love in her old relationship with him? Hedda will not commit herself – perhaps there was. She thought of them as being two good friends. So this is where that apparently unmotivated idea came from in her conversation with Mrs Elvsted in Act I. She was drawing on the terms that once defined her own relationship with Løvborg. There was an affair of sorts.

As the *tête-à-tête* continues that affair begins to look more and more strange. Hedda reminds Løvborg how candid he used to be when he told her about his dissipations, and he replies that it was at her request. She is quick to claim that she always questioned him with circumspection, but even now Løvborg is astonished at the kind of questions she asked: why did she do it? Her answer, and the circumstances in which this scene is played, suddenly knit together the pieces that so far have defied correlation.

Do you find it so impossible to understand if a young girl – when it can be done like that – in secret –
...That one would give a lot to take a little peep into a world which –
– which one isn't allowed to know anything about?

Hedda's vivid interest in Mrs Elvsted's affair, her obvious familiarity with Brack's way of life, her peculiar involvement in Løvborg's rackety youth are all explained. So is the relationship between this oddly depraved interest in scandalous behaviour and the apparently contradictory desire for propriety and aloofness for herself. The propriety cuts her off, but it breeds the depraved interest. Hedda is not a woman disinterested in life; her interest in life is vivid but depraved by the constraints that forbade her to engage directly in it. Depraved is not too strong a word for Hedda's behaviour; it is justified not merely by reference to her love of the unsavoury, but even more by the strangely vicarious way in which she has chosen to indulge it. She has used Løvborg to do her living for her while she sheltered behind a curtain, peeped at the world outside.

What forced her to shelter? When Løvborg describes how they used to sit in the presence of the General pretending to read a magazine together while they exchanged their surreptitious confidences, we feel the whole weight of Hedda's social position being brought to bear. She was like this because she was brought up as a young lady under her father's eye. Cut off from life by the fears attendant upon her exposed position as the local aristocrat's daughter. And the circumstances are repeated and reinforced in the present. For Hedda and Løvborg are still talking surreptitiously, over an album; the General is in the room; and they have to speak in the presence of others who sit only a few feet away, their duplicity forced upon them by the frequent interruptions of George and the beady eye of Brack. The scene enacts the kind of constraint Hedda has always lived under. She was then and is now a person who *can* only peep at life, cannot commit herself to it: who can bring herself to satisfy her heightened desire to participate in life only through other people because people are watching. She was a coward because she was afraid of scandal; now she is ready to confess that her worst cowardice was in not surrendering herself to Løvborg's love instead of defending herself with the pistol. Typically, she does not confess this *quite* openly, and she ends ambivalently by warning Løvborg not to assume that she was activated by what he calls a lust for life. She has said enough to encourage him to believe that she may have overcome her old reservations; but her last words set up the familiar barrier between herself and open commitment: 'Be careful. Believe no such thing.'

It is, to say the least, no bad accompaniment to the obscure mood of this scene that during it the light has begun to fade and continues to do so during the even more cryptic scene that follows between Hedda, Løvborg and Mrs Elvsted.

Hedda's determination to involve herself in this partnership shows when she places herself firmly between the lovers, and in her provocative reply to Løvborg:

LØVBORG ...Isn't she lovely to sit and look at?
HEDDA (*strokes Mrs Elvsted's hair lightly*) Only to look at?

She wants to egg him on. But the stroking of that hair recalls Hedda's fundamental and violent jealousy: it is controlled, but this hint of it calls in question the genuineness of Hedda's apparent friendliness. And what is more significantly and disturbingly called in question is the genuineness of Løvborg. There is something indicative about the slight pause before he embarks on his praise of Mrs Elvsted, and the praise itself is given in faintly embarrassing form; it is as though Mrs Elvsted were an object rather than a person intimately bound to him. Worse still, Løvborg begins to describe his relationship to Mrs Elvsted in terms directly borrowed from his relationship with Hedda. In fact he is not concerned with Mrs Elvsted; he is using his praise of her to offer a surreptitious challenge to Hedda, and Hedda's few interventions show that she recognises what is going on beneath the surface. It all happens in a short passage of dialogue:

LØVBORG Yes. Because we two – she and I – *we* are two real friends. We trust each other completely. And that's why we can sit and talk together so frankly.
HEDDA Without circumspection, Mr Løvborg?
LØVBORG Well –
MRS ELVSTED (*softly, clinging to Hedda*) Oh, how happy I am, Hedda! Because – just imagine – he says I've inspired him too.
HEDDA (*looking at her with a smile*) No, does he say that, my dear?
LØVBORG And then there's her courage to act, Mrs Tesman!
MRS ELVSTED Good heavens – courage! *me*!
LØVBORG Infinite, – where her friend's concerned.

HEDDA   Yes, *courage,* – yes! If only one had *that.*
LØVBORG   What then, do you mean?
HEDDA   Then one might perhaps be able to live one's life after all...

Løvborg uses the term that he has, we know, used in both his relationships – friends. Hedda, a few moments earlier in their *tête-à-tête,* had evoked this relationship; Løvborg's emphases *we* (stressed in the Norwegian) and 'real' implies that he finds Mrs Elvsted a truer friend than Hedda was. He claims for her the quality he once saw in Hedda – frankness (the word is the same). Hedda's reply refers back to her own claim that, however frank she was in her discussions with Løvborg in the past, she was circumspect; the repetition of the word shows that Hedda is deliberately pursuing the comparison between herself and Mrs Elvsted that Løvborg has initiated.

Hedda responds to Mrs Elvsted's claim to have inspired Løvborg with what looks like amused contempt, but she responds; and then Løvborg continues with his comparison. His praise of Mrs Elvsted's courage picks up the term used by Hedda in praise of her own relationship with Løvborg – she saw something courageous in it. But again Løvborg adds an emphasis damaging to Hedda. He praises Mrs Elvsted for her courage *to act* – something that Hedda, a self-confessed coward, never possessed. And to this implied rebuke, Hedda's response is suddenly no longer ironical and superior but strong and serious. Her words, stressed as they are in the text, show her to be sensitive to her own lack of courage, and to recognise that without courage life is not liveable. And at this instant of deeply serious self-appraisal, Hedda seems to come to a decision. The indications are slight but they are there. Her tone changes suddenly and she begins to try to exert her own influence over Løvborg and get him to drink. But this is no real departure from the earlier conversation; it is a testing out of another term of comparison. In Act I, Mrs Elvsted reported that Løvborg said she had a sort of power over him; in Act II he said that Hedda had a sort of power over him. It is clear from Hedda's reversion to this key term that she is trying to make *her* power dominate:

HEDDA (*laughing*) Haven't I got any power at all over you then, poor me?

She laughs, but from now on it is clear that she has discovered a determination in herself to prove Løvborg wrong in his comparison. She is determined to meet his implied challenge and in doing so supplant Mrs Elvsted.

Her goading of a reformed drunkard to drink again looks like the exercise of power for mere mischief, or at best for its own sake. She obviously enjoys her new control; she uses it both to make Løvborg drink and to stop him from drinking too much. It is not until the end of the Act that the true significance for her of what she has embarked on reveals itself. It is an astonishing passage:

HEDDA Ten o'clock, – then he will come. I can just see him. With vine-leaves in his hair. Flushed and bold.
MRS ELVSTED I hope to God it's like that.
HEDDA And then, you see, – then he will have gained power over himself again. Then he'll be a free man for the rest of his days.
MRS ELVSTED Oh God, yes, – if only he would come back just as you see him.
HEDDA He will come like that and not otherwise! (*getting up and drawing closer*) Doubt him as much as you like, I believe in him. And now we shall prove –
MRS ELVSTED There's something behind all this for you, Hedda.
HEDDA Yes, there is. For once in my life I want to have power over a human destiny.
MRS ELVSTED But haven't you got that?
HEDDA Haven't got it – and never have had it.
MRS ELVSTED But over your husband's then?
HEDDA [Yes] that would be really something, wouldn't it? Oh, if you could only understand how poor I am. And *you* have been granted such riches. (*throwing her arms passionately around her*) I believe I shall burn your hair off after all.
MRS ELVSTED Let me go! Let me go! I'm frightened of you, Hedda.
BERTHA (*in the doorway*) I've set tea in the dining-room, ma'am.
HEDDA Good. We're coming.
MRS ELVSTED No, no, no! I'd rather go home alone! Now, at once!
HEDDA Nonsense! You must have some tea first, you little blockhead. And then – ten o'clock, – then Eilert Løvborg will come – with vine-leaves in his hair.
(*She drags Mrs Elvsted almost by force towards the doorway.*)

It contains so much. It shows that there has suddenly appeared for Hedda an opportunity for satisfying a deep and categorical need – to exercise power over a human destiny. That it is not power for its own sake that she desires, but power for a purpose: to set Løvborg free so that he may exercise power over himself. That this purpose is not a discovery of the moment, a whim, but is connected with some of her most consistent ideas – power, and boldness, are terms of value that she used recently and in the past to Løvborg; the image of vine-leaves reminds us of the way she saw beauty in the old relationship. Hedda hopes to realise in this odd endeavour some of the values that have always been of tremendous importance to her.

The dialogue shows, in Hedda's confession of her poverty, how much she suffers from that feeling. Her jealousy of Mrs Elvsted's hair is expanded into, becomes a mere emblem of, a jealousy of the richness of Mrs Elvsted's life in comparison with her own. Her excitement at the thought of finding this way of filling up her poverty shows in her extraordinary physical violence, in her staccato sentences, in the very openness of her utterances – never before has she so revealed herself to another person. Hedda's passion is totally genuine; it terrifies Mrs Elvsted. It is no longer, like the spasm of frenzy in Act I, inarticulate and negative. It is less than fully articulate but it begins to take on definition. Hedda has at last discovered a vocation, a way of expressing, again through Løvborg, some of her most passionately felt values. The main stage is lit more brightly for this development – Bertha brings on a lighted lamp. Hedda has found something to live for. But what ultimately causes this terrifying intensity in this cool society woman, why that calm surface can suddenly erupt into such passion, why Hedda is as she is, is suggested by the fact that she drags Mrs Elvsted towards the inner room – her room. Hedda is still her father's daughter.

If the end of Act II marks the first real crisis that we have observed in Hedda's life, the beginning of Act III helps suggest what the immediate results are. The two women, fully dressed, are resting in the sitting-room. The atmosphere is close, dim – the curtains are drawn over the french doors and across the doorway to the inner room; the shaded lamp is turned half-down and the stove is almost out; its doors stand open. The mood is one of exhaustion, a kind of staleness, closeness.

It fits Mrs Elvsted well enough as she lies awake in misery; but the striking thing is the way Hedda has responded. She is first discovered sleeping. When she awakes she says she has slept quite well – an interesting little reference back to the beginning of Act I. There the young mistress claimed not to have been able to sleep in her comfortable bed; now she has slept easily on a sofa, fully clad. There is a kind of buoyancy in her mood that seems to be the result of her crisis – she can laugh. She is not worried about Løvborg; she finds it easy to explain to herself why he did not return; she can still imagine him with vine-leaves in his hair. When Mrs Elvsted questions her sincerity, Hedda puts her in her place: 'You really are a little mutton-head, Thea.'

Her mood is suggested by more than the words. The woman who in Act I demanded the closing of the curtains, and, when she herself threw them open, stared sullenly out at the world; who in Act II stood at the open french window actually firing a pistol into the garden; who described herself as a young girl longing to 'peep' into the outside world – she can now throw open the curtains over the french door and let in a stream of daylight. Her gesture has now become fully natural – no sign of repugnance, or tension or hostility. Hedda's crisis seems to have resolved some of the tensions between herself and her environment. The impression is reinforced by the way in which, without making any sort of fuss, she goes down on her knees to re-lay the fire in the stove. Hedda seems positively an invigorating force in the set, so much unlike the negative creature we met in Act I.

There is, however, a further effect created by the set. Hedda opens the curtains over the french window but those over the doorway remain closed. The inner room towards which Hedda has from time to time drifted, which contains her piano and the portrait of her father – which, in short, has become her sanctum – this is now cut off from view. The set is, as it were, opened outwards instead of inwards, but at the cost of shutting off that room. In reading the play we need to remember that this is the background to the whole of Act III.

Tesman's arrival – he plays so typically the role of a henpecked husband – is broad comedy but it serves a more important function. It provides occasion for further, though oblique, definition of what Hedda's new vocation means to her. It is clear that she has no curiosity about George's activities during the night, but as soon as he mentions Eilert she shows her interest – she sits down to listen, and says, 'Well! Let me hear about it then.' And yet she is not at all concerned, as George is, with the new book that Eilert read aloud. George describes it as a most remarkable work; Hedda brushes it aside impatiently: 'Yes, yes, I'm not interested in that.' She wants to hear about something else: did he have vine-leaves in his hair? The image clearly has deep significance for her. And it receives at least a partial definition when Hedda contradicts George's commonplace judgment on Løvborg:

TESMAN And to know that he – with all his gifts – unfortunately enough is completely past saving for all that.
HEDDA I suppose you mean that he has got more courage for living than the rest of them.

'Courage for living' [livsmot] is connected with the word she used to describe her affair with Løvborg in Act II – it clearly represents one of her key values. She also reveals an interest in what George has to say about the inspiration behind Løvborg. He relates how Løvborg delivered a long, incoherent speech about the woman who had inspired him in his work. The word 'inspire' is the one Mrs Elvsted used of her own influence on Løvborg and at the time Hedda reacted to it with something approaching contempt. She reacts now in a way that shows that she does not assume that Mrs Elvsted was indeed the source of the inspiration Løvborg was referring to the previous night: 'Did he say who she was?' When George gives his decided opinion that it must be Mrs Elvsted, Hedda's reply is noncommittal 'Well –' and then she changes the subject. We cannot feel that she has closed it.

She shows no great interest at first in the manuscript of the new book. Her first question is – why didn't George give it back immediately? But then she seems to find a purpose for the papers. She first enquires who else knows about them and then decides to get them into her own hands. She is much concerned to know whether the manuscript could ever be reproduced. She is struck when George uses again the word to which she seems to be sensitive:

> No, I don't think that would ever be possible.
> Because the inspiration – you see –
> HEDDA Yes, yes – that's exactly it, of course –

She changes the subject. But from these hints we may imagine the processes of her mind – the manuscript becomes the irreplaceable proof of that other woman's inspiration that Hedda wishes to supplant by her own. And that gives the papers a new importance in her eyes. When George leaves, she hastens to hide them in the bookcase before Brack can see them.

We are reminded of Hedda's peculiarly vivid interest in the less conventional side of life that she herself avoids when she encourages Brack to give her details of his 'lively' party, but there is clearly a more precise focus to her interest: Eilert Løvborg, and a special interest in him, namely the extent to which she has succeeded in influencing him as she intended. She shows no dismay when she hears that Løvborg went on with some of the others to another party 'of the liveliest kind'. She seems to take this behaviour as a sign of his having thrown off Mrs Elvsted's influence:

> BRACK ...But at that time he had refused the invitation. Because now, of course, he has put on a new man, as you know.
> HEDDA Up at Sheriff Elvsted's place, yes. But still he went all the same?

And when Brack says, with cynical mockery, 'unfortunately the spirit [ånd] moved him at my place last night', Hedda slightly modifies 'spirit' in a way that shows how persistently preoccupied she is with the idea of inspiration: 'Yes, he really was inspired [beåndet], I hear.' If no longer by Mrs Elvsted, then by herself, seems to be the implication. But then Brack describes the sordid events of the evening in a way that makes it impossible any longer to believe that Løvborg did respond to her influence in the way she expected. What actually happened was so sordid. There is no frivolity in her voice when she concludes, 'So that's how it turned out, then. Then he didn't have vine-leaves in his hair.' There is a flatness in her utterance and in her mood at this moment; she 'looks vacantly in front of her'. But that is all; she hastens to conceal her feelings by a sudden change of tone, as though she does not wish Brack to understand her involvement. But the subdued crisis has registered on us; Eilert Løvborg has failed to respond to Hedda's inspiration; she has not, so far, succeeded in shaping a human destiny in her way. And it hurts.

There is worse to follow. Brack may be quite unable to understand what Hedda means by vine-leaves, but he can appreciate that Løvborg is in some sense his rival. Now that Hedda has shown openly enough her interest in Løvborg, Brack feels himself to be at liberty to express his own interest in Hedda more openly and brutally than ever before. Hedda's smile fades as she says, 'You really are a dangerous person – when it comes to the point . . . I don't mind – so long as you never get the upper hand over me in any way', and when Brack leaves, she looks after him with a serious expression. We can sense the alteration in her position as we think back to Brack's first entrance 'by the back door' in Act II which found Hedda in a posture of aggression, firing her pistol at him, and compare his exit, again 'by the back door', with Hedda now defenceless against him. Hedda's direct intervention in a human destiny is laying her open to intrusion; and, in visual terms, her sanctum is not available; when she goes and peeps through the drawn curtains of the inner room (conjecturally, to make sure that Mrs Elvsted is not stirring), the movement has the force of an image.

She seems detached in her preliminary exchange with Løvborg; there are no indications to him of what she expected of him; and when Mrs Elvsted comes on for her emotional encounter with her lover, Hedda recedes into the background. But though she has little to say, there are indications of intense involvement on her part in certain aspects of the situation.

For example: when Løvborg tells Mrs Elvsted:

> It's that our ways must part now.
>
> MRS ELVSTED Part!

it means so much to Hedda that she cannot control herself:

> HEDDA (*involuntarily*) I knew it!

It means so much to her to have her hopes confirmed that she has been able to break Mrs Elvsted's hold over Løvborg as part of her mission to restore him to power over himself. It takes a lot to make Hedda respond involuntarily.

Something of the sort happens a little later. Mrs Elvsted insists on being with Løvborg when the book comes out. Hedda's words, spoken as though to herself, show her concern:

HEDDA (*half-aloud, tensely*) Oh, the book – yes!

She seems anxious to discover, from what the others say, the significance of the book for them. For Mrs Elvsted and for Løvborg it is *their* book, something shared; when Løvborg then declares that their book will never be published, it is Hedda who registers strong though unspecific, inarticulate emotion with a simple 'Ah!' She is anxious when Mrs Elvsted asks where the manuscript is, and almost gives herself away, again involuntarily, as she almost contradicts Løvborg's tale of destroying it. She is most deeply moved when Mrs Elvsted describes the book as a child, hers as well as Løvborg's:

HEDDA (*almost inaudibly*) Oh, the child –

It is the merest of hints but it is enough. It suggests the comparison Hedda is making between this intellectual child created under Mrs Elvsted's inspiration and the physical child, conceived by a process she hates by a husband she despises, that she is reluctantly carrying. It suggests that Hedda is seeing the book in this light, both as an essential bond and as a reproach to her, for the first time. Her almost voiceless expression suggests that she is deeply moved; this intervention, like the others in this strange scene, amounts to self-communion; Hedda is so much involved emotionally that the social creature has for a moment given way to a passionate introvert. And what has involved her has been the revelation of what the book means to the other two and to her.

And so she goes on probing. She keeps her conversation with Løvborg fairly cool, given the circumstances, but then he uses a word that touches her. He says that Thea 'has broken my courage to live'. It is the key word again, that Hedda has just used to define his superiority over the others at the party, the quality which she valued in their earlier relationship and which she thought she had reinspired in him. Thea has broken the strength that means most in Hedda's scale of values; thus there is a particular weight behind her response: 'That silly little idiot has had her fingers in a human destiny' – she speaks staring straight ahead. She is affronted not simply because Thea is a rival in power, but because that power seems to have destroyed what matters most to Hedda.

However, she seems not to be quite convinced that she has lost. She goes on prodding Løvborg to find out what the book really means to him. As much, it seems, as to Thea. It is a kind of child for him too; its loss means for him the end of that relationship, and the only thing left for him is suicide.

Hedda seems indeed to have lost to her despised rival. Yet she can see an opportunity for herself to step in again. At least Thea's influence is broken as an active force. This gives Hedda a chance: if she has failed to persuade Løvborg to live beautifully, she can still get him to die beautifully. It is all the same to her. She has never been concerned with him as an individual. She has always used him. Used him to do her disreputable living for her at second-hand in the past; used him within the play to live, again at second-hand, unconventionally in the way that matters most to her, expressing in action as she herself dare not her truly basic values of freedom, courage, independence, everything that goes into her term 'beauty'. Now that he is broken, she can still build him up for use again. She can as it were take over his decision to die and make that into a demonstration of her idea of beauty. She does not believe in vine-leaves any more – that Dionysiac image implies life – but she still holds to her values and she still must have them shown for all to see.

There is a feeling of ineffable certainty and assurance about Hedda when she produces her pistol. She is totally convinced that this time she must succeed. Løvborg makes us wonder whether she has, after all, chosen the right man. There has always been some doubt about his sincerity; something perhaps a little un-convincing about his proposal to kill himself. His reactions now do not quite match up to Hedda's serene self-confidence. When she gives him the pistol as a memento, he stares at it and says: 'That? Is that the memento?' And in the midst of that elevated exchange, where they both employ full names like hero taking leave of hero, his banal 'Thanks', and his equally prosaic tucking away of the weapon into his pocket seem vaguely inadequate to the occasion as Hedda conceives it.

But for Hedda there are no doubts. She is convinced of her man this time. And then the Act ends by demonstrating why she so desperately needs to be convinced of her power to inspire a man to act out her dream of beauty. The ending erupts again into astonishing violence of emotion as she burns the manuscript.

The action is in part a simple ritual of triumph over Thea. The burning does nothing that has not already been done; Thea and Løvborg have already been parted by the mere belief in its destruction; but Hedda clearly derives great satisfaction from this vindictive deed. But there is more to it than that. Hedda speaks as well as acts, and from her broken, agitated rhetoric, and from her fragmentary words we can sense the source of all her actions: 'Now I'm burning your child, Thea – you and your curly hair! Your child and Eilert Løvborg's. Now I'm burning – now I'm burning the child!' The words cannot be taken in isolation. In isolation they are absurd, but the broken rhetoric reveals the pressure behind them. This is a moment of blinding emotion for Hedda; and it matters so much to her because it is the culminating instant of triumph over many sources of humiliation and anguish that have tortured her in the past. She is expressing her intense jealousy of the intellectual child; behind that shows her disgust for her own physical child by an inferior man; her jealousy of Thea's influence over Løvborg and her sense of triumph at establishing her own influence; her more fundamental sense, current since her schooldays, of Thea's superior richness of being, symbolised for Hedda by that magnificent head of hair. It is a moment of destruction, related to other destructive moments in her life; but for Hedda one of tremendous fulfilment, a working-off of a terrible burden of inferiority resented not just now but throughout her life. She desperately needs this success.

It is also the first physical intervention in life, the first actual, compromising deed that we have seen Hedda perform. It makes her ecstatic; but from the stage we are still faced with the faintly disturbing circumstance that Hedda acts without the comforting presence of her father. The curtains still cut her off, visually, from her sanctuary, her inner room. Hedda has intervened in life, but at the cost of her privacy.

The stage picture that we see at the beginning of Act IV is significantly different from that of the previous Acts. The sitting-room lies in darkness. The inner room is lighted by a hanging lamp. The curtains are drawn over the french window but not over the doorway to the inner room. Hedda is in black. She paces the darkened room, goes into the inner room to play a few chords on her piano and returns to the darkened room.

Then Bertha brings a lighted lamp into the sitting-room and leaves again. Whereupon Hedda crosses to the french window, moves the curtain open a fraction, and looks out into the darkness. Shortly afterwards, Mrs Tesman enters in black and the dialogue begins.

This is quite a long pantomime, during which no word is spoken; it is left to our eyes to register our responses. Every detail is readily understandable in terms of actual events: Aunt Rina has probably died. Yet how much more the details suggest as images.

The balance of the set, for instance, has been emphatically reversed. In Act III it was, as it were, turned outwards: the french doors were uncovered and the inner room was curtained off. Now the opposite is the case. Not only that, but the lighting emphasises the inner room. There is no reason why the main room should not have been lighted from the beginning; the marks of mourning on Bertha merely reinforce those on Hedda and Mrs Tesman; they can hardly be the reason for bringing her on stage with a lamp.

Hedda's pacing the room and her fingering the piano are obvious enough signs of restlessness, but her movements are more significantly related to the set. She moves out of the main room into the inner room, her room – the sound of the piano, her piano, reminds us – under the eye of her father's portrait. But she does not remain there. Something makes her go to the french door and peep through a chink in the curtains.

The total effect cannot, of course, be precisely formulated. The business at the curtain is coloured by the many previous occasions Hedda has stood by them, and by our recollection of her description of herself as a girl who wanted to peep at a world she was not supposed to know about. The effect of the setting and the pantomime is to suggest a withdrawal, a falling-back on the inner room; and with it a renewed uneasiness towards the outside world that Hedda seemed so happy to intervene in during Act III. It is a strong and striking preparation for the events that develop.

They have forced Hedda into the background. Aunt Rina's death has brought Miss Tesman back into the house as of right, and the grief she shares with George leaves Hedda standing like an outsider while they talk. She says little. But one brief utterance is interesting. She listens to Miss Tesman's plan to take in another invalid to look after, and she seems faintly impressed by the old lady: 'Will you really take on a burden like that again?' It is only a momentary breach in her customary cool exclusiveness; she goes on to snub George when he tries to suggest that the three of them could get on well together, and is coldly unsympathetic towards his grief. But it is a breach.

Her main concern shows itself to be elsewhere. The mere mention of Eilert's name is enough to make her enquire 'quickly' if there is news of him. Soon she is involved in more than her own curiosity; her action at the end of Act III begins to threaten consequences. George has heard from Løvborg a tale he knows to be false about his destruction of his manuscript: Hedda is again 'quick' to ask whether George told Mrs Elvsted who in fact held the papers – her manner shows that her wits are having to work hard to find a way out of this difficulty.

The way she chooses recoils on her. She decides to tell the truth but in such a way as to make it impossible for George to make her crime public. She puts on an act: she cynically assumes the role of the little woman. She did it for love of her husband – she even manages to use his Christian name as she rarely does – and because she was pregnant.

At first she can treat this as a private joke, uttering these soft sentiments with an almost imperceptible smile. The scheme recoils as she approaches the point where she has to reveal her pregnancy. It is a necessary part of her scheme, yet her language shows that it is no easier for her now to contemplate her condition and to endure smothering, intimate solicitude than it was in Act I. There she fought hard to conceal the fact and to ward off the intimacy offered by Miss Tesman. Now, to stop George from revealing what he knows, she must lay herself open. It costs her a great deal. As she approaches the point of revelation, she cannot bring herself to utter the words:

HEDDA Well, I suppose you had better know – that just at this time – (*violently breaking off*). No, no, – you can ask your Aunt Julia. She'll tell you fast enough.

And when the inevitable result comes, and George capers in loud glee and proposes to spread the news, the old, strange, yet fully genuine anguish shows itself again:

HEDDA (*clenches her hands as if in despair*) Oh, this is killing me – all this is killing me.
TESMAN All what sort of thing Hedda? Eh?
HEDDA (*coldly, controlled*) All this – ridiculousness – George.

She cannot go back. This is part of the price she must pay for her intervention in Løvborg's destiny, this laying herself open to vulgar intrusion from the Tesmans, this acknowledgement of the pregnancy she hates and despises. She has had to sacrifice an important area of her jealously guarded privacy to achieve her supreme ambition.

Mrs Elvsted's return gives Hedda a chance of finding out whether she has succeeded. She is tense for news. Not too tense to register, for the second time in this Act, some astonishment at what another person is capable of:

MRS ELVSTED . . . And so I went up to his rooms and enquired after him there.
HEDDA *Could* you bring yourself to do that, Thea!

All of Hedda's regard for propriety is in her phrase, but it seems to indicate a certain respect too. Hedda seems to be realising that people she despises, first Miss Tesman and now Mrs Elvsted, are capable of acts of dedication that Hedda herself could not perform.

In consequence, Hedda is anxious to be reassured about the success of her own act. She questions Brack 'tensely', breaks in 'involuntarily' with 'So soon, then' when Brack informs them that Løvborg is in hospital, perhaps dead. She is convinced; and what it means to her to have succeeded in her vocation shows in the crescendo of feeling in her words. She broods over the manner of the death as she imagines it, savouring its quality. She becomes again the introvert, taking little part in the conversation. Then suddenly there comes another crisis. She breaks out of her self-communing to express the thoughts that mean everything to her. It is astonishing that this woman who has shown so strong an instinct for secrecy and privacy should suddenly burst out in a loud voice in a room full of people with: 'At last an achievement!' Her words are untranslatable. They are very simple: 'At last a *dåd*' – where *dåd*, without any inflating or defining adjective, means an action suitable to a hero. The nearest English words, 'feat', 'exploit' will not do; yet to expand the word into 'a heroic deed' or 'deed of courage' or some such makes Hedda sound merely rhetorical.

She is carried away by her success; she wants the significance of this action to be known. More than aesthetic beauty is involved. Beauty is just the comprehensive term for the values she sees exemplified in Løvborg's death. And again, as she expresses them, we recognise them as values with a long history in her life. There is the courage implied in the word 'dåd' – a quality she felt in her earlier relationship with Løvborg; there is beauty – another of those qualities; there is the freedom to exercise power over oneself implied when she says, 'I tell you there is beauty in this. Eilert Løvborg has had a reckoning with himself. He has had the courage to do – what needed to be done.' Hedda has succeeded. She has at last filled the emptiness of her life: she has perceived in Løvborg a man capable of a finer form of unconventionality than that implied by his youthful dissipations; she has set him free to shape his own life and, being a kindred soul, he has shaped it in accordance with her intensely felt values. He may have failed to live those values, but he has proved them in his death. And Hedda wants everyone to know, for this is the fulfilment and vindication of her secret self, and its private aspirations, the demonstration of her superiority.

It comes as a minor shock for her to discover that she has, after all, failed to destroy utterly the 'child' that made her feel so inferior; Mrs Elvsted has the notes from which the book might be reconstructed. Another mild surprise for her to realise that even George is willing to dedicate his life to the task; first Miss Tesman, then Mrs Elvsted, now her stupid husband – they all seem to be able to find a purpose for their lives. It makes it all the more essential that her own purpose should have succeeded, that she should not be, as she was at the beginning of Act II, tortured by her own emptiness. George and Mrs Elvsted occupy the inner room to begin their task at once. Hedda is not seriously perturbed – she retains her elation and goes on to expand her vision; but the way she uses language at this moment of crisis demands careful attention. Strung together, and set out in their natural rhetorical units, her speeches run:

> At last an achievement!
> I tell you there's beauty in this.
> Eilert Løvborg has had a reckoning with himself.
> He has had the courage to do – what had to be done...
> What a release it is,
> this thing of Eilert Løvborg's...
> A release to know
> that something really can happen in this world that shows courage and free-will.
> Something with a touch of spontaneous beauty to it...
> ...I only know
> that Eilert Løvborg has had the courage to live his life after his own fashion.
> And now –
> this great thing.
> This thing with beauty to it.
> That he had the strength and the will to take leave of life's feast –
> so early.

Her speeches prove that she speaks from the centre of her personality. The terms that ring out like refrains are ones that we have often heard before from her. The root word 'free' [*fri*] is in the word 'release' and 'free-will'; it sounds together with 'beauty' and 'courage'. This cluster of ideas, with the related ideas of spontaneity, of living after one's own fashion, of taking leave in one's own time – these are expressions of what we have come to recognise as Hedda's most fervent obsession, definitions of a way of living that is more than merely aesthetically beautiful. The obsession has content, serious content.

The terms are used with confidence and her series of speeches begins with an air of certainty. She opens with clear statements: 'at last an achievement'; 'I tell you there is beauty in this.' But then a significant vagueness begins to creep in. Within each rhetorical unit, the element that is meant to define fails to do so. The 'beauty' of what Løvborg has done is defined by a vague figure of speech – 'has had a reckoning with himself'. Hedda herself seems to find it hard to define his 'courage' – there is that significant little pause between 'to do' and 'what had...'; and when she finds the words they are vague. Indeed she returns for a second attempt at definition with 'the courage to live his life after his own fashion' but that is no clearer. She tries three times to define her sense of release, and each time falls back on 'something'. 'Thing' leads to the climax of her definition: 'this great thing. This thing...', but the climax itself, her most strenuous attempt to be specific, emerges as another vague figure of speech: 'to take leave of life's feast'; poetical and sentimental.

Hedda's vision cannot be dismissed as an empty one when it has such content; her sense of commitment and certainty cannot be doubted; but the vagueness of her rhetoric shows that Hedda is gesturing towards values that she cannot give full definition to. They are values that she believes so passionately in precisely because she has never experienced them in her own life. And yet her life is invested in her vocation, which is to give expression to them through Løvborg.

Brack's response shows how far he is from beginning to comprehend Hedda. For him her concern with 'beauty' is a 'pretty' illusion – the difference in stature between the terms is a measure of the difference between them at this point. He sets about demolishing what to him is a mere figment.

There was no free-will about Lovborg's death; Hedda has failed to destroy the bond between him and Mrs Elvsted in that he died still searching for 'the child'; he was shot, accidentally, without beauty, in the belly. Løvborg has failed Hedda in death as he failed her in life. Her one attempt to mould a human destiny to her ideal has failed. We know what it meant to her to have discovered a vocation in life; what it means to have failed in it comes through unmistakably:

HEDDA (*looking up at him with an expression of revulsion*) That too! Oh, farce and vulgarity, they lie like a curse over everything I so much as touch.

Her great vocation has collapsed into travesty.

Worse than that. Hedda has behaved throughout this Act with an air of confidence; she seems to believe, until this moment, that she has succeeded not merely in achieving her mission of intervening in life through Løvborg but in preserving her stance of aloofness. Now she discovers that by intervening she has laid herself open to gross intrusion from Brack; and during the scene which reveals this, her inner sanctum is physically occupied by Mrs Elvsted and George. The feeling grows into an ironical suspicion that Hedda cannot, after what has happened, simply retreat behind her defence of aristocratic privacy. She cannot even revert to her position of hopeless boredom. She is in process of being trapped by Brack.

She does not, however, surrender. She makes a strange and vehement reply to Brack when he suggests that Løvborg must have stolen her pistol:

HEDDA (*jumping to her feet*) Stolen! That isn't true. He did not!

Strange because Brack seems to be offering her an easy way out; yet, for some reason, she will not allow it to be thought that Løvborg stole the weapon.

It is so characteristic of Hedda's basic predicament that this crisis has to be bottled up, that her outburst of vehemence should be terminated by a warning 'Shh' from Brack as Tesman and Thea come out of the inner room to occupy Hedda's writing-table. In the presence of others, one must be decorous. Hedda's language changes abruptly to express trivialities. And yet we are in various ways made to feel the continuity of tension in her even during this brief scene of interruption.

Something prompts Hedda to remove all her belongings from the writing-table, including an object she is careful to hide, and carry them into her inner room now free again – her sense of privacy seems to be asserting itself in some ill-defined fashion. Then she returns to face Brack again; but not before she has shown, by lightly touching Mrs Elvsted's hair, that the old jealousy is still active, mixed with the old contempt. This kind of poise, displayed so soon after the shocks she has received, attests to her sheer nerve.

Brack, leaning over Hedda, seems to dominate her. He instructs her in the significance of the pistol. If it was not stolen from her, the police will want to know who gave it to Løvborg. Brack, as the only person to recognise the pistol, is prepared to hold his tongue. Yet again, before he actually names his terms to an apprehensive Hedda, he seems to offer her an escape:

BRACK (*shrugging his shoulders*) Well, there's always the way out that the pistol was stolen.

Brack seems not to wish to press too hard, but Hedda resists even this pressure. Again she shows that she will not allow the idea of mere theft to be entertained. There is great violence in her determined: 'Rather die!' There is no further explanation, but it seems as though Hedda will not allow her transaction with Løvborg to be entirely vulgarised. Whatever he may have done with the pistol, her giving it to him remains for Hedda a vastly important thing. And she maintains this when a simple lie could give her an escape route from the situation closing in around her.

But she has not yet fully appreciated how dire that situation is. Brack smiles at her threat and uses the phrase that Hedda herself has used earlier in the play, the phrase of social conformity he is confident they both subscribe to: 'People may say such things. But people don't *do* them.' The threat has not impressed him. He can go further. When Hedda says explicitly that the pistol was not stolen, he has her. Since it was not stolen, Hedda will have to explain in court why she gave it to Løvborg. She is threatened by the thing she has most feared in her life, exposure to public scandal. She has not worked out her situation clearly after all; she had not thought of being implicated. She lowers her head; for an instant it looks as though she is beaten at last. But almost at once her head is raised again. As Brack insinuates a tender alternative to public disgrace, Hedda rejects it violently. Her words show why she does so:

HEDDA (*looks up at him*) So I'm in your power, judge Brack. You've got the upper hand over me from now on.

BRACK (*whispers more softly*) Dearest Hedda, believe me, I shan't abuse the position.

HEDDA In your power all the same. Dependent on your demands and your will. Not free! Not *free* (*rising violently*) No – that's a thought I shall never tolerate! Never.

These terms have, by now, long genealogies. Hedda was jealous of her power over Løvborg; it was a power she intended to use to give him power over himself. For that is the only power that matters. In Act II she was glad that Brack had no power over her. Now he has and one of Hedda's most jealously nurtured ideals is threatened. The other is freedom, a *leit-motif* in the rhetoric she expended on Løvborg; it is the foundation of her philosophy of beauty; now her own is threatened.

Her reaction is not one of mere pique. It is a response appropriate to this threat to her one intense, positive desire, for a different kind of living. She has invested everything in getting that desire turned into reality for her by Løvborg; not only has she failed with him, but she can no longer hope even to maintain her ideals for herself in her peculiar kind of aloofness. Brack is forcing her to endure, in her own person, the rape of her own essential values. Hedda, who sought vicariously a way of life that seemed to her beautiful because free, finds herself offered a life of ugly servitude.

Her recovery of poise is astonishing yet her manner does not quite conceal her feelings. As she drifts around the room we are given as it were a *résumé* of Hedda. Her involuntary smile and her mimicry of George's intonation reminds us of her social snobbery, her contempt for this bourgeois pedant. Her stroking of Mrs Elvsted's hair recalls that fundamental sense of inferiority in Hedda that has produced such violent jealousy: contempt goes with that too. Her question 'Is there nothing useful you two can find me to do here?' and George's answer 'No, nothing at all. . .' remind us of the aimless state she was in before she discovered her vocation and is in again now that it has collapsed. And the very poise, the control she can exert to keep those feelings concealed from the others in this terrible crisis of her life reminds us of what has always been Hedda's fate: to live and behave within the strict constraints of social propriety, to keep her private self hidden and aloof from vulgar observation.

She has little more to say, but the *résumé* continues. She enters the inner room; we remember the strong impulses that have constantly drawn her into that sanctum. She closes the curtains and cuts herself off, physically, from a hateful world as she did at her first entry. Plays a wild dance-tune that reminds us of the violence that has appeared from beneath that cool surface; puts out her head for one brief, insolent moment and reminds us of the young girl who was only allowed to peep at life.

Here the *résumé* ends, and a last astonishing, new dimension is revealed. Hedda is not defeated. She defies Brack with insolence again. She has withdrawn into her own, aloof, aristocratic world to realise her own values through her own actions. That is the new dimension. There is no vicariousness now. Hedda believes in her values so totally, rejects so utterly their negation by Brack, that she can bring herself to meet her own demands. She breaks through the crippling impediments of cowardice to find at last the courage to *act*, to act for herself, to act in fulfilment of her own demand for beauty. 'People don't *do* such things.' That phrase once character-ised Hedda too. Brack cannot appreciate it, but Hedda has changed; she has become precisely a person who *can* do such things. Absurdly, destructively, but with a strange kind of integrity, Hedda has broken through in the only way she can.

Ibsen's own preliminary note (one amongst many): 'With Hedda, there is a deep poetry at bottom', epitomises Hedda's complicated condition; it also provides a means of gauging the distance travelled since *Love's Comedy*.

What that condition is has been explored in the course of the analysis. Hedda is caught in the contradiction of being simultaneously a person whose deepest urges are towards a poetry of living – defined at least approximately by her recurrent use of key terms – but whose social position has educated her to accept as, at times, of equal or even superior validity the restraints demanded by society. The basic conflict, broadly definable as being between the essential self and society, is the same as it was in all the other plays that have been discussed. What is different is Ibsen's sense of what is involved in that conflict.

Ibsen's 'deep poetry at bottom' gives the answer. Falk was a poet out in the open; one, moreover, who is allowed by Ibsen's imagination at the time to go on living as a poet; the cost of this freedom, in terms of superficiality of involvement, has already been discussed, but the implications are clear: poetry, poetry of living, can in some sense be autonomous and inviolable even in the modern world. Brand, though more fully committed to the society he must live in, remains free to articulate his moral poetry in words and in actions; even though Ibsen now recognises that his very power must make his achievement irreconcilable with actual living he, too, can resist contamination by society; moral poetry also can remain inviolable even when it is mistaken. Mrs Alving is the first character whose very poetry is infected by the social conditions it is directed against; her moral poetry is tethered by a social habit of thought so that her vision expresses itself in the cadences of social rhetoric and in actions that are at best ambiguously free.

Hedda represents an enormous extension of Ibsen's sense of how deep the infection can penetrate. In a strange way we can feel that for all that has happened and does happen to Mrs Alving, nothing affects her integrity of soul. This is more than an assessment of her as a person; it is an indication that Ibsen's scrutiny itself does not yet penetrate into the depths of personality. Nothing happens to Mrs Alving that does not remain accessible to her mind and to articulation through measured words – not, that is, until the last scene. That scene demonstrates that the final experience, at least, is beyond the kind of comprehension that Mrs Alving has hitherto shown, but Ibsen does not explore the nature of that experience. Mrs Alving is not understood at that depth.

Hedda Gabler carries out just that kind of exploration. Hedda is a poet deep down because that is where social conditioning has driven her poetic impulses. Not merely her intellect but her secret recesses of being have been invaded by the social conditioning she has been subjected to. If we label as her essential self that source within her which provides her peculiar and personal drive towards a poetic style of living, then we may say that for much of the play the imperatives issued by her social self have at least equal validity with that. Her feeling for decorum, her fear of what people will think or say, seems as fully natural to her as her impulse to breach that decorum. Thus Hedda is not a radical intellect that can survey, however imperfectly, its own relationship to a hostile environment, as Mrs Alving was, but a person whose essential being can no longer be separated from what threatens it. Ibsen has discovered that modern society penetrates below the intellect to the deepest sources of personality. Mrs Alving is at war, after her fashion, with society; Hedda is racked by internal civil war between her social and her essential self; she is both Pentheus and Dionysus.

And this kind of strife calls everything into question because it leaves nothing in its pure form. Hedda's aspirations, her actions, her language are all turned into fragmentary vagueness by the pressures that have driven them so deep. We have no clear achievement to respect, no clear statement to admire. There is not even the impressive wholeness of character that carried Mrs Alving through all the stages of her agony. Hedda is unpredictable, spasmodic, hectic, a poet rendered almost inarticulate and incomprehensible by her inner contradictions.

The play also shows how Ibsen has matured in his assessment of the society that exercises pressure upon the individual. *Love's Comedy* presents it as an easy target for ridicule by representing it through characters who are, for the most part, caricatures; and the broadness of touch, the certainty that these figures do stand for readily recognisable absurdities in modern life implies that such absurdities are as readily recognisable in real life as in art. Society is for the most part egregiously bad in egregious ways. Something of the same simplicity of judgment produces the Sheriff, Schoolmaster, Dean and so on in *Brand* and persists even into *Ghosts*.

Manders, who epitomises the operation, both as agent and as victim, of social coercion, is given few merits to offset his poverty of intellect and spirit; through him, society is roundly and confidently condemned. And in a way this is comforting; it is reassuring to be made to feel that some areas of difficulty (they diminish, of course, in the passage from *Love's Comedy* to *Ghosts*) are amenable to ready diagnosis and implied cure; the clarity reduces the tension. On the other hand it does not breed conviction in the reader. It is precisely where Ibsen seems most confident in his diagnosis of society as evil that we are likely most to suspect him of oversimplifying. To reverse what was said parenthetically above, the sense of conviction grows from *Love's Comedy* to *Ghosts* as the certainty of diagnosis diminishes.

In *Hedda Gabler* it well-nigh disappears. Society is not caricatured. It is true that it contains George, but there is Miss Tesman too, and, above all, Thea. They have their weaknesses, but in every conceivable way but one they are superior to Hedda as people, and thus a challenge to any claim that might be made for the intrinsic superiority of Hedda's poetic vision of life. Thea can do as much as Hedda and more – inspire, have power, reform, love, act, show courage, and all this positively. She is a product of society and thus society may be credited with her as well as debited with George and Brack. It is no longer a foregone conclusion that society does not stand comparison with the integrity of the isolated individual; the merits and demerits are nicely presented through characters who are far from being caricatures; they have become human.

An effect follows from this closer approximation to the relativity of judgment in actual life – an effect on us, the readers. We are made to work – think and feel harder – to get our bearings. We have to define for ourselves the one way in which Hedda, for all her deformities, is a strangely superior being – through her residually creative sense of human potentiality as against the basic conformity of Thea's mind. Ibsen no longer believes that simple assertions can be made. The more delicate and complex balance presents a greater challenge to understanding.

Another effect is on Hedda. If society cannot be diagnosed in

terms of black against white, then it becomes even more difficult
for Hedda than it was for Mrs Alving to identify the ultimate
deadness of society and the critical moment when society threatens
the living truth. Mrs Alving slipped unawares into her pit but
soon recognised it for what it was. Hedda never slips and can
never become aware. No one moment marks her entry onto the
path of tragedy. Her fate was to be born as daughter to the General;
all else follows. Hedda is never given the chance to challenge her
circumstances because they have commended themselves to her
in a way that obscures their falsity. Life as the General's daughter
may have proved disastrous, but it has its manifest attractions
which prevent Hedda from ever revolting against it. And insofar
as this is true, she is more totally and irrevocably trapped than Mrs
Alving; trapped from birth where the glamorous, stifling cocoon
began to be woven around her.

The point can be reinforced by reference to the set. There is no
ostentatious gloom. The setting is so normal, so attractive; we
come only gradually to the awareness that the very seemliness is
part of the trap Hedda finds herself in; it is not even called in
question, to the extent that it was in *Ghosts*, by anything so readily
indicative as mist and rain beyond the windows. Neither we, the
audience, nor Hedda the protagonist, are given any grounds for
suspicion, still less for rapid identification, of the nature of her
situation. *Ghosts* provided less obvious, less reassuringly clear
warnings than *Brand* or *Love's Comedy*; *Hedda Gabler* provides
none at all – it merely presents a handsome room. Ibsen's imagination has recognised not only that society penetrates into
the recesses of personal identity, not only that it does so with
pervasive subtlety of penetration, but that it does so in so
attractive a guise that it will be embraced and not rejected by
the victim.

And yet it is in the final event repulsed. And here we need to
revert to the other emphasis in Ibsen's deceptively simple note.
However deep Hedda's poetry may be driven by her social
conditioning, she remains a poet. The content of the poetry is
significantly vague, its utterance fragmented, its translation into
action disastrous, and yet the impulse behind the absurdity is

genuine; genuine enough to make Hedda choose to die rather than tolerate the ultimate surrender of her values.

Ibsen presents Hedda as, in the most marginal sense, a hero. Marginal because every affirmation by her and about her is contradicted by contrary affirmations. Contradicted, but not denied. She is a heroine pared to the bone, stripped of moral force, of forthrightness, of courage in the accepted sense, of positive action; she is muddled, inarticulate, destructive, trivial, and yet... We can respect her hard and late-won integrity for those very reasons. For it is demonstrated in circumstances which seem to make any degree of integrity impossible. The power of society to invade and corrupt has been so strongly realised that any gesture of independence from that power seems almost miraculous.

It does not diminish the gesture that it must be meaningless to other people. Brack is spokesman for the general incomprehension, but what does he amount to as a witness? It is an additional quality of Hedda's peculiar, vitiated kind of poetry that she acts, finally, in a terrible isolation. The vision she dies for has no backing. There is behind it no system of values endorsed by tradition; no group, not even a person who she knows can fully share her vision. The only validity it possesses for her is her own intense passion of conviction. To die for a certainty that depends entirely upon the promptings of one's isolated essential self demands a kind of courage.

But the courage, the vision, the poetry are never allowed to cancel out the absurdity, the destructiveness and the triviality. Ibsen may wish to present this peculiar kind of achievement as the final resultant of the contradictions inseparable from Hedda's condition, but it is essential to his understanding that the achievement should be recognised as a peculiar one and that it should, by that recapitulation of imagery in the last scene, be located alongside all that qualifies it. Hedda is not a heroine in a heroic play but a heroine in a specifically modern tragedy. This, Ibsen seems to feel, is the most that modern heroism can be and can achieve. It is not much; as tragedy, this play brings the genre almost to its extremity, close to the loss of that sense of human potentiality that I take to be one of its essential components. But it remains tragedy, and Hedda remains in a strictly limited yet genuine sense heroic. She dies for a vision of human potentiality superior to the reality to which life condemns her. Surround that statement with all the qualifications that Ibsen insists on, and we have one of the most impressive recreations in drama of the experience of what it means to have heroic aspirations in an age that almost, but not quite, denies all possibility of heroism.

It is from Ibsen's insistence on the fineness of balance between contradictions that the serious critical disagreement about the play reasonably stems. It does not seem to me reasonable to accuse the play of being non-dramatic – it has often been described as a novel *manqué*. It is inseparable from its nature as a study in enforced reticence that it should avoid explication, and an essential part of its vision that such attempts at articulation as are made should be fragmented by the inhibitions they must overcome. Yet the inarticulacy, and that which strives for articulation are both created in fully dramatic form. To know more about Hedda would be to make her character and her situation different from what they are.

Once we are prepared to respond to that character and that situation, it must be the case that each one of us has to weigh the contradictions against our own sense of values. All tragedy comes perilously close to comedy, or lends itself to parody. No other protagonist is so open to the objections of commonsense as Hedda because Ibsen invites the application of commonsense. He presents the contradictions so scrupulously, and makes his own judgment so marginally, that it is no wonder that serious critics have come down on the other side of the fence. I believe it is wrong to see Hedda as a study in absurdity, but I cannot see how Ibsen could have remained true to his sense of her ambiguousness without leaving that open as a possible reaction. It is not easy to present an experience of great complexity and at the same time point to the resolution of it. *Hedda Gabler* may have advanced far beyond *Love's Comedy*, but the old ironical fascination with the complexity of modern living is still strong, and so is the fascination with the heroic.

7

'LITTLE EYOLF'

Few of Ibsen's plays open with a scene of such opulence. We see a pretty, richly furnished room with plants and flowers in it; there is a wide view out over the fjord and of forest-clad slopes; the sun is warm, the sun of an early morning in summer; and Rita herself, wife to Alfred Allmers, is a pretty, voluptuous blonde of about thirty wearing a light-coloured dress. Even the situation is cheerful; she is unpacking her husband's walking-gear and chatting happily to Asta, Alfred's half-sister, about his welcome, early return.

Both women are excited and happy at Alfred's unexpected return, yet the mood is far from simple. Little nuances begin to hover about the straightforward narrative. There is, for instance, that little index of the relationship between the wife and the half-sister in Rita's return of Asta's greeting – a mere turn of the head, a nod, but no warmth in response to Asta's 'Good morning, Rita dear'. Their ways of talking about Alfred are different. Asta has been drawn to the house by a strong instinctive feeling she cannot analyse; there is no doubting the warmth of her devotion but she lacks the tone of intimate certainty, befitting a wife, that Rita has. And though Rita has sanction and motive for speaking about her passion for Alfred as openly and vehemently as she does, she takes advantage of her position when she tells Asta that it is easy for *her* to talk about more freedom for Alfred; it's a way of gently putting her in her place.

These are, however, minor nuances compared with others that have also begun to cluster. Against the grain of the opulence, of the happy, excited talk of the women, a few impressions of Alfred himself begin to form. And these are not what we might expect. He seems to be not a man of warmth himself but in some ways the opposite: a man who sends a short, cold telegram an hour before his arrival, a man often troubled with a cough; the word 'tired' attaches itself to him; his first thought on his return has been to set

his son to his book-work again, his 'poor, pale little boy', Eyolf.
Already there's a potential discrepancy between the women's
estimate of Alfred and the kind of man he seems to be.

And this brief, oblique preparation serves to concentrate our
attention on him at his first appearance. Some kind of meagreness
is evidently suggested by his slender and delicate build, gentle eyes,
thin hair and beard, his serious, thoughtful expression. Not all
negative qualities but in combination they suggest a lack of vitality.

And Alfred's entry cannot be separated from Eyolf's; he enters
leading the child by the hand. Thus it is a corporate impression
that is created; and Eyolf contributes a good deal more to it than
mere lack of vitality. He seems to show that, and other qualities of
his father, to a magnified degree: he is positively undersized and
looks weakly. He is strikingly intelligent too, with his beautiful,
clever eyes. But he is also a cripple, dressed in a sort of soldier's
uniform; and this is a striking indication, not elaborated or
explained, of some kind of discrepancy. Although we cannot be
sure, the possibility remains open that this too may be as much an
index of the father as of the son.

Alfred's initial mood is buoyant enough. He has returned without adding a word to his book, but that is because he has lost
interest in writing – he is quite happy about it. But then there
comes a sudden, striking dislocation of tone. They have been
chatting in a neutral enough fashion when Alfred says, in reply to
Eyolf's childish admiration: 'But believe me, someone will come
after who will do it better.' The Norwegian sets a problem here.
Alfred says, 'der kommer en bakefter som vil gjøre det bedre.'
This seems a direct echo, almost an exact quotation, of Mark i. 7,
in Norwegian translation. An English translation, to strike the
echo, would have to tap the words and style of the Authorised
Version: 'There cometh one mightier than I after me', with all its
distancing, isolating archaism; by doing so it would give to
Alfred's words a degree of elevation or prominence the Norwegian
does not give; for there is not the same distance between the idiom
of St Mark and the idiom of Ibsen in Norwegian.

The Norwegian gets its effect in fact not from an elevation of
style at this point but from the astonishing presumption behind

the reference. For the words reported by St Mark were those of John the Baptist. This little man has, without any sign of self-mockery, asserted some kind of similarity between himself and John, and between Eyolf and Christ who will come after. The self-aggrandisement is remarkable; and it is repeated, less emphatically to be sure, when Alfred says that when his successor comes he himself will return to the mountains 'up on the heights and on the great moors'. And this he says 'seriously'. Alfred is making large gestures but he means them.

But this elevated mood is not secure. Not only is it challenged by his insignificant appearance and by the initial impressions of him, but it is broken by sharp indications of pain and unease. It hurts him, obviously, that Eyolf is a cripple, unable to live the active life of an ordinary boy. What is likely to impress us is the verification of the general impression of some kind of discrepancy exemplified in Eyolf. This cripple wants to climb in the mountains, to swim and to become a soldier. It is pathetic, this discrepancy between ambition and capability, pathetic and emphatic. And it helps form our assessment of the father; as this John the Baptist shows his pain and then flares into resentment, threatening to show the beach-brats who is master, his self-elevation begins to look suspect.

Another effect of this brief episode is to show that beneath the opulence and the happy semblance of things there are hidden tensions; all of them, so far, deriving from Eyolf's disability. Then the old ratwife comes on to give a tremendous enlargement to these tensions.

Her real name signifies 'wolf' but she looks more like one of her own victims; she is small, thin and shrunken; her hair is grey but her eyes are piercingly keen. Her predominant colours are vaguely sinister – black and red. In part she is substantial; we can imagine a cross between a gipsy woman and an old peasant woman. the sort of person Ibsen remembered from his boyhood days; but in part, and perhaps obtrusively and damagingly, she seems to exist in order to promote a function within the play. Her language gives her away.

It is quite different from anything that we have heard. Her

flowery civilities – or servilities – we might expect from an itinerant worker, but not the sustained and deliberate ambiguity of her terms. For a rat-catcher, she is remarkably reluctant to name the creatures. She refers to them (often using the neuter form of the adjective, no noun) as 'any[thing] that gnaws here in the house', 'poor, wee [things]', 'sweet little mites', 'the blessed wee creatures', 'the lovely little [things]'. When she does name them as rats, she half-humanises them: 'because of the rats and all the little rat-children'; her own sweetheart is 'down where all the rats are'. She seems to speak in this way so that she may be used to set up resonances between herself and the main issues of the play.

And this she begins to do. Her first speech links back to a recent one of Alfred's. He said, 'Oh, Rita, how this gnaws [*nager*] at my heart, all this.' She says, 'have the master and mistress got anything that gnaws [or 'torments' – *gnager*] here in the house?' They have, it seems, although they do not recognise it. Everybody has; or so seems her story of the plague of rats to imply. Her strange neutrality of language permits, even encourages us to translate 'rat' into vaguer torments. Her speeches generate a whole web of images deriving from water – sea, depths, darkness, sleep, death; and her narrative of the rats and of her own sweetheart defines as a common contradiction in human relationships the sharp antitheses of fear and attraction, persecution and peace, restless activity and stillness, hate and love.

She does more than suggest the hidden tensions of human relationships in general. There are one or two touches which make her parable (for so Ibsen seems, for once, to employ one of his characters) apply directly, though imprecisely, to the situation here in the house. The echoed *nager/gnager* is one instance. Another is 'the poor, wee things' – Asta called Eyolf 'a poor...little boy'. She and her dog are 'tired' like Alfred. Less obvious, yet striking, is the fact that the old woman slips into the biblical idiom just as Alfred did. She refers to 'poor wee things that are hated and persecuted so cruelly' – an echo of 'bless them that hate you and pray for them which despitefully use you and persecute you' or 'And ye shall be hated of all men for my name's sake...But when they persecute you in this city' – the combination is honoured in its associations.

It is not easy to be true to one's feeling of what the old woman does in this scene. That she is obtrusive can hardly be denied; she is different from the others in more than class and function. Yet she is not a symbol. Perhaps she is best described as generating in us a sense of potential complexity which is not yet fully identifiable in the main situation where the characters can imagine themselves to be on the whole wealthy, comfortable, happy and high in mood. She ends, appropriately enough, with a speech in which she ties together the two words used separately by Alfred and herself earlier: 'If the master and mistress should notice anything here that gnaws and torments [*nager og gnager*]...'

She creates this disturbing effect, and physically she disrupts the happy family circle; Rita goes out on to the veranda for fresh air, Eyolf slips away. But the scene between Alfred and Asta, alone on stage, seems to glide into a mood of relative tranquillity in spite of her intervention as they discuss the family letters Asta has brought. It is only when Rita returns that the ratwife figures again.

Rita's first words are ominous: 'Ugh, it seemed to me the weird old woman brought a sort of smell of death in with her', and jerk our minds back. But the old woman remains effective in another way. She has stirred something in Alfred's mind. He claims to understand the power of attraction that the sea and its dark peacefulness hold for the rats. But he goes on to filter her ideas through his own mind, to clothe it in his own imagery, which is an imagery antithetical to hers. She spoke of peace in the depths, Alfred, consistently with his earlier imagery, says: 'Besides I can understand well enough the compelling and attractive power she talked about. The solitude up there amongst the peaks and on the high moors has something of the same.' He retains the imagery of exaltation but shows that he is responsive to that longing for darkness, death and peace in the depths. It is a curious mingling. And on the face of it, only a momentary acknowledgement of the old woman's vision, for Alfred goes on to explain the change that has come over him in buoyant terms again. Life has been wonderfully kind to him.

This is the gist of what he says, but the vague feeling persists that there is some kind of discrepancy within this man. His language does not quite convince – it strives after emphasis and elevation in ways that seem suspiciously easy. He says – and the pointing is Ibsen's own, though I have myself changed the format in order to make my point more easily:

> When I think back over my life – and my fate –
> during the last ten or eleven years,
> it almost seems to me like a fairy-tale or like a dream.
> Don't you think so too, Asta?...
> When I think what we two used to be, Asta.
> We two poor, wretched orphans – ...
> And now here I sit in comfort and style.
> Been able to follow my vocation.
> Been able to work and study, –
> completely to my own liking.
> And the whole of this great, unbelievable happiness –
> that we owe to you, my dearest Rita.

So many of the natural rhetorical units (which I hope I have reasonably indicated by the way I have set the speeches out) end in overemphasis – 'life – and my fate', 'fairy-tale or like a dream', 'poor, wretched orphans', 'comfort and style', 'work and study', 'great, unbelievable happiness' – that Alfred gives the impression of striving for a facile effect. And the impression is strengthened by the way he seems deliberately to elaborate and intensify; there is self-consciousness in that brief pause before he adds the pompous 'and my fate' to 'my life' and before he adds 'We two poor wretched orphans' to 'we two'. He begins to generate an indistinct smell of inauthenticity – made all the stronger when, immediately afterwards, he lapses from this level of speech to the banality of: 'Of course I only mention this as a sort of introduction.' Nonetheless he seems settled in this mood of self-elevation as he describes the great change that has come over his life. He has abandoned what was once his life's work, his big, thick book on 'Human Responsibility' – a title which, incidentally, makes it all the more remarkable, in retrospect, that he, the secular humanist, should have likened himself to John the Baptist – but in favour of a more important task, that of becoming a true father to Eyolf.

It seems characteristic of him, by now, that he should solemnly refer to his sense of 'the higher responsibilities that made their demands' on him; but there is little to prepare for the rhetoric that breaks from him when he speaks of his plans for Eyolf. It makes a strong impression.

> I mean that, with all my might,
> I shall try to make the irreparable as light and easy for him as it can conceivably be...
> I shall try to bring light to all the rich possibilities that are dawning in his infant soul.
> All the noble seeds stored up in him
> I shall bring to growth –
> make blossom and fruit. (*more and more warmly, rising*)
> And I shall do more than *that*.
> I shall help him achieve harmony between his desires and that which lies attainable in front of him. Because that is just what he isn't at this moment. All his longings go out towards things that, for his whole lifetime, will remain unattainable by him.
> But I shall create a conscious happiness in his mind. (*He paces the room a few times. Asta and Rita follow him with their eyes.*)

There is no mistaking the fervour; it is there in his physical excitement and in the uncharacteristic flow of his sentences; they are the longest to come from him or any other character. And yet he fails to be quite convincing. He aims so directly at emphasis – 'with all my might', 'as it can conceivably be', 'rich', 'noble'; speaks in such sweeping, unqualified terms – 'all the rich possibilities', 'All the noble seeds', 'All his longings'. He may begin with the caution of 'I shall try...' but it soon changes to the forthright 'I shall...'. He adorns his speech with evocative imagery but it is shortwinded – 'light' and 'dawn' in one sentence, 'seeds', 'growth', 'blossom and fruit' in the next; 'harmony' in the next. The images serve as local adornment; they break up rather than unify the speech; they are, in the worst sense of the word, inevitable in such development as they are allowed. This is poor rhetoric. Indeed, as we watch Alfred pace the room under the eyes of his adoring womenfolk, it looks like a piece of private self-display, the cock among the hens. What comes across most forcibly is something not intended by Alfred; he speaks of Eyolf, but the phrase that echoes like a refrain throughout is 'I shall', 'I shall'. The devotion is self-devotion and nowhere does it show more blatantly or more unconvincingly than in the resounding conclusion to his peroration: 'I cannot share myself in this matter. And so I withdraw. Eyolf shall be the complete man of our race. And I shall make it my new life's-work to turn him into that complete man.' We listen to the words but remember the pale little cripple. Afred may himself speak of helping the child to reconcile his wishes with the inexorable future, but his rhetoric undercuts the caution and the proclaimed modesty. And the rhetoric sweeps on: there is a remarkable egotistical involvement in Alfred's sense of his own place in the scheme of things, as the thinker who has achieved fellowship with the cosmos, no less:

> Yes! And then I went up into the infinite solitude.
> Saw the sunrise shine over the mountain-peaks.
> Felt myself nearer to the stars.
> Almost as if in sympathy and in community with them.

It is not merely the vocabulary, with its insistent imagery of elevation and grandeur, it is the very structure of the speech that helps create the impression. And the man himself is slight, thin-haired and so forth.

Altogether the scene fulfils the earlier hints. There is in Alfred a discrepancy between aspiration and capacity like that so signally portrayed in his son. Or so we are well justified now in suspecting. His rhetorical gestures are so broad, and so simple; he entertains no thought of impediment, and this seems over-simple in a play in which the ratwife has created so powerful a suggestion of hidden, tormenting tensions and even the main characters have shown, from time to time, that such tensions may exist.

Alfred himself seems quite secure in his new vocation. Living 'human responsibility' must now totally occupy his energies; the book must be abandoned, for he cannot divide himself between two tasks. He is happy and convinced; he seeks to draw the women into his vision.

But at once one of the hidden tensions manifests itself. He takes his wife's hand, but when he reaches out the other to Asta, Rita breaks away bitterly, 'So you can share yourself after all.' No more than that, but it amounts to a minor crisis – suppressed by the arrival of Borgheim.

The road-construction engineer is obviously meant to contrast at many points with Alfred. He is only a few years younger – 30 to his 37 – but he is young and vital. Alfred walks in the mountains, Borgheim cuts his roads through them. Alfred has just abandoned a major task, Borgheim has just successfully completed one. And yet, for all the differences, there is a similarity too.

Like Alfred he looks cheerfully ahead to his new prospects – to more roads, and, obviously enough, to Asta. And of these he speaks in a mood and style of simple, elevated enthusiasm 'Oh you great big beautiful world – what joy it is to be a builder of roads!' There is no ground for questioning this enthusiasm. Borgheim looks the part, his achievements justify him. And yet the simple enthusiasm sounds brittle after the sinister intimations that have been stirred up. Borgheim reinforces a mood of optimism and of elevation – he contributes to the mountain-imagery – in a play that also accommodates the ratwife and the imagery of depths and darkness.

This elevation of mood then crashes down as some of the tensions shake the apparent stability of this domestic world. When Rita and Alfred are left alone together, her possessive jealousy flares out. She wishes Asta would never come near the house again. She tries to get physically close to Alfred, to capture him in her arms, but he repulses her; she says she hates him and finally wishes that she had never given birth to her son. She tries to seduce Alfred physically there and then but arouses only stubborn hardness in him and furious resentment in herself. But clearly her passions are the obverse of her true feelings. She expresses hatred because she loves Alfred; she is physically demanding because she is physically neglected; she threatens infidelity because she wants her husband's attention; she resents Asta and Eyolf because they stand between Alfred and herself. The scene amounts to more than a hostile portrayal of Rita; it suggests the circumstances that have made her what she is. It helps define Alfred, as a man and as a philosopher – his sense of human responsibility does not seem to extend to the most obvious responsibilities of a husband. It defines some of the tensions.

The scene is marked by several abrupt fluctuations of mood and sentiment so different from the apparently settled cheerfulness of the opening. Rita, for instance, is from moment to moment bitter, hateful, tremulous, threatening – and then speaks half-laughing of her threat to seduce Borgheim. The sudden changes, the inseparable contradictions are a verification in this actual relationship of what the ratwife implied. These people, like other people, are indeed plagued; and part of their malaise spreads from the contradictions of love and hate.

Alfred is too Olympian still to be seriously shaken by this display. If there are tensions he can rationally explain them away by his philosophy. It is, he says, part of the human condition that the years bring change. Physical passion fades; it is natural that he should now wish to share himself between his wife and son. But the rationality does not work; it drives Rita beyond bounds, to the very verge of wishing that Eyolf were dead. Alfred's philosophy, that made everything seem so clear and simple, has run headlong into something obscure, even though he seems not to appreciate the fact.

And the same turns out to have happened to Borgheim when he returns from a stroll with Asta. That happy prospect has been closed, it seems. There is no elaboration or explanation, but his enthusiasm has been dashed. Rita knits together his frustration and her own, welds the two situations into one by her wild talk about the evil eye that spoils happiness. Her vehemence makes her the central figure for the moment; here the hidden tensions, or some at least, threaten not just to disturb but to shatter the semblance of unity and happiness. And at that moment the alleged cause – alleged, that is, by Rita – is removed from the play. The awful probability emerges that Eyolf has drowned; the Act that opened with the family coming together ends with its panic dispersal – Asta and Borgheim dash off, Alfred follows them, and we are left with Rita in a state of collapse on stage.

There is no discrepancy in Act II between the appearance of things and the hidden reality. The setting is unequivocally one of

gloom and sadness, a reversal of the imagery of height and elevation that permeated Act I, a physical representation of that
alternative, and as it then seemed alien, imagery generated by
the rat-woman. Alfred sits in a narrow little glen overhung by
trees. It flanks the fjord, but there is no broad view now, only
glimpses through the tree. No sunshine, only heavy, threatening
weather with driving mist.

Alfred's mood is reversed too; in Act I, life seemed a wonderful
dream; now the dream has become a nightmare: how marvellous
it would be if he could only wake up. And yet, natural as such a
mood might seem to be, he does not so much mourn for Eyolf as
brood on the situation. His thoughts are slightly tangential. There
is more resentment than direct sorrow in his description of the
water: 'How pitiless the fjord looks today. Lies so heavy and
sluggish. Lead-grey – with flashes of yellow – and it reflects the
rain-clouds.' The aesthetic description seems out of place. And
again direct sorrow gives place to a kind of angry determination
to analyse intellectually and in his own humanistic terms when he
says to Asta:

On the surface, yes. But down deep, that's where the undertow runs fast...Do
you really believe he's lying just off here, my dear? But he isn't. Asta. You
mustn't believe that. Because you have to remember how fierce the current
runs out here. Right out to sea...That's why little Eyolf has gone so far – far
away from the rest of us now...Why, you can work it out for yourself...
In twenty-eight or twenty-nine hours – Let me see – ! Let me see – !

His grief sounds like affronted egotism when he describes his loss
as 'something done against me and Rita'. In this mood he seems to
feel not simple grief but resentment at a situation which his
philosophy cannot cope with. He cannot see where human
responsibility applies. Eyolf did not deserve this fate; he was kind
to the old woman and to her dog. His intellectual response is
feeble, but it is all he is capable of, and it leaves him in a mood of
sullen despair that seems not to be quite the grief it offers to be.
Eyolf's death, as a human event, does not truly occupy his mind.

Clearly not as his talk with Asta develops. He is easily led away
by his interest in her. And as they not only talk about their warm
attachment in the old days but re-enact it as they sit closely and

intimately while Asta sews on crepe, Alfred shows that he can relax and indeed forget his son. He can even smile. And yet what makes him smile is something much stranger than the conventional manner of these two might suggest. For their past life was extraordinary. Two youngsters left prematurely to make a home together, with the half-sister given a boy's name and dressed in boy's clothes. The explanation given – that Alfred was ashamed of not having a brother – seems absurdly inadequate to the situation; especially when we register that the real son was, years later, given the name of the fictitious brother. That relationship between brother and sister, and the disguise adopted for it, has lived powerfully in Alfred's subsequent life. And the nature of the disguise, a denial of sex, suggests the real nature of that relationship. The fiction was a device, unconsciously adopted, to control an affection that they show no signs of ever having identified, a protection against innocent incest.

Some such interpretation seems needed to explain the story of the past and the remarkable warmth of affection that Alfred has consistently shown towards Asta. And there is additional proof in the power their attachment has to drive the real boy out of Alfred's mind. He may recoil in self-recrimination, but once again his words do not quite carry conviction: 'No, no, no – that's just what I mustn't do. I have no sanction to. No right to – And no heart to either.' The repetition 'no sanction. No right', and that slight pause before the addition of 'no heart' manages to make this sound self-conscious and contrived. He seems to be driving himself to feel what otherwise he would not feel when he says: 'All I must do is contemplate the spot where he lies and drifts down there in deep water.' His proposal to row out to the spot in a boat seems a mere wild and pointless gesture, indeed mere posturing when he allows himself to be dissuaded so easily by Asta. For all his insistence on his grief, he soon allows his mind to drift back to the person who really concerns him, not the dead boy but the living girl: 'It's good that I've got you, Asta. I'm so glad of that. Glad, glad – in the midst of sorrow.' There's no doubting where the balance of emotion lies.

This strange, strong, unacknowledged love excludes everybody else, so far as Alfred is concerned. Not merely Eyolf, but Rita too. The marriage has had none of the substance of that adolescent attachment. Alfred begins to show what really lay behind the light hints of Act I when Asta urges him to go and find Rita. His response is extraordinarily vehement:

(*vehemently, pulling away from her*) No, no, no – don't talk to me about *that*! Because I can't, do you see? (*more calmly*) Let me stay here with you.

Not only does the fictional Eyolf mean more to him than wife or son, but 'he' makes the marital relationship a matter for revulsion and disgust. The real nature of this marriage is coming to light.

Alfred makes one more attempt to express the feelings appropriate to his loss:

(*grips her hand and holds it fast*) Thanks. (*gazes for a while over the fjord*) Where has my little Eyolf gone now? (*smiles sadly at her*) Can you tell me *that* – my big, clever Eyolf? (*shakes his head*) Nobody in all the world can tell me that. I know just this one, terrible thing, that I haven't got him any longer.

but the banal questioning, the sad smile, the grasping of the hand of the girl while he thinks about the boy, the clumsily symmetrical compliment ('little Eyolf. . . big, clever Eyolf') and the unconscious egotism of the last sentence all contribute to an impression of spuriousness. With the entry of Rita the unreal decorum is shattered again.

She is greatly changed. In Act I she hung about her husband, embraced him, tried to seduce him into love-making. Now, as she enters restlessly, she brushes past him. In this mood she is left to confront Alfred while Asta tactfully withdraws with Borgheim.

Unlike Alfred, Rita seems to be suffering agonies of sorrow caused directly by Eyolf's death. It suggests the awful immediacy of the event that she should be haunted by the thought of the great, open eyes of her son as he lay on the bottom. The actuality still seems not to touch Alfred. He does not translate her words into thoughts of the horror of what happened to the boy; instead he distances her phrase, turns it into a simple moral accusation against her by throwing up in her face the words she used in her fit of resentment at the end of Act I: 'Were they evil, those eyes, Rita?' It seems more important to him to pin responsibility, to justify his abhorrence for Rita, than to feel for his son. He makes no more pretence of fondness as he did earlier. He is entirely harsh and cold when he says, 'Sorrow makes people wicked and hateful' – an excuse not for Rita but for himself, and by now his sorrow is suspect.

They go on to rip their marriage apart. That is their theme, their marriage and the impediments to it. It is becoming more and more apparent that although Eyolf may have seemed the cause of hidden tension, the real cause lies elsewhere. It is remarkable how little of Act II is directly concerned with the boy.

Rita brings the real cause a little further out into the open. Not just by reminding us of the consuming egotism of her passion for Alfred that makes it impossible for her to share in love, but by accusing Alfred of never truly loving his son. She begins to see through his elevated vocations to the soft centre of this man. Both the great book on Human Responsibility and the great practical experiment in human responsibility were really disguises for self-mistrust: 'Because you had begun to be consumed by mistrust of yourself. Because you had begun to doubt whether you had any great vocation to live for in the world.' And this is convincing. It tallies with what has already been hinted at, it verifies the strong images of discrepancy between ambition and capacity. And we respect Rita's perceptiveness even more when she juxtaposes that other set of hints. She feels that in some way Asta has monopolised Eyolf's affection. She almost manages to say that Alfred has been sexually estranged from her.

But that is all she can do, juxtapose elements in the situation. Alfred is not unmoved by her attack. He half-acknowledges the self-mistrust; he avoids her gaze when she seems to touch on their sexual relationship as she urges him to look into himself and into everything that lies beneath and behind appearances; but he is able to produce an answer that fits his own predisposition towards rational analysis and the attribution of human responsibility. He defends his loss of passion by his deterministic 'law of change'. He turns Rita's story of Eyolf's laming into another simple accusation. She enticed him, therefore the baby fell, therefore she is responsible for his lameness, his inability to swim, therefore for his death. He is willing to share the blame, but he seems to be seeking comfort by reaching that neat, rational conclusion 'And so there *was* retribution in Eyolf's death after all.' Yet in the context it is something else that registers. Alfred may be applying his humanistic mind to an analysis of a situation that had painfully defeated his powers of explanation earlier, when he could discern no grounds for retribution in the death, but his words connect with the imagery of forces not susceptible to that kind of explanation. He reminds Rita that she came to him when he was watching over the baby and 'lured' him. The word is that used with such effect by the ratwife – it serves to connect this row, ostensibly about a rational accusation about responsibility for a dead boy, with the vague complex of dark, hidden, irrational tensions indicated by the old woman. Alfred's neat formulation may satisfy him for the moment, but not us.

It does not satisfy him for long. His humanism can find no positive value in this experience and he has taught Rita not to believe in the solace of religion. Their subsequent conversation reveals two people who are in fact lost. In the intervals of destructive recrimination they search desperately for something, anything, that will give them peace or the illusion of purpose: forgetfulness, travel, resumption of work on the book that has lost its significance. Anything will do, but nothing will serve. Their moods change as rapidly as their fragmentary plans, from accusation to bitterness to hardness to mildness to violence, within a few moments. Yet in all this vacillation their fundamental dispositions are not changed; Rita remains insistently possessive, Alfred stubbornly insists on what begins to emerge as the thing most important to him, that there can no longer be any kind of relationship between himself and his wife. The point is made with especial emphasis:

ALFRED (*slowly, looking at her steadily*) There must always be a barrier and a wall between the two of us from now on.
RITA Why must there – ?
ALFRED Who knows if a child's big, open eyes aren't watching us night and day?
RITA (*softly, with a shudder*) Alfred – that is a horrible thought!
ALFRED Our love has been like a consuming fire. Now it must be put out –

RITA (*moves towards him*) Put out!
ALFRED (*hard*) It is put out, in *one* of us.
RITA (*as if turned to stone*) And you dare say that to me!

Alfred is not talking about their one act of physical love as the cause of Eyolf's death; he is revealing his revulsion from physical love in itself; he imagines Eyolf's eyes watching them *night* and day: their love has been a consuming fire. And it is only after he has been able to make his cardinal point clearly and brutally, that so far as he is concerned their love is finished, that he can relax into a measure of kindness and suggest, in milder tone, that perhaps out of their common guilt and longing for atonement may result a kind of resurrection.

Once again Alfred's vocabulary is disturbing. In Act I the humanist invoked the words of John the Baptist; in Act II he gave praise and thanks to God in a dream; now, a few minutes later, his language is full of religious terms. His secular philosophy seems not to provide him with his vocabulary, which is drawn from a religion he has renounced. The impression is of a waverer, a man not substantially based on any kind of belief, secular or religious, but using the arguments of rational philosophy or the mysticism of religion as occasion demands. Alfred no longer impresses as a philosopher.

Rita rejects his ideas. She has no use for any resurrection – she is a warm-blooded human being, not a human fish. Her passionate sorrow at the loss of physical love produces another revelation about Alfred's relationship with her and with Asta. He denies that he ever loved her.

RITA   What did you feel for me then at the very beginning?
ALFRED Terror.

There is no English word that I can think of capable of applying the whiplash of the Norwegian 'skrekk'. Alfred's single word needs to be felt almost as a physical blow because the revelation is so vital for all its brevity. It rips aside the last tatters of what at the beginning has seemed a marriage based on affection even if that affection had now somewhat faded. Instead we have suddenly revealed to us a marriage entered into in terror by the husband;

terror mitigated for a while by physical infatuation, and subdued by something quite different, the need to provide for Asta. When Rita says, bitterly, 'So it was really Asta who brought us together', we can feel that she is coming close to the truth. For what is indicated here is a man so obsessed by his strange attachment to his half-sister that he is incapable of entering into the mature responsibilities of marriage. He was terrified yet attracted by his wife physically; now that the attraction has faded, he has demonstrated his revulsion; and, furthermore, his incapacity to meet any of the actual responsibilities of marriage, whether as husband or as father. Rita has brought into the open the fact that Alfred has tried to conceal, from himself as much as from others, of a crippling immaturity created by that abnormal, precocious intimacy between the two young orphans.

Eyolf the boy has long ceased to be the centre of interest. He has been the occasion for discovering these terrible tensions, but, more important, he has been one of the defences Alfred built against real contact with life.

Rita senses this. She taunts him with his old fantasy. She forces together that innocent-seeming relationship and the physical realities of marriage when she reminds Alfred that he told her the secret of Little Eyolf during a delicious moment of love-making. Alfred cannot bear to recall the love-making: 'I don't remember anything! Won't remember anything!' He recoils as if in horror. Rita presses her advantage: he told her the secret at the instant when Eyolf became a cripple. Alfred is shattered; he has to support himself against the table when he says, in a hollow voice, 'Retribution'. Rita rounds the episode by repeating, in a tone of menace, 'Yes, retribution'.

One of the things that makes this so striking a scene is its reversal of roles and its redefinition of a key term. Rita has become the aggressor, the accuser. What has happened is more than a repetition of the circumstances of Eyolf's crippling – we already knew about the facts. It is a reassessment of the event with the inclusion of Asta as a factor, and it is this inclusion that seems to make 'retribution' mean something different now from what it meant earlier when Alfred levelled it against Rita. Nothing is explained, yet Rita clearly feels that now she can justly accuse Alfred, and Alfred is deeply shaken by the insinuation. And because of the very imprecision, because neither seems able to explain Asta's role in the disaster of their lives and yet both feel it so strongly, we feel that the word 'retribution' emerges now not from the rational application of Alfred's secular philosophy but from levels of feeling not accessible to it. If his term is to be retained, it must be used now with a different, more comprehensive meaning.

At this moment of shock and redefinition, the truly central figure in the situation returns with Borgheim – Borgheim who again, though so unlike Alfred, serves to amplify his predicament in simplified terms. For Borgheim too has run into obstacles he cannot surmount or overcome in his pursuit of Asta. But Alfred soon contrives to get rid of him and Rita so that he may be alone with Asta.

Alfred has discovered an answer to his problem. He cannot endure to remain with Rita; a thought that has come over him only this very day. But he will return home to Asta. The pressure of emotion is strong, it breaks up the flow of his language into brief, emphatic units. Behind the feeling we can begin to glimpse an at least partial definition of what his love for Asta means to him.

It is defined when Alfred says he needs to be 'cleansed and ennobled' by Asta after his life with Rita; when he describes their relationship as 'one high holiday from first to last'; defined not merely by the ideas but by the elevated vocabulary which seems to reach out towards the resources of a very different kind of belief from his own. Here, we may feel, is the source of that peculiar elevation of phrase that Alfred has adopted so often, here in the one relationship that he does not subject to the rigour of his secular intelligence; for he claims that love between brother and sister, the love that moves him so deeply and drives him into religious exaltation of phrase, is the only relationship that is not subject to the law of change.

Pure, ennobling, high holiday, elevating, exempt from natural law – Alfred has revealed what value lies in his attachment to Asta/Eyolf. Just in time for this second Eyolf to be taken away from him. Asta is not his half-sister; she is no relation. Their love is no longer protected by kinship; indeed Asta hints that what before seemed chaste and pure might itself change into love between her and Alfred as between any man and woman. The old fiction, focussed in the imaginary Eyolf who protected the real Asta, is no longer possible to maintain.

It feels like another death. Coming at the end of Act II it balances the death of the other Eyolf at the end of Act I. Asta says a last farewell to the relationship with flowers. Their beauty suggests purity – they are waterlilies. We are not being invited to judge Alfred's obsession simply as a weakness; it is, in its way, beautiful. But it is a beauty that has grown up from the deep bottom; the image recalls the imagery in which the ratwife defined the human condition; it joins Asta and Little Eyolf and Eyolf all together as persons who have, in one way or another, populated the hidden recesses of Alfred's soul, preventing him from facing the real world and real relationships and real responsibilities. Now, at the end of Act II, Alfred's third defence of his emotional privacy is taken away; first his book; then the boy, now the fictional boy. Alfred is left naked, whispering the three names that have so intertwined in his feelings 'Asta. Eyolf. Little Eyolf.' He whispers them in a narrow little glen under a heavy sky; at the end of an Act whose imagery has, unlike that of Act I, been almost exclusively an elaboration of the ratwife's imagery of depth and darkness and death. We have watched the exposure of Alfred's subconscious being, and he has turned out to be not a man with a mission but a man with an obsession which makes any mission a mere façade. Act II confirms the hints of Act I that Alfred's high claims are discordant with his capabilities.

The change of mood in Act III is remarkable because there seems nothing to justify it. The scene is set on an elevation in Alfred's garden; there is an extensive view over the fjord. It is a late summer's evening with clear sky. The play has moved up out of the close gloom. Though not decisively; the light is beginning to fade and before long Borgheim hoists a flag, but only to half-mast.

Borgheim shows his persistence. For all his disappointments, he has not changed. Nor, it seems, have Alfred and Rita. Borgheim reports that they are keeping apart. The conversation limps along in short, frustrated sentences. Because nothing has changed, nothing is possible. Through Borgheim and Asta we listen to what sounds almost like a rehearsal in slightly different terms of what we have heard before.

For Borgheim is like Rita and Alfred. He too wants one person to share his life and only one. Rita wants Alfred; Alfred wants Asta; Borgheim wants her too. Like Rita, and like Alfred, Borgheim refuses to accept the operation of the law of change in the relationship that means most to him. Like them he argues with insistent vehemence for his love. He is caught in much the same toils as the others, though his are fewer and less complicated.

Since this is a kind of repetition, an enlargement of what is already known, it does not engage the attention so much as Asta's quieter contribution. She seems wiser than anybody else in the play. She has tried, like them, to live for one person alone and can remember the delights of that experience. Unlike them she has discovered that even such a relationship must be subject to the law of change. Her pain shows when she recalls the moment of change: '(*with suppressed emotion*) Well, Alfred got married.' But the defining quality about Asta is her ability to accept experience and to learn from it. She is free from vehemence and egotism; she remembers the beauty that once was, even though it has been subject to change. It was, she says, 'delightful', and Borgheim echoes the word twice more as he asks about her past. The little cluster of repetitions draws attention to the fact that the word has been frequently used in the play and has become an element in its colouring. In the earlier, relatively happy part of Act I, it has been used of the present; but in the latter part, and throughout the whole of Act II and now here in Act III, it is used of the past: delight has become a matter for nostalgic recollection only. But Asta does recollect with gratitude; she seems to have escaped from the contradictions of love and hate forewarned by the ratwife and lived out by Rita and Alfred. Asta has learned to accept without bitterness. But Borgheim cannot learn from her.

Nor has Alfred learned anything. He is still anxious to avoid his wife. He talks to Borgheim about his departure but his interest is in Asta – is she to go with him? He is desperate at the thought of being left alone – Asta is the only person who counts. He presses her to stay in the house; forbids her to go further than the town; urges her to return before long; then proposes to meet her in town. He is, in his own way, as obsessive as Rita. And there can no longer be any doubt as to the nature of his feelings for Asta when he concludes his conversation with: 'Yes, because you can never be sure who you might happen to meet later. On the way... The right travelling-partner. When it's too late. Too late.' The imagery indicates how he sees Asta; not as the half-sister he grew up with, but as the woman he met too late, whom, indeed, he has in a sense only just met at the moment when he realised that they were not related. Alfred has been in love with Asta all the time but has only now realised it. He says nothing about the ostensible cause of all these disasters, Eyolf. He is still obsessed with Asta.

And yet even after this display of his real feelings, he cannot acknowledge them and face the consequences. He begs Asta to remain and Rita joins her supplications to his. They both need her to shelter behind; they cannot bear life with just the two of them. Rita begs Asta to stay and take Eyolf's place; Alfred goes further and asks her: 'Stay – and share life with us, Asta. With Rita. With me. With me – your brother.' A great deal is compressed into those brief clauses. Asta is being asked to live out a fiction to protect this pair from reality. And the most blatant fiction is that proposed by Alfred. He is inviting her to resume their old relation-ship of brother and sister even though he knows it to be false. He cannot break loose from the strange intimacy of his adolescence and face real relationships. He needs shelter from his wife, he needs shelter from his feelings for Asta as a woman.

Asta does not say much but Alfred's words finally drive her to decisive action. When he says 'your brother', she snatches her hand away from Rita and says, with decision, 'No, I can't.' She is running away from Alfred and from herself, from a reality that she can perceive but which the others cannot acknowledge. There is no attempt by her to erect a fiction to hide behind; indeed it is Alfred's attempt to preserve one that finally makes up her mind. Her brief words, and above all her decision, show that she has faced the situation as it is and has chosen the only action possible in the circumstances. She has broken the knot and she is the only person capable of doing so. Asta is wise.

Her escape from being used as fiction has its own dangers. She goes off with Borgheim and marriage is certainly what he sees in prospect. For her it would be marriage with a person as possessive as Alfred or Rita. There is a possibility that the disastrous human situation that has been enacted will be repeated. And yet there are strong indications the other way. Borgheim is not an Alfred; he is a man capable of straightforward achievement; his love for Asta needs no disguises; and Asta is so mature. The marriage may not be perfect, but it will be more than a mere means of escape.

The other two are left to face reality alone together. The only sign, so far, of development in them has been their professed readiness to share – Rita will share Alfred with 'Eyolf', Alfred will share Asta with Rita – but there is more desperation than conviction in this. Left to themselves they thrash about in spiritual agony, little changed. But the difference between Rita and Alfred becomes more distinct. There is a directness in her response to her son's death. The ship's lights remind her of his staring eyes; she feels it as an outrage that boats should be moored over the site of the tragedy; the ship's bell rings out for her the heart-breaking refrain 'the crutch is floating'. The event, and details from the event, are haunting her.

By contrast Alfred remains oddly uninvolved in the actual death. For him lights are only lights, a mooring is a mooring, there is no refrain. It is partly his intellect, his way of thinking, that makes him so rational, but the very rationality prevents us from feeling that his emotions are engaged. His feelings are elsewhere. For him the climax of the episode is involved with the other Eyolf; it is significant that when the ship leaves with Asta on board, he uses the phrase he once used of Eyolf's death: 'Asta has gone.' That relationship is now irrevocably ended and it is this that occupies him.

By now Rita has come to recognise his obsession though not all the complexities that go into it. She supposes that he will soon follow Asta. The assessment seems correct. Their conversation is bitter and negative. Life is pitiless, says Alfred; people are heartless, says Rita. Their only response to their situation seems to be complaint against others and against each other. But then Alfred begins to show that the removal of the last of his beautiful fictions is having some effect on him after all. He himself begins to redefine another of his key terms: 'The law of change might hold us together after all, perhaps.' Before, he used the law to justify his longing to sever the bond with Rita – life with her was something he needed to be cleansed of. Now he acknowledges that his life with Rita has bound him to her, not separated; he sees that the law can work differently. And now it is apparent that they have indeed begun to change. Rita can feel it in herself; and though she defines it as painful, as the wreck of every single joy in life, she can also see it as a kind of birth too. Alfred goes too far in the same direction:

Yes, there is. Or a resurrection. A pass into the higher life...
That loss, that is precisely the gain.

That is too much for Rita who accuses him angrily of playing with words – we are, after all, creatures of earth; but he is moving.

It is noticeable that the old, elevated vocabulary of Alfred's has re-entered after a long silence. The biblical echoes (from Philippians 3. vii), the hint of mountain imagery, remind us of the fake philosopher of earlier scenes. It surges abruptly out of the simple, flat dialogue. It shocks rather than impresses, and yet Rita's angry dismissal of it as 'words' does not seem quite justified now. The terms are not encrusted in rhetoric as they were earlier in the play; they stand in brief statements that suggest some kind of sincerity. And in any case, Alfred is no longer making an egotistical claim only for himself; he is speaking of mankind; he is trying to redress, not deny Rita's estimate. When she replies with, 'Good God, we are creatures of earth as well', he agrees; he wants merely to remind her that we have other dimensions too: 'We have some kinship with sea and heaven too, Rita' – she more than she knows. Unobtrusive though it is, the exchange creates an important development to one of the most emphatic and persistent chains of imagery in the play. In Act I Alfred imagined himself a creature of heaven, close to communion with the very stars in the great solitudes of the high mountains; in Act II he collapsed into a hope-less misery defined by the fjord and sea. Each mood seemed exclusive and exaggerated. His language in Act III suggests that he is emerging into a more balanced, less exalted or depressed, assessment of his own and the general human condition. Man has something in him of earth and sea and heaven.

Rita may not understand this intellectually, but her behaviour shows some such maturing process to be at work in her too. She makes no more demands of her husband; she simply asks, without vehemence, that he should remain near her. She offers to share him with his book; this may be just another straw that she grasps at – the book, we know, no longer matters to Alfred – but it is the shift in attitude that counts. She wants to help him to live now, not insist that he live for her.

Yet Alfred, though he has moved out of his exclusive and self-deluding moods, has not moved far. He cannot see how to translate his new forbearance into action. He still hankers after separation; though he acknowledges that he can never return to his old refuge from reality, Asta, he can propose nothing more than a return to the portentous setting of the mountains – he reintroduces the imagery of Act I. But now there is a difference, for he knows now, as he did not seem to then, that he cannot survive there. Yet he must go because he is drawn to solitude.

The word 'drawn' taps the other vein of imagery which counterpoised Alfred's imagery of exaltation in Act I. The rats were 'drawn' to their deaths in the sea. Alfred could recognise the fascination because of his own obsession with the heights and solitude, but that connection between him and the rats was left undeveloped. Now it is pursued as he tells Rita of his experiences in the mountains.

It is a strange episode and strangely located in the play. Alfred presents his narrative as a logical sequence leading to a logical con-clusion: his path was blocked by a lake he could not cross, he was baffled by the terrain, got lost, found his way again by chance, and therefore decided to return home to devote himself to Eyolf. It is late in the play to be offered this explanation for the vocation he declared in Act I; and the explanation comes long after the vocation has been revealed as spurious. What Alfred seems to be saying is no longer interesting. But in consequence, attention can focus on the narrative in a different way, on various discrepancies between its conscious intention and the unconscious revelation it provides.

Alfred speaks as though he could perceive a logical progression from his being lost to his decision to return to his son. The assumption shows in the form of his climax: 'That night raised me to a decision. And it was then that I turned round and came straight home. To Eyolf.' Yet what he describes is a deeply illogical and irrational experience. It describes the man himself, the man as he was when all familiar circumstances and relationships had been stripped away. Alone for the first time in his life, faced with difficulties and dangers that were real, the self-confident rationalist abandoned reason. During his night of ordeal he did not, he says, think. The energetic man of vocation, as he presented himself in Act I, showed no energy of decision; he lapsed into passivity. He luxuriated in the thought of death as an end to his perplexities. Although Alfred seems to see the experience as one that led logically to a decision by him, the story itself suggests something different. The lake is a symbol of a difficulty to which there is, for him, no solution – his love for Asta; in consequence he is incapable of solving any other difficulties; instead he surrenders himself to a longing for peace in death; he is crippled in his power to decide and act by this impediment which blocks all real decisions and all real actions. But his habit of mind makes him project onto events which simply happen to him in his state of passivity the form of logical justification and conscious purpose. There is no logical connection between his experience and his decision to devote himself to Eyolf. The decision is a function of emotion, not of mind; he hits upon it as he hits upon his lost route. It is a way out of his unacknowledged dilemma and as such he seizes upon it, but the ostensible process of solution is very different from the actual. The very vagueness and basic incoherence of his story is the medium through which his inner, central confusion is conveyed.

Return to Eyolf is thus not the vocation he represents it to be but an obscure justification for evading the central predicament in his emotional life and the tensions caused by it. Through his narrative and his method of narration, Alfred assumes a new place in the patterned imagery of the play. For in his irrational passivity, Alfred becomes the human equivalent of one of the rats, perplexed beyond endurance by the endless contradictions of love and hate, unable to resolve them because the solution is itself excluded; his love for Asta can never be acknowledged, far less enjoyed. It is, for him, a kind of restful surrender which can never involve action. He does not consciously define it as such, and indeed it is indicative that he is not able to do so; but he reveals as much when he describes death, 'a good travelling-companion', in the same terms as he had used, by implication, of Asta, when he lamented to Borgheim that the 'right travelling-companion' had presented herself too late. Asta and death co-exist in his imagination.

But, as he goes on to reveal, when death came and took Eyolf away, 'Everything inspired horror. Everything.' Again, Alfred expresses more than he can explain, but what is depicted is the agony of a man whose unconscious device to control the tensions of his relationships has been destroyed by the removal of the main piece in his design, Eyolf the 'respectable' substitute for the forbidden Asta/Eyolf.

He has not controlled them yet. After his moment of emergence he falls back into chaos. He can find nothing to respond to with conviction. Both Eyolfs have gone. He acknowledges that he is as 'earthbound' as Rita, but to be earthbound is to be nothing. When Rita pleads with him, 'Oh, let's just live our life together as long as possible', he can only shrug. Life seems a desolate waste. The words are significant: 'desolate' was his description of the mountain lake that blocked his route, which he could not get round or across; 'waste' evokes the mountain wilderness in which he wandered. Alfred is confronting now, in his struggle with his relationships, what he faced in the mountains; and his response is the same. In the mountains he drifted; here, all he can suggest is that one day he may drift away, leave his wife. He has not yet discovered any other way of coping with difficulty.

Both of them are locked in this barless prison of Alfred's emotional entanglement, until the mood of introspection is

shattered by the sounds of crudely real events. The boys down at
the beach yell as their drunken fathers beat them.

Alfred's reaction to this other world is very poor: 'The whole
beach settlement should be cleared away... All the old hovels
should be torn down... Have the whole place down there razed
to the ground – when I am gone.' There is no advance, in these
unfeeling sentiments, over the harshness he showed in Act I when
he threatened to teach the boys who was master. The philosopher
of Human Responsibility is still grossly deficient in his own
exercise of responsibility. And the tight-minded seeker after cause
and effect is still trying to define in those terms the untidy but
human problems of other people: because the local children
refused to help Eyolf, they do not deserve to be helped; therefore
his hardness is justified. But now he speaks under pressure. The
logic is clear but the emotion behind it verges on hysteria. Alfred
speaks in abrupt, dogmatic sentences broken down into single
clauses. Even his language threatens to disintegrate.

Rita, meanwhile, gradually begins to grow in stature over him.
She can feel for the wretched boys, she reproaches her husband.
She at least has broken out of the bond of egocentricity that once
confined her: when Alfred makes it clear that he will leave her, she
turns her mind resolutely outwards towards other people. Her
language reflects the expansion that has taken place within her. Instead of the staccato vehemence of her earlier speeches, so similar
in their barely restrained violence from the mode Alfred has just
fallen into, there comes a warmer, more controlled voice:

(*slowly and resolutely*) As soon as you have left me, I shall go down to the beach
and have the poor, neglected children back here with me to our place. All the
naughty boys –

Her speech even grows into a pattern, which is something new in
Rita:

> Yes, in our little Eyolf's place.
> They shall live in Eyolf's rooms.
> They shall be allowed to read his books.
>   Allowed to play with his toys.
> They shall take turns to sit on his chair at table.

Pattern suggests control. Something other than her devouring egotism is at work here. She does not intend to feed it by using the local boys, willy-nilly, as substitutes for her lost son. She is proposing the opposite; she wants to violate, systematically and voluntarily, the kind of exclusiveness she once lived for; she wants these boys to enjoy what she once preserved jealously for her own son. Unlike Alfred, Rita has broken out of her prison.

She has chosen to do so in a way that seems concrete and actual and yet in the extreme prosaic and small in scale. Yet her language begins to suggest otherwise. It is while she talks of what she must do to prepare herself that Alfred's imagery of elevation begins to emerge paradoxically from her lips, not as quotation or parody, but as her own expression, new-coined by herself. The point is obscured in translation: 'I shall have to educate myself. Train myself. Develop myself.' What is lost is the strong repetition in the Norwegian of the prefix 'opp-', meaning 'up' or 'upwards'. Rita says, '...oppdra meg. Opplære meg. Oppøve meg.' Her words redefine the concept of elevation, relating it to the ordinary and the unremarkable. Her humble vocation begins, without any self-consciousness on her part, to take on stature, to emerge as an alternative form of elevation.

Rita now leads and Alfred begins to respond. He reverts to the 'law' that he has so often used to justify himself, but he redefines it: 'then a change must have taken place in you'.

A difference has come over his understanding of 'change'. This is a change he did not foresee; it is invoked not to justify himself but to acknowledge new growth where he never expected to find it, in Rita. His language begins to smoothe itself out and take on the quality of Rita's, until eventually and for the first time in the play, they collaborate in dialogue, sharing a set of feelings and ideas without antagonism in a kind of shared ritual of words and sentiment:

ALFRED ...The fact is we haven't done much for the wretched people down
there.
RITA We've done nothing for them.
ALFRED Hardly even thought about them.
RITA Never thought about them with any sympathy.

ALFRED And we had 'the gold and the green forests'.
RITA And we had our hands closed to them. And hearts closed too.

Alfred has broken out of his circle to join her in this new fellow-ship of feeling. He revises his account of cause and effect, of responsibility, to take his own share of the blame: 'So perhaps it's reasonable enough, after all, that they didn't risk their lives to save little Eyolf.' When Rita suggests that perhaps they themselves might not have risked their lives either, Alfred rejects the idea: '(*with an uneasy gesture of aversion*) But never doubt *that*, Rita!' but the sheer vehemence, verbal and physical, of his reply suggests a doubt within himself. Alfred is no longer clad in the armour of callous self-righteousness.

The scene continues to redefine key terms used earlier in the play, to retain them yet endow them with a new significance. The word 'noble' or 'ennoble' has hitherto been reserved to Alfred; now Rita takes it over as she took over the imagery of elevation: 'I suppose I must do my best and try to soften – and ennoble their lot in life.' Finally she makes her own the most central term of all. What she aims to do is translate human responsibility into action. In her mouth the term ceases to be a large, evasive gesture as it was in Alfred's. It expresses a deep and openly acknowledged sense of personal responsibility for her son's fate.

All of this paradoxical transfer of what one might call moral authority from Alfred to Rita gives her a new peace of mind: she finds she no longer need fear the big, open eyes; she can try to make friends with them. In comparison Alfred dwindles in stature. As Rita takes over his moral authority, so he falls into her earlier role and asks questions, asks whether he can help her. But only for a moment; then he begins to grow again. He renounces his idea of drifting away. Under his wife's influence, and with his attention filled by something other than himself and his problems, he appears ready to face a problem for the first time in his life.

With this development in both characters the mood of Act III has at last grown into harmony with the physical setting: the elevation within the garden, the relative wideness of the view, the gentle fading of a summer's day. When Alfred asks and is allowed to share his wife's new vocation, he hoists a flag but the sense of achievement is coloured by the setting. It is an achievement, this breaking out into direct relationship with life, but it involves loss too; yet achievement it is for these two people. Not an abrupt change; it has been brought about through the gradual redefinition of key terms, not just in words, but in their minds. The last few lines of dialogue define it – Rita and Alfred contemplate the long, hard struggle ahead, he at first as sheer unremitting labour. But then his language begins to swell again with the old kind of elevation as he resumes the initiative:

ALFRED Then we shall sense the visitation of the spirits, perhaps.
RITA Where shall we look, Alfred – ?
ALFRED (*fixing his eyes on her*) Upwards.
RITA (*nods approvingly*) Yes, yes – upwards.
ALFRED Upwards, – towards the peaks. Towards the stars. And towards the great silence.
RITA (*giving him her hand*) Thank you!

The words fly up but Alfred now speaks with his eyes fixed upon the wife he once evaded, sharing fellowship with her, winning her gesture of comradeship. He uses the old imagery of mountain and stars but in a new relationship. It is an unobtrusive but crucial point that his last words redefine his sense of the spiritual geography of his life. He no longer speaks of walking among the peaks, of feeling nearer to the stars and in communion with them. That vague and evasive grandiloquence is not being repeated. Instead his imagery gives him a different location within the scheme of things. The peaks are there, the stars are there, not for him to dwell among but to strive towards, strenuously, intermittently. The key word is 'towards'. Alfred has discovered where he really stands once the central distorting fiction of his life has been removed. He stands on prosaic but solid ground at last, on a slight elevation in his own garden, about to take his wife's hand and embark on this small, ungrateful task. Alfred has discovered that he is a creature not just of heaven, or of sea, or of earth, but of all three, and he has discovered in what proportions he is truly made. And that, not in any absolute sense, but for this man, in his situation, is the kind of achievement signalled by a flag hoist against a fading summer sky.

Little Eyolf is an astonishing play. It goes beyond the limits of exploration plumbed in *Hedda Gabler* to the point of presenting an action whose real source is never defined. No character in the play is able to focus clearly on the central predicament, Alfred's incestuous affection for Asta. It is like a deep crater on the sea bed: its presence and its dimensions can only be conjectured by tracing the points at which it impinges on the more accessible and acknowledgeable sectors of experience in the various characters. The play itself does not try to do the work of definition that is beyond the individuals in it. The ambiguous obscurities of involvement are not defined or explained, they are recreated through a range of imagery itself ambiguous and obscure. The play succeeds in expressing the inexpressible.

It is not as though Ibsen could not bring himself to a frank confrontation with the theme of incest. *Ghosts* and *Rosmersholm* disprove that. His reticence is in part a respect for the intense privateness of Alfred's emotions or of any person caught in so intimate a trap, but it is also an indication that he is responding not to a general notion of idealism but to the particular predicament of this particular man. For Alfred is different from Mrs Alving and Rebekka West. Each of these is, in varying degrees, tough-minded. They can bring themselves to talk about incest. Alfred does not have that kind of toughness. Where they confront, he tries to evade.

The argument becomes circular, because character cannot be separated from situation. Mrs Alving talks of incest as a possibility for other people, not for herself; Rebekka West faces it as an act already performed in ignorance. Alfred has to cope with it as a potentially real relationship involving himself. It is the inspiration of his life, yet by its very nature it cannot be acknowledged, still less responded to in any way that could lead to fulfilment. Thus the source of his will is blocked; he cannot be tough-minded in this or in any other relationship because of his situation; and because he cannot be so, the situation must remain forever beyond his power to change it. He does not try. His energies are diverted, always (until the end) unconvincingly, in other directions but all bear some relationship to what it is that he feels impelled to skirt around.

The play presents the spuriousness that must mark the thoughts, speech and actions of a man as crucially frustrated as Alfred. His various vocations reveal themselves as the insubstantial substitutes they are, inflated, unrelated to actual performance, spiritualised and dignified by a vocabulary that is at variance with the values he consciously professes. Alfred is like a poet making fine phrases on a theme he cannot approach directly and honestly.

Yet for all that the controlling interest in the theme is neither diagnosis nor judgment. Incest is a necessary component, but the play does not make its climax out of the identification of that as the prime cause; it is incidental to the main interest. Nor does the play invite easy condemnation of a weak and confused emotional cripple, of a man who fails to be a hero. There is no doubt about the failure. Ibsen's earlier protagonists burst through the encrustations of the commonplace in stubborn pursuit of their ideals even when their lives were put at hazard. Alfred's reaction is not spiritual intransigence but capitulation, the surrender of his vision and the adoption of a different one provided for him by his wife. He is a fake poet of living, a failed hero, a Falk who discovers that he is really a Guldstad. But he is not offered for judgment on this score, only for understanding.

This failure is unusual in Ibsen's galaxy of protagonists. Indeed only one other play resembles *Little Eyolf* in this respect, *The Lady from the Sea*, where Ellida, wedded to the ideal of Freedom, grows to recognise its insubstantiality as she defines it and to accept from her commonplace husband the redefinition 'Freedom with responsibility', which means the shouldering of domestic responsibilities. *The Lady from the Sea* is, however, different from *Little Eyolf*. Ellida's predicament can be defined in the terms used of the rest of Ibsen's plays, as a contradiction between her sense of the poetry of life and the deadening weight of society. The need to marry, to be provided for, overrides her strange attraction towards her demon lover, and it is out of the internal tension produced by that initial surrender that the action develops. *Little Eyolf* contains a theme describable in similar terms – Alfred married the wrong woman for social reasons – but it is no longer this situation that motivates the play. In both *The Lady from the*

Sea and *Little Eyolf* the direction of movement normal in other plays by Ibsen is reversed: Ellida and Alfred both struggle with the distorting imperatives of their personal ideals and come finally to accept social obligation in their place; in *The Lady from the Sea* these imperatives are invested with a kind of nebulous power of inevitability but only by dint of forced and overemphatic imagery. That Ellida herself should use language in this fashion is entirely appropriate to her hectic condition, but the play itself employs imagery independently of her though in the same way to create the figure and the significance of the figure of the roving lover. He becomes that rare inhabitant of Ibsen's mature work, a character created almost entirely for a purpose. The final impression is that Ibsen has tried to portray a woman who is caught in a compulsion but has not been able to define for himself what that compulsion might in fact originate in. The result is that the play bears the taint of melodrama.

In *Little Eyolf* Ibsen has discovered an impediment that is truly and inherently unassailable. Alfred's love for Asta is what might be called an accident in nature brought about by a conjunction of events beyond his control; it is, moreover, a love that cannot, for quite elemental reasons, be acknowledged or fulfilled. Thus Alfred is placed in a situation which inhibits at source any resolute striving to achieve what he most desires. Frustrated at its centre, his will becomes defective in all circumstances, and having become fixed in that condition it is no remedy to find that his love was not incestuous after all. He has become habituated to evasion and cannot change even when the situation changes. And yet, in the end, he proves capable of diverting his muddled energy into the new channel of social responsibility where the old predicament will not be active.

We are not invited to judge Alfred, but to respond to the experience of following him through the self-deluding maze of his reactions to the point where he succeeds in redefining his life. The play calls on sympathy and understanding, and a certain admiration for the man who, given his apparently hopeless involvement, nonetheless succeeds in finding this new purpose for his existence, a purpose moreover which does not reject the ideal that once seemed essential to the poetry of living; he finds an essential place for it in the new scheme of things; the memory of Asta will survive as his inspiration.

And this is no mean achievement. Alfred is no hero, but he is not far short of one, may indeed, at the end of the play, be capable of becoming one, and his deficiency must, to repeat the essential point, be assessed in the context of his impossible predicament. He is a Falk caught in a real vice; Ibsen has imagined a situation where there are no voids left for escape. The mountains are there for Alfred as for Falk, but Ibsen can sense both that Alfred will not be left with the vitality to escape into them and that in any case such escape is meaningless; his poetry of word and action must be contaminated by his condition, his present by his past. Alfred is a Falk fully and precisely located within and confined by his situation.

Although the play works towards the climax of redefinition, it is mainly a representation of frustration and waste. All relationships in the play have been in some degree falsified and deformed by the central relationship. This is the keynote of the last three plays, but what is wasted needs to be defined. In the earlier plays, up to and including *The Master Builder*, Ibsen's imagination was caught by the waste of exceptional quality through social pressures of one kind or another; now it is more sensitive to the waste in social terms caused by people who believe themselves endowed with exceptional quality. He was always sensitive to the unavoidable danger that exceptional quality would go hand in hand with a kind of inhumanity, intentional or unintended; little people are damaged by contact with superior natures; but he did not let his understanding diminish his sense of the ultimate value of distinction. He comes much closer to doing so in the last plays.

It is partly a matter of proportion. In the last plays the greater part of each work explores not merely the waste to the soul of the hero and the degradation of his pretentions to be a hero but the waste to those with whom he lives. Alfred has become an unconscious poseur, Borkman a financial crook, Rubek a commercially minded artist. It is their present spuriousness that fills most of each play. We do not witness the slow but steady rebirth and growth of fundamental ambition in them as we do in Solness or Hedda Gabler; instead there is offered only a late and sudden flare of integrity at the very end of the play. It is an essential element in any final assessment, yet it does not constitute the final statement. His last heroes have only this much of their old integrity and vitality left.

And yet it is there. Even in these sad plays which mourn the waste of opportunity not merely for distinction but for ordinary fulfilment through human relationships, distinction remains the one quality in people that never fails to make Ibsen's art tingle with excitement. By the end of his career he had explored the relationship of heroism to modern life with a steadily deepening sense of its fragility and susceptibility to deformation. The easy assumptions behind Love's Comedy have been abandoned long ago. Heroism is virtually impossible in the modern world. Yet the very phrase admits that it is possible; even in the most adverse circumstances, just possible. And because it continues to inspire some people in the intricately fateful complexities that Ibsen had come to sense in modern living, because it manifests itself against such odds as these, the affirmation, though small, is resounding. It amounts to an assessment that, after the toughest and most ironical testing of human weakness and human aspiration, man cannot be written off as the victim of naturalistic conditioning. Conditioned he is, externally and internally, under enormous pressure from society, but he, or some of us, retains the freedom and the will to aspire after poetry, to reach for his ideal, to be a hero.

8

THE RELEVANCE OF IBSEN

For many readers, especially the younger ones, Ibsen is no longer, to use the cant term, relevant. The challenge deserves to be met and it can be; for in one very simple and straightforward sense his relevance is beyond dispute. He is one of the first and greatest of those who sensed in the nineteenth century what was to become perhaps the dominant shaping force of the twentieth, namely man's feeling of alienation from his own society. He grasped through his imagination the fearsome fact that by the inevitable closeness and intricacy of its organisation modern society had become, to an extent never before felt or acknowledged, a force insidiously hostile to self-fulfilment. In play after play he explores the subtle power of society to work through its agencies, formal and informal, and to act not simply as an external force upon individual integrity, but by deep, insidious penetration.

His appeal from that social coercion is directly relevant too. It is, at least in the plays which mark for me his finest achievement, from *The Wild Duck* to *The Master Builder*, to the intuitive and emotional, rather than the moral and rational sources of energy that exist in at least some people. The distinction is not as simple as the terms imply, since it is from the deepest emotional recesses of the individual's being that Ibsen comes, in his maturity, to believe that at least the intimations of the highest, because more fully alive, morality can emerge. But in his perception that the reaction to a life-denying society must come from the individual's sense of certainty and not from some alternative form of systematisation, social or moral, Ibsen ought to be relevant enough to catch the interest and approbation even of his younger audience nowadays.

His larger claim to relevance is, however, a more oblique one which rests not upon what he directly shares with us but upon what, for all these similarities, is different. Ibsen should be highly and most significantly relevant for the corrective severity that challenges the various kinds of sentimentality (with the callousness that goes with it) and complacency that we are in danger of failing to recognise in our own current assessments of life. He is a protection against the habit of broad and dogmatic classification into good and evil, against facile despair at man's apparent helplessness and against the equally facile optimism that by revolution or radical social engineering man can remove all restrictions to self-realisation. Feelings that we tend to separate for the comfort such simplification may afford us he insists on holding in tension, testing one value against another, demanding that we become aware, above all, of relationship which is the heart of his vision of life: if, in Ibsen's world, little coheres, everything impinges and his plays force us to experience that complexity. Ibsen is relevant as one of the last, as well as one of the finest, creators of tragedy for a world not so far removed from our own that we can afford to dismiss his tragic vision as meaningless to us.

Ibsen's heroes and heroines are all, in one way or another, extraordinary individuals, but that does not limit their power to expand into types of experience. All tragedies deal with extreme cases. Ibsen's protagonists are extraordinary, in comparison with the secondary characters in their plays, by virtue not of obvious pre-eminence but of special endowment; they are possessed by aspiration, different for each, after some ideal, be it a moral principle, an emotional desire, a way of life, that for them comes to represent the essential goal of their being. This personal drive, seemingly autonomous, hurls them eventually into conflict with something else in the scheme of things which seems to frustrate or repress or deform it. They become acute examples of that condition, of which most of us are at one time or another made painfully aware, in which we sense that we are in some degree free to choose our destinies and be responsible for them, and yet simultaneously must exist with forces that infringe and deflect that freedom. This is a common enough sense of predicament; the extraordinariness of Ibsen's characters serves to bring it into sharp focus.

For Ibsen, that other power which is beyond the control of individual will and aspiration is society. Not society merely in its institutions or its official representatives but in the embracing form of that vast and intricate web of relationships and reciprocal influences into which, inescapably, we enter by the mere fact of being born – environment, parentage, social class, upbringing, education, marriage, range and type of acquaintanceships and so on. Ibsen demonstrates his sensitivity to the intricacy and cryptic power of society in this sense, to the myriad means by which it can, in one way or another, insinuate its values upon the individual.

This society, for all its power, is, in Ibsen's view, dead. It is true that he ceased to judge it to be merely evil; he came to recognise that society was the context within which and only within which certain valuable qualities could be generated and developed: simple love and loyalty, respect for other people; yet it is his basic estimate that society by its very nature is not a source of creative energy. It is a structure made up of decayed truths, Mrs Alving's 'ghosts'. Society requires continuity, and thus clings to values long past their period of true vitality; by doing so it necessarily becomes hostile to the creative aspirations of some individuals. Ibsen's best plays present the collision between just such individuals and just such a society. He avoids sentimentality in presenting the conflict. He does not offer us heroes of inviolate and inviolable integrity defending their pure idealism against the external on-slaught of a corrupt society. He insists upon the extent to which his protagonists must themselves be permeated by the very power that they, consciously or instinctively, oppose. Even they are subject to conditioning by society and it penetrates deep into their personalities. Thus Ibsen presents his heroes as inwardly torn; each has a special endowment, an essential self, the source of his or her particular individuality; yet at an almost equal depth there operates the social self. The conflict that fascinates Ibsen, the testing which proves or disproves the heroic quality of this or that individual, is internal. It is within the character and mind of individuals that the tensions of living in a modern society are best explored.

The power of society to permeate in this way and challenge the intimate integrity of Ibsen's heroes is connected with a particular quality in modern life. Ibsen's world is small and unobtrusive in scale. It does not seem to threaten spectacular crises that are self-evidently crises for those involved. Moreover when choice is required between what a character feels, as a matter of living truth, should be done, and what society demands should be done, social conditioning can not only obscure the presence of a moral crisis but dictate the outcome; it is all too easy, faced with what appear small-scale dilemmas, to accept the social imperative as a matter of course. Society, as Ibsen sees it, is a trap into which an individual can fall unawares – even, like Hedda, be born into without one identifiable moment of surrender.

Yet none of them, not even Hedda, seems thereby to be relieved of the responsibility for that surrender. Ibsen may persuade us of the presence and the pressure of society with strong, sometimes overwhelming power, but he displays on stage the most vivacious representations of people going about their own lives and making their own decisions, whether it be to oppose or submit to social conditioning. It is they who permitted, at some stage, the viola-tion of their own integrity, though it is made difficult to see how they could have done otherwise. They are at once victims of compulsion yet responsible for choice within that compulsion. Like Aeschylus's Agamemnon, they themselves 'put on the harness of necessity' by allowing social values to condition their personal values. That is their tragic flaw.

But Ibsen did not write to identify responsibility and allocate blame. The tensions are too complex to be simplified in this fashion. His concern is to communicate the experience of living through the tragic paradox in the modern world. If there is a resultant attitude it is an excited, though heavily qualified, admira-tion for the heroic figures who refuse, in spite of all that is ranged against them, to be totally conditioned. He exposes their limita-tions so nakedly that they often seem open to the charge of being merely morbid or maladjusted, and indeed in part they are. The development traced in this book of Ibsen's expanding sense of modern tragedy is a movement away from pure idealism and pure heroism towards a recognition that such unblemished integrity is an impossibility in the conditions of nineteenth-century living. And yet these weaknesses are also indices of strength. His heroes are maladjusted to an imperfect society, and their morbidity is, at bottom, an extreme and desperate reassertion of that personal and superior vision or ideal that they once allowed, without full awareness, to be debased.

It is an essential part of their extraordinariness that Ibsen's heroes cannot remain in a state of unawareness. For them, and only for them, an infringement of their essential selves is something which must inevitably have consequences. Unaware or not, they have suffered damage at the very centre of their personalities and that centre of experience cannot, because it is essential, simply accept suppression. It must at some later stage, reassert itself. A man or woman of special endowment must at some time feel the need to be true to it, and feel so all the more passionately the longer that endowment has been allowed to remain frustrated and unexpressed. The essential self cannot be silenced.

All tragedies begin with some outrage, some breach in the rightful order of things; it is from this that the consequences flow. The feast of Thyestes, the killing of Iphigenia, the rejection of Cordelia are typical examples. The equivalent in Ibsen is, again, unspectactular, but it is no less, in his terms, outrage and no less productive of consequence. For to Ibsen the signal outrage in modern life is the falsification of the essential self, the blinding of the personal vision, the repression of the individual's drive towards his supreme value. It is outrage when Mrs Alving submits her radical honesty to social convention, when Hedda suppresses her poetry of living through social cowardice, when the Master Builder diverts his creative energies into building suburban houses for money and social status – outrage because of what that kind of falsification does to the individual. For since they cannot fulfil themselves, everything in their subsequent lives suffers obscure corruption: judgment becomes perverted, feelings distorted, careers and relationships debased; character is warped, even language suffers. And the consequences spread wider, outwards from the heroes through the effect they have upon those amongst whom they live. Hedda is a blight on her society; Solness devastates his. They cause this damage without necessarily intending it, but it is done, and it is another form of sequel to the initial surrender of the essential to the social self.

Ibsen picks on a moment when a new crisis occurs. His heroes feel the necessity of thrusting through the crust of social slag which has piled up over them and of being truly themselves at last. The more vehemently they try to break free, the more clearly the web of cause and consequence, the pattern behind unobtrusive events, shows its strength. Ibsen's heroes have entered the trap long before he begins to tell their stories, and consequences have been developing unchecked because unsuspected. Thus they have become victims of necessity; it is too late for them to escape. For Ibsen can see that no man can turn back the pages of his life and start afresh. It is impossible to go back to the suppressed alternative and become fully what one might once have been: a real radical, a fine creative artist, a genuine poet of living, a pure idealist.

Paradoxically part of our sense of the stature of Ibsen's heroes comes from this dire and irreversible involvement. They are people who will not, this time, surrender. They face the final test of their ultimate integrity of devotion to their ideals and they would rather die or risk death than give them up. They are destroyed but they affirm something about the potential of the human spirit.

Their stature is enhanced in another way. Ibsen's vision of man involved ambiguously with a power that limits and distorts but never finally destroys our sense of the dignity of men is one that can be related to Shakespeare's or to the Greeks'. Yet his is tragedy specifically of a more modern age. The Greek heroes share the world with gods; the plays generate faith that the gods, if only they could be fully perceived and comprehended, would be seen to relate in some kind of harmony with what is finest in man. The terms are necessarily vague because tragedy does not presume to explain the mystery. In Shakespeare men share the world with a remotely effective system of moral and spiritual order with which they come most closely into accord when they are at their finest. The ultimate source of value exists in the second power, not in man. In Ibsen the second power, society, is not the prime source of value. His heroes share their world with a decaying structure that is hostile to perfection; and it is upon his individual that the burden is thrown of creating living value. Only they, by their special endowment, can try to break new ground, to grope beyond what society offers towards a different, enhanced kind of living. It may be that grope is all that they can do, grope on all fours towards what even they cannot distinctly see, yet they do it. And they do it alone. There is no valuable solidarity of tradition or shared belief in Ibsen's plays that can give spiritual support to his heroes; they must act alone, or at most with one like-spirited individual, doomed to incomprehension by the rest. And yet they act. They are still, in however limited a sense, heroic. That is the vision of Ibsen's maturity. The limitations are insisted upon by Ibsen. He probes and questions the integrity of his protagonists to reveal so much absurdity mixed with their authenticity, so little effective power at their disposal, such confusion in their minds resulting from the inner tensions that rend them, that it is no wonder that some readers accept his ironical demolition as the final intention. It is not surprising that he himself should from time to time, in Gregers, in Ellida (from *The Lady from the Sea*) and in Allmers, cross the narrow divide and portray characters whose idealism is in fact insubstantial and unauthentic, a kind of spiritual substitute for personal deficiency rather than a positive drive. It is not surprising that in the three plays of his old age, *Little Eyolf*, *John Gabriel Borkman* and *When We Dead Awaken*, his sense of the capacity of some individuals to keep alive their spark of integrity becomes very limited; yet even in these sad plays, whose emphasis is on the wastage of lives through frustration rather than the rekindling of almost smothered fires, the spark is located and celebrated.

The form of what is for me Ibsen's mature work reflects his assessment that the essential components of modern life are the individual and the society that envelops him. He recreates both: intricate, suggestive portraits of the inner and social lives of his characters, and substantial representations of their insidious milieu. The pattern that he perceives behind the small particulars he communicates through patterns of imagery, and draws these together through concentration into symbolism. In his best plays the symbolism grows out of the particular and is not imposed or applied.

To those who believe that there is no pattern in life, that personality is an illusion, or that individuality is a trivial component in a world now analysable only through large and general concepts; to those who believe that modern man can do anything he has the will to commit himself to, as to those for whom man has dwindled to the level of impotence; to those who imagine themselves forever immune from the kinds of frustration and tension that his protagonists experience, Ibsen will never have much relevance. For the rest of us he will remain the great poet of the contradictions inherent in modern society, one who explored despair yet moved beyond it by virtue of a tough-minded, ironically sceptical yet finally convinced faith that whatever society may be or do, some men at least will refuse to succumb to its deadening power. I do not believe that his faith is misplaced even when transposed into our later generation. The signs are there in our worship of at least revolutionary heroes and in our celebration of natural instinct and feeling. Understanding of Ibsen does not mean accepting his vision and his form as things to be reproduced now as interpretations of our age. It means absorbing and testing his faith, with his kind of scrupulous severity, against our experience. In that sense he should always be relevant.

BIOGRAPHICAL TABLE

Year	Works	Related events
1828		Born SKIEN, 20 March, son of a general merchant.
1835		Family, in financial straits after a period of prosperity, moves out of Skien to a small house in the country. During this period in or near Skien, Ibsen had opportunities of seeing performances of plays by Oehlensläger, Kotzebue, Scribe and Heiberg (Hegelian philosopher and theoretician of the 'vaudeville') – relevant to *Catilina*, *The Burial Mound*, *St John's Night*, *Peer Gynt*.
1843		Ibsen leaves Skien to become apprentice to an apothecary in GRIMSTAD. A period of considerable loneliness and hardship. Reads Kierkegaard? Introduced to works of Shakespeare? Reads Schiller's *William Tell*, Sallust's *Catiline*, Cicero's *In Catilinam*.
1846		Fathers an illegitimate son.
1848–		Stimulated by European revolutions and wars.
1849	*Catilina* written. Work begun on *The Burial Mound*.	
1850	*Catilina* privately printed, largely unsold. *The Burial Mound* completed (May), performed (September) at the Christiania Theatre. *The Grouse in Justedal* written (2 acts only, second incomplete) – first	Moves to CHRISTIANIA (Oslo) to prepare for university entrance. Fails in Greek and arithmetic but enjoys status of student. Active interest in radical causes. Scribe dominates the theatre in

229

Year	Works	Related events
	treatment of theme of *Olaf Lilje-krans* (see 1856).	Christiania during this period.
1851	*Norma*, political satire in parody of Bellini's opera.	Student journalism and poetry. Moves to BERGEN as 'dramatic author' at the Norwegian Theatre.
1852	*St John's Night* written during study tour.	Sent on study tour of theatres at Hamburg, Copenhagen, Dresden. Could have seen productions of *Hamlet, King Lear, Romeo and Juliet, As You Like It* in Copenhagen. Impressed by Hebbel's *Maria Magdalena*. Read Hettner's *Das moderne Drama*?
1853	*St John's Night* performed at Norwegian Theatre in Bergen – failed.	
1854	*Lady Inger of Østraat* written. Earliest plans for *The Vikings at Helgeland* (in verse).	
1855	*Lady Inger of Østraat* performed in Bergen – failed. *The Feast at Solhoug* written.	Reads Petersen's translation of Icelandic sagas and Landstad's collection of Norwegian ballads (relevant to *The Vikings at Helgeland* and *The Feast at Solhoug*). Camilla Collett's *The Sheriff's Daughters* published (relevant to *Love's Comedy*).
1856	*The Feast at Solhoug* performed at Bergen and Christiania with success. Published. Work on *Olaf Liljekrans*.	Meets future wife, Suzannah Thoresen. Considerable acquaintance, over this period in Bergen, with works of Scribe.
1857	*Olaf Liljekrans* performed at Bergen – little success. Work on prose version of *The Vikings at Helgeland*.	Moves to Norwegian Theatre in CHRISTIANIA (created in opposition to the Danish-dominated Christiania Theatre). Bjørnson publishes *Synnøve Sölbakken* and *Mellem Slagene*.
1858	*The Vikings at Helgeland* produced	Marries.

Year	Works	Related events
	by Ibsen at the Christiania Norwegian Theatre, successfully. Other productions follow. Published. Preliminary work on *The Pretenders*. Earliest work on *Love's Comedy*, in prose.	
1859	Publishes poems.	Only child, Sigurd, born.
1860	*Svanhild* written, early prose fragment of *Love's Comedy*.	Public attacks on Ibsen's competence.
1861		Attacks increase.
1862	*Love's Comedy* published – little success.	After several rejections, Ibsen awarded a small grant to collect folk-songs and stories in Western Norway. Norwegian Theatre in Christiania goes bankrupt, placing Ibsen in severe financial difficulties.
1863	*The Pretenders* published.	Appointed (at low salary) literary adviser to the Christiania Theatre (now reformed). Awarded further small travel grant (not used for the purpose intended); refused a state pension. Fêted at student festival in Bergen; important press notices of his work begin to appear.
1864	*The Pretenders* produced by Ibsen at the Christiania Theatre – moderate success. Early notes for *Julianus Apostata* (see 1869). Early notes for *Brand* in epic form.	Awarded a grant for travel abroad, supplemented by friends. Leaves Norway for ROME.
1865	No headway on *Julianus Apostata*. Begins work on *Brand* in verse.	Awarded an additional grant. Unspecific references to 'Greek tragedy'. 'I read nothing but the Bible.' Bjørnson publishes *The Newly-Wed*.
1866	*Brand* published as a 'dramatic	Awarded an annual stipend and

Year	Works	Related events
	poem' – successfully. *Peer Gynt* 'already fully developed in my mind' but work delayed by financial worries. 'Inclined to start in earnest on *Emperor Julian*.'	further travel grant. Present at reading of Bjørnson's *The Newly-Wed*. First letter to Georg Brandes, Danish critic who greatly influenced Ibsen. Denies debt to Kierkegaard in *Brand*.
1867	*Peer Gynt* written and published – successful. First ideas for a modern comedy (*The League of Youth*?).	Denies any systematic knowledge of Heine and Kierkegaard. Refers to Asbjørnson's *Book of Norwegian Folk Tales*; and to Goethe's *Götz von Berlichingen*.
1868	Rapid progress with *The League of Youth* after 'wrestling with it all summer without writing anything down'.	Moves to new home in DRESDEN. Asks for Brandes' *Aesthetic Studies*; later acknowledges the influence of the essay on comedy on *The League of Youth*.
1869	*The League of Youth* published – sells well. Performed at Christiania – controversial but popular. Preoccupied with *Emperor Julian*. First ideas for *Pillars of Society*?	Decorated in Sweden. Represents Norway at the opening of the Suez Canal. Reference to 'Holberg's Comedies, which I never tire of reading'. Hartmann's *Philosophy of the Unconscious* published.
1870	Work on *Emperor Julian*. Notes and first draft for *Pillars of Society*.	
1871	Poems published. Serious work on *Emperor Julian*.	Receives a Danish decoration.
1872	Work on *Julianus Apostata*.	References to Horace's *Ars Poetica*, Dante's *Divina Commedia*, to Byron and to Goethe's *Hermann und Dorothea*. Begins to read Brandes' *Main Currents in 19th C. Literature*.
1873	*Emperor and Galilean* published successfully.	Receives a Norwegian decoration. Hostile reference to J. S. Mill's *Utilitarianism*.
1874		Visit to Norway.
1875	Work on *Pillars of Society*.	Moves to MUNICH. Reads and sees Bjørnson's *A Bankruptcy* and *The Editor*.

Year	Works	Related events
1876	Work on *Pillars of Society* interrupted.	Decorated by the Duke of Saxe-Meiningen.
1877	*Pillars of Society* completed and published.	Honorary doctorate from Uppsala.

By now Ibsen was established as an important dramatist. Since publication and performance, even of his less popular works, now became automatic and on a scale far exceeding that of his earlier successes, no further reference to these events is necessary. The year of completion is the year of publication unless otherwise stated.

Year	Works	Related events
1878	Plans for a new play; notes for 'the tragedy of modern times' – *A Doll's House?*	Moves temporarily to Rome, October.
1879	*A Doll's House* completed at Amalfi.	Summer in Amalfi. Returns to Munich, October.
1880	Plans for *An Enemy of the People?*	
1881	Postpones preliminary work on a play (*An Enemy of The People?*). Rapid completion of *Ghosts*.	Moves temporarily to Rome for the winter.
1882	*An Enemy of the People* completed. Preliminary work on *The Wild Duck*.	
1883	Intermittent work on *The Wild Duck*.	Refers to Brandes' *Main Currents*, vol. v (*The Romantic School in France*).
1884	*The Wild Duck* finished quickly.	
1885	Preliminary work on *White Horses* (*Rosmersholm*) from the autumn.	Travel in Norway, summer. Meets Carl Snoilsky, probable model for Rosmer. Returns to Munich.
1886	*White Horses* revised and completed as *Rosmersholm*.	
1887	Preliminary ideas for *The Lady from the Sea*.	Summer visit to Denmark and Sweden; impressed by Danish coastal scenery. Refers to Strindberg's *The Father*.

Year	Works	Related events
1888	*The Lady from the Sea* written rapidly summer – early autumn.	Reference to Brandes' essay on Zola and to Tolstoy's *The Power of Darkness*.
1889	Plans for a new work – *Hedda Gabler*?	Summer in Gossensass; makes acquaintance of Emilie Bardach and Helene Raff, thought to have served as models for Hedda and Hilde (in *The Master Builder*). Die Freie Bühne in Berlin opens with *Ghosts*.
1890	*Hedda Gabler* completed after very slow progress.	Théâtre Libre in Paris produces *Ghosts*.
1891	Preliminary ideas for *The Master Builder*?	Independent Theatre in London produces *Ghosts*. Ibsen leaves Munich; after a cruise to North Cape, he settles in CHRISTIANIA. Makes the acquaintance of another young girl, Hildur Andersen, a pianist; many links with Hilde.
1892	All draft material for *The Master Builder* destroyed? Busy on the new version May–September. Completed.	
1893	Begins laying plans for a new work (*Little Eyolf*?).	
1894	*Little Eyolf* finished after concentrated work in the summer.	
1896	*John Gabriel Borkman* begun April, finished October after rapid progress during the summer.	Reference to Brandes on Shakespeare; denies artistic debt to G. Sand and A. Dumas.
1897	First indistinct ideas for a new play (*When We Dead Awaken*?).	
1898	'I still have various wild ideas in stock' – *When We Dead Awaken*?	Seventieth birthday; world-wide congratulations.
1899	*When We Dead Awaken* completed.	

Year	Works	Related events
1900	Uncertain about further writing: 'but if I continue to keep the vigour of mind and body that I enjoy at the moment, I do not think I shall be able to keep away permanently from the old battlefields. However, if I do appear there again, I shall appear with new weapons and in new armour' (6 March).	15 March, Ibsen suffers his first stroke.
1906		Ibsen dies 23 May.

SELECT BIBLIOGRAPHY

Biographies

Bergliot Ibsen, *The Three Ibsens*, translated by G. Schjelderup (London, 1951).
Henrik Jaeger, *The Life of Henrik Ibsen*, translated by Clara Bell (London, 1890).
Halvdan Koht, *Life of Ibsen*, second and revised edition translated by Einar Haugen and A.E. Santaniello (New York, 1971).
Michael Meyer, *Henrik Ibsen: The making of a dramatist 1828–1864* (London, 1967).
Henrik Ibsen: the farewell to poetry, 1864–82 (London, 1971).
Henrik Ibsen: the top of a cold mountain, 1883–1906 (London, 1971).

Letters, speeches and articles

The Correspondence of Henrik Ibsen, edited by Mary Morison (London, 1905).
Speeches and New Letters, translated by Arne Kildal (Boston, 1910; London, 1911).
Ibsen: Letters and Speeches, edited by Evert Sprinchorn (New York, 1964; London, 1965).
Ibsen, vol. 1: *Early Plays*, edited and translated by James Walter McFarlane (appendices II, IV) (London, 1970).

Translations

The Oxford Ibsen, 8 vols., general editor James Walter McFarlane (London, 1960–).
(lacks vol. VIII: *Little Eyolf, John Gabriel Borkman, When We Dead Awaken*).
The Plays of Ibsen, translated by Michael Meyer (London, 1960–): *The Pretenders, Brand, Peer Gynt, Pillars of Society, A Doll's House, Ghosts, An Enemy of the People, The Wild Duck, Rosmersholm, The Lady from the Sea, Hedda Gabler, The Master Builder, Little Eyolf, John Gabriel Borkman, When We Dead Awaken.*

General studies

Eric Bentley, *The Modern Theatre* (London, 1948).
In Search of Theatre (London, 1954).

M.C. Bradbrook, *Ibsen the Norwegian*, new edition (London, 1966).
Georg Brandes, *Eminent Authors of the Nineteenth Century* (New York, 1886).
  Henrik Ibsen, Bjørnstjerne Bjørnson (London, 1899).
Brian W. Downs, *Ibsen: the intellectual background* (Cambridge, 1946).
  A Study of Six Plays by Ibsen (Cambridge, 1950).
  Modern Norwegian Literature 1860–1918 (Cambridge, 1966).
Francis Fergusson, *The Idea of a Theatre* (London, 1949).
Henry James, *The Scenic Art*, edited by Allan Wade (London, 1949).
John Northam, *Ibsen's Dramatic Method*, reprint (Oslo, 1971).
Ronald Peacock, *The Poet in the Theatre* (London, 1946).
  The Art of Drama (London, 1957).
Elizabeth Robins, *Theatre and Friendship – some Henry James letters* (London, 1932).
P.F.D. Tennant, *Ibsen's Dramatic Technique*, reprint (New York, 1965).
M.J. Valency, *The flower and the castle* (New York, 1963).
Raymond Williams, *Drama from Ibsen to Brecht* (London, 1968).
  Modern Tragedy (London, 1966).